A Theory of Individual Behavior

A Theory of Individual Behavior

Robert Wichers
Department of Economics
University of Pittsburgh
Pittsburgh, Pennsylvania

Academic Press
San Diego London Boston New York Sydney Tokyo Toronto

This book is printed on acid-free paper. ∞

Academic Press, Inc.
525 B Street, Suite 1900, San Diego, California 92101-4495, USA
http://www.apnet.com

Academic Press Limited
24-28 Oval Road, London NW1 7DX, UK
http://www.hbuk.co.uk/ap/

Library of Congress Cataloging-in-Publication Data

Wichers, Robert.
A theory of individual behavior / Robert Wichers.
p. cm.
Includes index.
ISBN 0-12-748450-7 (alk. paper)
1. Microeconomics. 2. Rational choice theory. I. Title.
HB172.W584 1996
338.5--dc20 96-26266
CIP

PRINTED IN THE UNITED STATES OF AMERICA
96 97 98 99 00 01 QW 9 8 7 6 5 4 3 2 1

CONTENTS

Preface vii

1 **Introduction** 1

PART I

PRELIMINARIES

2 **Mathematical Preliminaries** 17

3 **Methodological Preliminaries** 48

4 **Economic Preliminaries** 63

PART II

MODEL ONE

5 **Introduction** 89

6 **Model One** 106

7 The Short-Response Function 122

PART III

MODEL TWO

8 Model Two 141

9 The Long-Response Function 158

10 A Test 168

11 Afterword 174

Answers 181

Index 197

PREFACE

The aim of this book is to present a new theory of individual behavior, with emphasis on testable implications. Discussed first is individual economic behavior—roughly, the subject matter of utility theory and the theory of the firm. The book then widens its scope to formulate a theory of individual behavior in general.

The mathematics is confined almost entirely to multivariate calculus and elementary linear algebra, both at a level that should be comfortable for all graduate students and many upper-level undergraduates.

In preparation is a successor volume, *A Theory of Social Behavior*. That book, too, begins with economic behavior—social or interactive behavior this time—and ends with social or interactive behavior in general. Topics in social economic behavior, such as price formation, competition, and general equilibrium, are discussed in that book rather than this one.

It is a pleasure to thank Cynthia Browning, Jim Cassing, Francis Chan, Ed Green, Jack Ochs, Phil Reny, and Al Roth for helpful discussions and encouragement. Special thanks go to P. de Wolff and J. S. Cramer, of the University of Amsterdam, who back in 1967 and 1968 supervised the dissertation that became this book's Model Two.

1

Introduction

The aim of this book is to develop a new theory of individual behavior, economic and otherwise. Particular attention is paid to testable results.

Presented first is a theory of individual *economic* behavior, to be called Model One. ("Model" and "theory" are used interchangeably throughout.) Generalization then leads to the main theory, concerning all individual behavior. The main theory is called Model Two.

Individual economic behavior, the subject of Model One, includes both market behavior, the subject of utility theory, and producer behavior, the subject of the theory of the firm. You could thus view utility theory and the theory of the firm as the beginning point, Model Two as the endpoint, and Model One as the connecting bridge. Put another way, the primary purpose of Model One is to clarify where Model Two stands relative to traditional microeconomics.

Once Model Two is begun, Model One is no longer needed, and discarded.

As said, the emphasis is on testable results. Model One has nine, including the long-sought demand function; Model Two has ten. These being unusually large numbers, some discusion is in order.

In the two hundred years of its existence, traditional utility theory has produced only one (nontrivial) empirically verifiable result, namely, the Slutsky equation (1915). Apparently, searches for testable results are unlikely to bear fruit. This is why most theorists direct their attention elsewhere. Their books and articles rarely aim for testable results; typically, they seek to construct more and better mathematical descriptions of economic reality, or to enlarge the scope of economic theory, or to refine existing theories, or other things of this sort. Important though such goals may be, they should not be allowed to obscure that *the chief purpose of positive economic theory remains the production of testable results.* Failure to meet this objective may not always be a weakness, but it is never a strength.

More than any other factor, it is the search for testable results that determines the organization and development of what follows. If now and then you wonder where the argument is going, most likely it is in the direction of some testable result.

In case your interest lies with the art of model building, rather than with empirical verifiability, you may still get something out of this book. For example, you will encounter the first positive theory of behavior that successfully incorporates continuous time, and the first theory that fits consumers and producers alike. You will also find a demonstration that equilibrium, including general equilibrium, is both theoretically and practically irrelevant; equilibrium is a will-o'-the-wisp whose introduction into traditional theory is the unfortunate consequence of a mistaken assumption.

Some characteristics of the two theories follow. First, Model One.

(*i*) Like neoclassical utility theory, Model One is based on a utility function, *u*, and a constraint. Like neoclassical utility theory, Model One takes *u* to be independent of time. Like neoclassical utility theory, Model One leaves *u* unspecified. Model One does not say, for example, that *u* is quadratic or has the Cobb–Douglas form.

(*ii*) Yet, unlike neoclassical utility theory, Model One produces nine testable results—specific, analytical forms of nine functions that economics has long sought. They are

- (*a*) The consumer's own-price demand function—e.g., the demand for bread as a function of the price of bread
- (*b*) The consumer's cross-price demand function—e.g., the demand for bread as a function of the price of butter
- (*c*) The consumer's own-price supply function—e.g., the labor-supply function
- (*d*) The consumer's cross-price supply function—e.g., the supply of labor power as a function of the price of housing
- (*e*) The producer's own-price demand function—e.g., the (derived) demand for steel as a function of the price of steel
- (*f*) The producer's cross-price demand function—e.g., the demand for steel as a function of the wage
- (*g*) The producer's own-price supply function—e.g., the supply of output as a function of the output price
- (*h*) The producer's cross-price supply function—e.g., the supply of output as a function of the price of capital
- (*i*) The *quasi-Engel function,* which describes how the consumer's demand for a good depends on the consumer's *wage.* (In the traditional Engel function, the independent variable is the consumer's *income.*)

Since the beginning of economic science, the Holy Grail of microeconomic theory, or at least one of its grand prizes, has been the consumer's own-price demand function. But the search has come to nothing; it is now well established that if *u* is unspecified, and given the assumptions of utility theory, the analytical form of the demand function cannot be found. One therefore has to settle for second best—the Slutsky equation.

It does not follow that the search for the demand function is bound to fail. What does follow is that so long as u remains unspecified and the assumptions of utility theory are left intact, the demand function cannot be derived. More positively put, if the demand function is to be found, you must either specify u (and, more important, justify the specification) or change the assumptions of utility theory. A search for a justifiable specification of u is likely to end in failure, seeing that two centuries of effort in that direction have brought no success. Model One therefore chooses the alternative. Model One deletes one assumption of utility theory—the "mistaken assumption" mentioned a moment ago—and puts another in its place.

The deleted assumption is that the consumer maximizes utility—the very cornerstone of utility theory. The replacing assumption is, quite loosely speaking, that the consumer *tries* to maximize utility. A little less loosely speaking, the consumer transacts so that his endowment, which is a point, at all times moves in the direction in which utility increases fastest, budget constraint permitting. *The consumer thus does not choose a bundle. He chooses a direction. His main and never-ending business is steering—steering his endowment in the direction he likes best.* You could say that the consumer maximizes the *slope* of the utility function, rather than the utility function itself. The utility function is thus not a maximand but a crescend.

Once the new assumption is in place, it is a simple matter to derive the consumer's demand function, thereby rendering the Slutsky equation obsolete. The function turns out to be

$$\frac{Bp + C}{Dp^2 + Ep + 1} \qquad (p \geq 0). \tag{1}$$

In (1), B, C, D, and E are parameters whose values differ from commodity to commodity and from consumer to consumer. Depending on those parameter values, the demand curve either slopes downward, as in Figure 1, or has the backward-bending shape associated with Giffen goods, as in Figure 2. Note that the p-axis is horizontal, in both diagrams. The reason for this break with tradition is explained later.

All people are different—Tom likes tofu, Tim likes tea. All goods are different too. It is often concluded that a single demand function, like (1), cannot possibly fit every consumer and every good. If that argument were sound, (1) would be of little or no use. Then again, if the argument were sound, Newton's theory of gravitation would be useless too, for it would follow, since all objects are different, and all objects behave differently, that no single theory can possibly fit every object in the universe. Actually, Newton never held that all objects behave *the same way*. Newton held that all objects behave *according to the same principles*. Similarly, this book

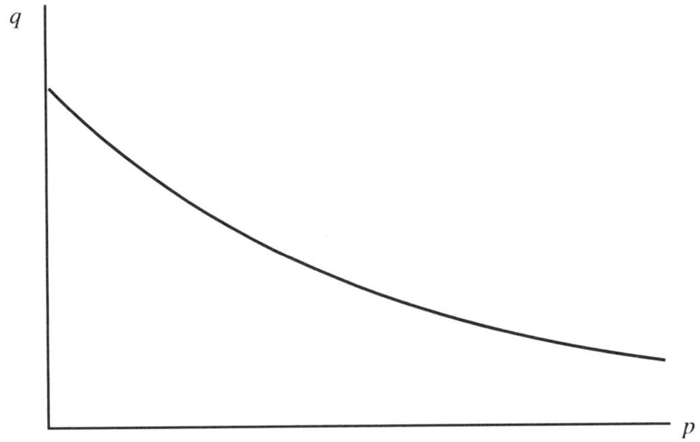

Figure 1. Downward-sloping demand curve.

rests on the premise that all people behave according to the same principles, rather than in the same way.

But is not all this a matter of opinion? Less so than you might think. For one thing, everyone's behavior is ruled by the mind, and the workings of all minds are governed by the same electrochemical laws. It is difficult to avoid the conclusion that all people behave according to the same principles.

But suppose you are not convinced; suppose you believe there are at least two essentially different categories of people, and therefore two essentially different types of behavior, calling for two essentially different theories. By the rule that all concepts must be defined, it is then necessary to define the two categories, or at least the difference between them. In the absence

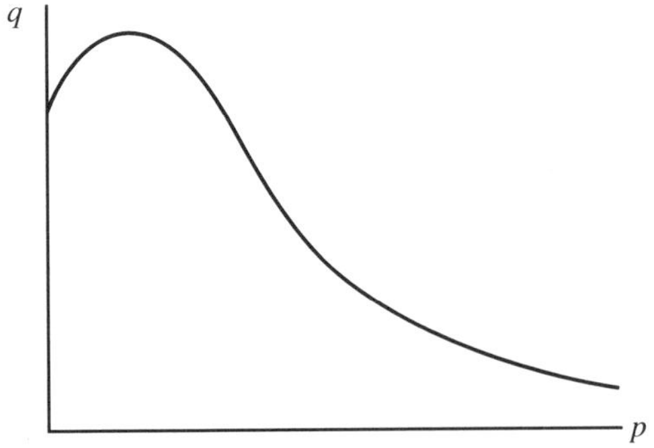

Figure 2. Giffenesque demand curve.

of such a definition—and to date, no adequate one exists—economic theory should treat all people with complete symmetry. Model One does so: whatever it has to say for one person, it says for all. By the same reasoning, the set of all goods may be dichotomized only if one defines the resulting subsets, or at least the difference between them. In the absence of such a definition—and to date, no adequate one exists—economic theory should treat all goods symmetrically. Model One does so: whatever it has to say for one good, it says for all. The premises of Model One thus imply that if (1) is *a* demand function, it is *the* demand function.

Similar remarks apply to the other eight testable results.

More features of Model One:

(*iii*) The theory is positive, rather than normative. Model One uncritically accepts that people lie, cheat, steal, make mistakes, lose money, stumble and fall. A normative theory might describe such forms of behavior as irrational or inefficient or suboptimal, but a positive theory does not have that option. To a positive theorist, the idea that a person can behave irrationally is as unacceptable as the idea that the moon can behave irrationally.

(*iv*) Model One is dynamic. It treats time as a continuous variable, rather than as a sequence of periods. Model One is, even so, not an exercise in control theory. Control-theoretic models have a normative outlook; Model One does not.

The shift from period analysis to continuous-time dynamics is more than a mere change in the theoretical treatment of time. It engenders a new way of looking at some issues of economic interest. It changes some answers. And it changes some questions.

In traditional utility theory, the consumer begins each period with an initial endowment, $\mathbf{x}(0)$, ends each period with a final endowment, $\mathbf{x}(1)$, and uses the time in between to transform the one into the other. We thus see him as undertaking a well-defined *project,* as having a well-defined *task.* Many of the questions asked by traditional theory implicitly view the consumer as an undertaker of tasks and make sense only so long as one accepts both that view and its period-analytical matrix.

At the instant where two periods abut, time is reset to zero, and $\mathbf{x}(1)$ is reset to $\mathbf{x}(0)$. Since $\mathbf{x}(0)$ and $\mathbf{x}(1)$ are usually taken to differ, this puts a jump discontinuity into the endowment's time path. It is a puzzling discontinuity, without counterpart in the real world.

When time is a continuous variable, there is no period, no period beginning, no period end, no final bundle, no theory-generated jump discontinuity. As periods disappear, so does the temptation to see the consumer as one who undertakes projects, a completer of tasks. This, more than anything else, accounts for the differences between questions posed by traditional theory and questions posed by Model One. An example follows.

Neoclassical theory asks what bundle the consumer will choose, given the utility function and the budget constraint. If the question sounds reasonable it is because neoclassical theory adopts period analysis and views the consumer as one who performs tasks, among them the choosing of a bundle. The question does not sound reasonable at all in the context of Model One, which knows no periods and, in virtual consequence, does not regard the consumer as a completer of tasks. Model One asks, instead, which *direction* the consumer will choose. Choosing directions—steering the endowment—is not a project with a start and a finish. It is a ceaseless job. Imagine yourself sailing around the world in a sloop and you have some idea: you have to steer, day in, day out.

(*v*) In its approach and its methods, Model One is much closer to the natural sciences than to the social sciences. This is particularly true when it comes to definitions. Traditional theory as a rule defines its concepts interpretively; Model One defines them mathematically and makes a clear distinction between the definitions and the interpretations. It is customary, for example, to define a stock as a commodity quantity possessed, and an endowment as a collection of stocks. In Model One, a stock is *interpreted* as a commodity quantity possessed, but *defined* as a point with a single, nonnegative coordinate. Likewise, an endowment is *interpreted* as a collection of stocks, but *defined* as a point with n coordinates, all nonnegative.

(*vi*) Because Model One uses only mathematically defined terms, its vocabulary is much smaller than that of traditional theory. Apart from "utility," the core notions are only four. Two of these are "stock" and "endowment." The other two are *flow* and *action.* By interpretation, a flow is the difference between two commodity stocks. By definition, a flow is the difference between two one-coordinate points; equivalently, a flow is a one-element vector ("1-vector"). By interpretation, an action is something you undertake—a transaction perhaps, or a production activity. By definition, an action is the difference between two n-coordinate points; equivalently, an action is an n-vector. Just as each endowment coordinate is a stock, so is each action element a flow. "Undertaking an action" means adding an action to an endowment. The outcome of this undertaking is not fatigue, or satisfaction with a job well done; the outcome is another endowment.

Mathematically, actions are indistinguishable from what activity analysis calls *activities.* Connotationally, there is a difference: "activity" suggests producer behavior; "action" refers to all economic behavior. But connotations do not matter. Mathematics is what counts. And mathematically, an action is the same as an activity. Each is a difference of two endowments.

Undertaking an action whose ith element is positive will increase the stock of the ith good; undertaking an action whose ith element is negative will decrease the stock of the ith good. Take the action "buying a loaf of bread." It is a vector with a negative money element, a positive bread element, and, if no other goods are involved, $n - 2$ zeros. Buying bread thus decreases the money stock, increases the bread stock, and leaves all other stocks unchanged. As is probably clear from this example, the term "action" covers not only all production activities and all transactions, but also all nonmarket activities that affect commodity stocks, from paying taxes to baking cookies.

Actions may have any number of positive elements, any number of negative elements, and any number of zeros. Suppose, for example, that gasoline is rationed and that you need a coupon for every gallon. "Buying a gallon of gas" is then an action with at least two negative elements, a money flow and a coupon flow. In the same way, any trade with nonmonetary transaction costs is represented by a vector with two or more negative elements, and so is every production process that uses two or more inputs. A production process with two or more outputs is an action with two or more positive elements. So is every *joint purchase.* If, for instance, you buy the supermarket's Special Offer, a package consisting of a toothbrush and a tube of toothpaste, you undertake an action with two positive elements. If the Special requires not only cash but also a coupon, the transaction is, from your point of view, a *joint sale* as well.

(*vii*) Among the nonmathematical notions that Model One avoids are (*a*) all anthropic terms, (*b*) all institutional terms, and (*c*) all cognitive terms. Amplification follows.

(*a*) *Anthropic terms* like "consumer," "producer," and "agent" are used throughout the book, but only to enliven the story. They are not part of the model proper. Indeed, the protagonist of Model One is not a consumer, producer, agent, or person of flesh and blood, and the behavior that Model One seeks to describe is not that of a living being. *The protagonist of Model One is the endowment, which is a point, and the behavior of interest is the behavior of that point.* Among the things we wish to know are the time path of the endowment; the time path of the actions that account for the endowment's motion; and, if at some instant there is a change in a price or some other parameter, the effect of that change on the various time paths from that instant on.

The endowment, then, acts as the representative of its owner, and the owner himself is not involved. This is nothing new. Although interpreters of neoclassical utility theory have a great deal to say about the consumer, the theory itself mentions neither him nor his behavior. To be sure, neoclassical utility theory is interested in behavior. But the behavior of interest is not that of the consumer. The behavior of interest is that of the consumer's endowment, or possibly his demanded bundle.

The endowment, an inanimate point, is not very good at representing its owner, a living being. In fact, it plays the role so badly as to cause what may be called the Problem of the Intrusive Consumer: intuition is constantly tempted to let the consumer himself come onstage. But the consumer has no business there. He should stay in the dressing room while the lead actor—the endowment—is out in front saying his lines.

The Problem of the Intrusive Consumer besets traditional economics as much as it does Model One. Traditional economics selects a proxy for the consumer (endowment or demanded bundle), but then keeps inviting the consumer himself into the story. It assumes *the consumer* capable of ranking bundles. It says that *the consumer* plans and chooses and decides and allocates. It holds that *the consumer* acts rationally. It asserts that *the consumer* is able to maximize utility. It depicts *the consumer* as plagued by uncertainty. In the end, however, none of these assumptions is given mathematical expression, and none finds its way into economic theory proper. In the end, the Intrusive Consumer's only contribution is an unwanted one: he confuses the issues. He should leave the stage to his proxy. It is what proxies are for.

Unfortunately, highlighting the Problem of the Intrusive Consumer is not going to make it go away. Nothing is going to make it go away so long as its cause—the huge gap between a living being and its inanimate representative—persists.

Model Two resolves the difficulty by choosing as the agent's proxy not his endowment but his brain, thus reducing the width of the gap to nearly zero. But Model Two is still far away. Is there anything that will work right now?

Neoclassical utility theory itself offers a solution. For an explanation, consider that living beings do not have utility functions—if they did, medical science would have found them by now. Thus, when neoclassical theory says that the consumer has a utility function, it is not referring to a living being. What it is referring to is perhaps best regarded as a kind of robot, placed midway between the flesh-and-blood consumer and his endowment. The robot-consumer is neither as animate as the former, nor as inanimate as the latter; but he is just animate enough to serve as a proxy for the living consumer, and just inanimate enough that the endowment can serve as the proxy's proxy.

The robot-consumer follows, at all times and to the letter, the rules that economic theory has programmed into him. It means, among other things, that he is incapable of acting either rationally or irrationally. (The only one who can conceivably be rational or irrational is the living consumer—the intrusive one.) Nor does the robot-consumer have the ability to choose. True, we usually say that he *chooses* the utility-maximizing bundle. But we also usually say that he makes this *choice* every Monday, rain or shine; and that reduces "choice" to a mere figure of speech.

Seeing how long the robot-consumer has been part of economic theory, he seems to be making himself useful. More to the point, the very fact that utility theorists have not yet abandoned him suggests that, in their eyes, his behavior adequately represents that of a living consumer, and the behavior of his endowment adequately represents that of the living consumer's endowment.

In one way, however, the robot has not done so well. He has been largely unsuccessful in keeping the Intrusive Consumer out. The consumer is often said to predict, plan, optimize or fail to, act rationally or irrationally, behave consistently or inconsistently, allocate his time efficiently or inefficiently, anticipate the future, have expectations, have an aversion to risk, cope with uncertainty, have preferences, be capable of ranking bundles. Since robots do not have such abilities, the consumer being referred to can only be the intrusive one.

In this book, the Intrusive Consumer does not intrude. When he is mentioned, as he is from time to time, it is only to put some realistic meat on the theoretical bones. His representative, the robot-consumer, is mentioned a bit more often, but he plays no role in the theory, either.

Because the robot-consumer has no choice but to obey the rules of theory, the time path of the endowment is completely and uniquely determined. It is a path without forks. If there were a fork, the robot would have to choose whether to go right or left; and robots do not choose.

(*b*) Model One avoids *institutional terms* for not one reason but two. The first was already mentioned: institutional terms are likely to be mathematically undefinable. The second reason is both more cogent and of greater scope: no theory of behavior should refer to institutional notions like *contracts, banks, government, laws, rights, possession, property, ownership, country, state, border, financial instruments,* or even *cars,* for the simple reason that there was behavior long before any of these things had been invented.

An institutional concept of particular interest is *money,* which throughout this book means nominal money. Because there was behavior before there was money, no theory of behavior should refer to money. Indeed, Model One does not. Model One mentions (and mathematically defines) *goods,* of which money is one; but it does not mention money or any other good by name.

Since money is an institutional concept, every monetary notion is too. Examples are *income, profit, cost, revenue, expenditure, savings, taxes*—arguably even *demand* and *supply.* None of these terms is included in the formal vocabulary of Model One. What Model One does mention, and define, and have something to say about, is a *flow rate.* Each of the just-listed notions is a flow rate.

(*c*) Living beings play no role in Model One, and so *cognitive notions* do not either. Among them are *knowledge, intention, purpose, decision, choice, preference, expectation, prediction, planning, rationality, optimization.* The protagonist of Model One does not know "his" utility function, or "his" indifference curves, or the price of flour, or how much money he has in his pockets. After all, the protagonist is an endowment, and an endowment does not know anything.

It may seem that stripping away all anthropic and cognitive and institutional elements will destroy the very essence of economic behavior, leaving nothing of economic interest. Actually, what is stripped away is a layer of terminological irrelevancies. The essence of economic behavior is not thereby destroyed; it is exposed. Witness the nine testable results.

This is not to say that it is easy to learn to live with an economic vocabulary consisting of a mere handful of terms. To find out how hard it is, try doing a three-minute monologue on microeconomics without once mentioning consumers or producers, preferences or optimization, money or prices, profit or income, revenue or cost. It is difficult enough to make you long for a return to the traditional vocabulary. But then you would have to give up nine testable results.

Still more features of Model One:

(*viii*) The uniqueness of the endowment's time path—the absence of forks in the road—implies that there are no multiple equilibria in Model One. If there were, the endowment would have to choose, which it does not know how to do.

(*ix*) *Uncertainty,* being a cognitive notion, is among the concepts that Model One avoids. But there is something else. It is often argued that "randomness" is the mathematical equivalent of "uncertainty." Without necessarily subscribing to this idea, Model One does make room for randomness. It depicts the endowment as affected by exogenous factors and allows for the possibility that those are random.

It is worth noting that "behavior under uncertainty" sounds a good deal more plausible in a period-analytical theory than in the continuous-time dynamics of Model One. At some point, after all, uncertainty becomes certainty, thus ending a period: sooner or later you find out whether the lottery ticket wins or loses, whether the bread you bought is fresh or stale, whether or not your car is stolen or your house burns down before the policy expires. Events like these are quite difficult to model in continuous time. Increasing the difficulty is that uncertainty often disappears gradually, rather than all at once. The main problem, however, lies in the meaning of uncertainty. So long as uncertainty is mathematically undefined, a coherent mathematical theory of behavior under uncertainty remains out of reach.

(*x*) Model One regards the utility function as neither cardinal nor ordinal. Cardinality and ordinality are properties of measures. Utility can therefore be cardinal or ordinal only if it is a measure—a measure of usefulness, for example. In Model One, utility is not a measure of anything. It is just a function, unrelated to anything found in the real world, unrelated to anything concrete enough to be measurable. (Chapter 6 drives the point home. You will find there that if u were taken to be a minimand, or a decrescend rather, the testable results of Model One would remain the same.)

So, since u does not represent anything measurable, it would be meaningless to characterize the utility function of Model One as cardinal or ordinal. The terms simply do not apply.

(*xi*) Given that there are neither consumers nor producers in Model One, who does the consuming and the producing? According to Model One, actions do. An action is said to *produce* good i if its ith element is positive and to *consume* good i if its ith element is negative. Thus, buying bread consumes money and produces bread.

(*xii*) Because people have no utility functions, it is futile to seek the analytical form of the utility function by observing the behavior of human beings. The only way to "find" the utility function is to specify it. And the only way to assess the realism of the specification is to see whether the implied behavior of the (utility-driven, theoretical) endowment resembles the behavior of an endowment belonging to a living being.

Is it difficult to specify u? Not at all. What is difficult is justifying the specification. In his 1854 book, Heinrich Gossen took the utility function to be quadratic, his sole reason being that a quadratic u is algebraically easy to manipulate. Economists everywhere berated him for it, saying things like "Mathematical convenience is no justification at all" and "Shame on you, Heinrich." Actually, if Gossen had taken the trouble to demonstrate that his specification had realistic implications, his choice of a quadratic utility function might well have been tolerated. After all, the Cobb–Douglas production function, too, was plucked out of thin air, but found acceptance because Cobb and Douglas showed that their function fitted actual observations. On a more monumental level, the same can be said about Newton's inverse-square law: at the time of its creation, its sole justification was that it applied so well to the real world.

In conclusion of the outline of Model One, a few words about *preferences.* Over a hundred years ago, Vilfredo Pareto observed that he could always tell which of two endowments carried more utility; but he could not think of a way to measure *how much more* utility the winner carried. Actually, Pareto made a much stronger statement. He declared—without offering proof—that it is *impossible* to measure the utility difference. A few decades later, John Hicks took this one step further. Accepting Pareto's declaration on faith, he concluded that "utility" was a tainted notion, and should therefore be banned from economic theory. To see what this means, imagine a three-dimensional picture illustrating the consumer's adventures in a two-goods world. Utility is measured along the vertical axis; goods 1 and 2 are measured along the other two axes, which lie on the floor of the diagram. Hicks in effect proposed that economics do away with the vertical axis, fix its eyes on the floor, and never look up. Of course, once the vertical axis is removed, all statements involving utility become illegitimate and must be reformulated without mention of the word "utility." A statement like $u(\mathbf{x}) > u(\mathbf{y})$, for instance, becomes "Endowment **x** is preferred to endowment **y**."

And so began a concerted effort to purge economics of "utility" in favor of "preference." From the beginning, the language of preferences consisted of a good deal more than just "Endowment **x** is preferred to endowment **y**." Theorists saw right away that if the preference ordering was to have realistic implications, it was necessary to impose a few restrictions, like transitivity and continuity. Over time, a small collection of such restrictions came to be generally accepted.

Matters stood there, to everyone's satisfaction, until 1959. That year, Hirofumi Uzawa proved that if you are going to burden the preference ordering with that small collection of generally accepted restrictions, you might as well introduce a utility function—the two are equivalent. Utility immediately began a comeback, not least because utility functions are mathematically easier to manipulate than preference orderings.

The preference apparatus has been central to economic theory for so long that it is easy to overlook the shaky premise on which it is built. The shaky premise is Pareto's unproved assertion that it is impossible to measure utility differences—impossible to give empirical content to the slope of the utility surface in any direction.

Contradicting Pareto, this book gives empirical content to the slope of the utility surface in certain directions. Recall that Model One has the endowment move in the direction in which utility increases fastest, constraint permitting. Model One also assumes—this was not mentioned before—that the speed with which the endowment moves is proportional to the slope of the utility surface in the direction of the endowment's motion. The consumer thus acts faster when the potential utility gain is larger. Or: the endowment's speed reflects "preference intensity." The two-goods picture must thus be given back its utility axis; events are no longer confined to the floor of the picture; the diagram is three-dimensional again. With that, the language of utility and the language of preference cease to be equivalent. No doubt it is possible to redefine the preference ordering so as to restore equivalence, but nothing like that is attempted here. Preferences therefore play no role in what follows.

Next, some features of Model Two. Most are the same as those of Model One. The main difference is in the objective function.

All utility-based theories seek to condense the workings of the mind, and the way in which the mind drives behavior, into the single number u. Judging this too tight a corset, Model Two uses m numbers rather than just one, with m possibly very large. The m numbers are the coordinates of a point called the *state of mind.* The objective function of Model Two is defined over the set of all possible states of mind. Movements of the state of mind determine what the agent does. The determine, for instance, which goods he buys and sells over time, and at which rates. They also determine how these rates are affected by changes in prices and other parameters.

Note the difference with Model One. Model One is like traditional utility theory in that it effectively represents a living being by the *endowment.* In contrast, Model Two represents a living being by the *state of mind.* This is a good deal easier on the intuition.

The objective function of Model Two is analytically specified (and a justification is given). Specifying the objective function is attractive in that it leads to more, and more detailed, testable results. There are ten. One of them is that the effects of a change in a price or other parameter wear off exponentially. The other nine are the dynamic versions of the testable results of Model One. The dynamic version of (1), for example, is

$$\frac{B(t)p + C(t)}{Dp^2 + Ep + 1} \qquad (p \geq 0). \tag{2}$$

In the most elementary case, $B(t)$ and $C(t)$ have the form

$$\begin{aligned} B(t) &= B_0e^{-\gamma t} + B \\ C(t) &= C_0e^{-\gamma t} + C, \end{aligned}$$

with $\gamma > 0$. For an illustration, let p be the price of milk, and suppose p changes. Choose the instant of change as the origin of the time axis, $t = 0$. At the instant of change, $B_0e^{-\gamma t}$ and $C_0e^{-\gamma t}$ begin to converge to zero; $B(t)$ and $C(t)$ thus begin to converge to B and C; and the demand rate for milk begins to converge to constancy, its limiting value given by (1). Note that, although the demand rate begins to respond immediately to the price change, it never quite finishes responding: $e^{-\gamma t}$ is never quite zero.

The book concludes with a test of Model Two. The test uses 156 laboratory-generated observations, each of which is a three-coordinate point. The three coordinates are time, price, and quantity. Fitted to the 156 points is a surface with an equation closely related to (2). The fit is, by the standards of the social sciences, most satisfying ($r^2 = 0.97$).

The rest of the book consists of three parts and an afterword. Part I deals with preliminaries. Part II presents Model One. Part III presents Model Two. Each part has three chapters.

Questions

(Answers are in the back of the book.)

1. Sketch the demand function (1) if $B = C = D = E = 1$.
2. (Continuation) Replace p with $p - \frac{1}{2}$, recompute B, C, D, E, and sketch the result.
3. Is inactivity an action?
4. Write in mathematical symbols: "John's endowment consists of 2 bottles of beer and 5 dollars. Then he buys another bottle of beer, for a dollar."
5. A utility-maximizing consumer works for the phone company by day and, to make some extra money, bakes cookies several evenings a week. Every Saturday he sells his cookies to a few local bakeries. Does his baking make him a profit-maximizing producer, at least in the evening, or does he remain a utility-maximizing consumer at all times?
6. "The neoclassical consumer is able to rank all market baskets that he can afford and then choose the best of these bundles." Discuss.
7. "Consuming a good is the same as buying that good." Discuss.
8. "Microeconomics is about decision making." Discuss.
9. "The purpose of microeconomics is to show how scarce means should be allocated to maximize the satisfaction of desires." Discuss.
10. "Property rights are prerequisite for market exchange." Discuss.
11. "The formal meaning of 'Consumer Jones is indifferent between bundles $\mathbf{x}$ and $\mathbf{y}$' is that bundles $\mathbf{x}$ and $\mathbf{y}$ give the same satisfaction." Discuss.
12. "Representing all actions by vectors is too simplistic. It does not, for example, allow us to distinguish between voluntary actions like buying beer and involuntary actions like paying taxes." Discuss.

Part I

PRELIMINARIES

2

Mathematical Preliminaries

This book uses a good deal of linear algebra, a middling amount of calculus, and a very small bit of real analysis. Some of the mathematics used is assumed to be familiar. The rest is covered in this chapter.

Regarding linear algebra, it is assumed that you know

How to add and multiply two matrices;
How to multiply a matrix by a scalar;
How to add two vectors, both when they are columns and when they are arrows;
How to multiply a vector, whether column or arrow, by a scalar;
How to transpose matrices and column vectors;
How to compute a determinant by expanding with respect to a row or column;
How to determine the rank of a matrix;
How to solve a simple linear system, both with and without Cramer's Rule;
What the inverse of a (nonsingular) matrix is;
That $(\mathbf{AB})' = \mathbf{B}'\mathbf{A}'$ (the prime denotes transposition);
That $(\mathbf{AB})^{-1} = \mathbf{B}^{-1}\mathbf{A}^{-1}$ if $\mathbf{A}$ and $\mathbf{B}$ are invertible;
That $(\mathbf{A}^{-1})' = (\mathbf{A}')^{-1}$ if $\mathbf{A}$ is invertible;
That the standard norm of a vector $\mathbf{a}$ is $\|\mathbf{a}\| = \sqrt{\mathbf{a}'\mathbf{a}}$;
That the standard inner product of vectors $\mathbf{a}$ and $\mathbf{b}$ is $\mathbf{a}'\mathbf{b}$.

Among the linear-algebra topics covered below are

Vector spaces and subspaces;
Point spaces;
Linear combinations;
Linear dependence and independence;
Basis of a vector space;
Dual space of a vector space;
Nonstandard norms and inner products;

Angles and orthogonality;
Orthogonal projection.

Regarding calculus, it is assumed that you know

How to find the first- and second-order partial derivatives of a function of several variables;
How to expand a function of one variable in a Taylor series around a given point;
How to perform integration by parts.

Among the calculus topics covered below are

The Taylor expansion of functions of more than one variable;
The directional derivative;
The direction of steepest ascent, unconstrained and constrained;
The differential-equation system $\dot{\mathbf{y}}(t) + \gamma\mathbf{y}(t) = \mathbf{z}(t)$;
Delta functions.

The very last topic of this chapter uses real analysis—just enough to prove a single result. Since you are likely to find that result intuitively obvious, you can skip the real-analysis part without harm to your understanding. And if you are altogether unfamiliar with real analysis, skipping it is very much the recommended course.

Each Mathematical Topic has its own subsection. For ease of reference, the subsections—27 in all—are labeled MT 1, MT 2, and so on.

MT 1

Algebra is built on three operations. They are multiplication (including division), addition (including subtraction), and multiplication by a scalar. Actually, since there are several ways to define addition, several ways to define multiplication, and several ways to define scalars, it would be more accurate to say that algebra is built on three classes of operations. In this chapter, each of the three operations has its most common meaning.

MT 2

First, multiplication. A set is called a *set with multiplication* if (*a*) any two of its elements, not necessarily different, can be multiplied and divided (provided the divisor is not zero), and (*b*) all thereby obtained products and quotients also belong to the set. Property (*b*) is usually expressed by saying that the set is closed under multiplication.

For an illustration, take the set U of measurement units, such as the dollar, d, the erg, e, the foot, f, the gallon, g, the hour, h. Products of units, like f^2 and kg-m, and quotients of units, like d/g and miles per hour, are themselves units. It follows that U is a set with multiplication.

Among the elements of U is the quotient of a dollar and a dollar, that is, 1. Thus, 1 is a unit too.

For uniformity, all quantities expressed in some unit (other than 1) will be written with the unit last. Three feet thus becomes $3f$, and \$5 becomes $5d$.

Quantities measured in the unit 1 are said to be *dimensionless.* Most quantities of economic interest are *dimensioned,* are measured in units other than 1. If, for instance, Smith buys 4 gallons of milk for 12 dollars, he buys not 4 but $4g$, he spends not 12 but $12d$, and the price of milk is not $12/4 = 3$ but $12d/4g = 3d/g$.

Another set with multiplication is the set of real numbers. Still another is the set of nonsingular 2×2 matrices. In the set of real numbers, multiplication commutes: $ab = ba$. In the set of nonsingular 2×2 matrices, multiplication does not commute: $\mathbf{AB}$ does not always equal $\mathbf{BA}$. This illustrates something said a moment ago, namely, that there are several ways to define multiplication.

An example of a set *without* multiplication is the set of *locations in the plane,* like the point (3,4). The set of locations in the plane is traditionally denoted E^2. (The E is in honor of Euclid.) That E^2 is a set without multiplication is obvious: multiplying locations is meaningless. Multiplying *instants,* like 3 P.M. and 4 A.M., is meaningless too. The set of instants is thus also a set without multiplication. The set of instants will be called the *time line* or *time axis,* and denoted T.

MT 3

Addition is next. A set is called a *set with addition* if (a) any two of its elements, not necessarily different, can be added and subtracted, and (b) all thereby obtained sums and differences also belong to the set. Property (b) is usually expressed by saying that the set is closed under addition.

For an example, consider the set of *dollar flows.* The $4d$ you spent on apples yesterday is a dollar flow; so is the $5d$ you spent on pears; so is the $4d + 5d = 9d$ you spent on fruit. Other dollar flows are the $50d$ you earned yesterday, the $10d$ you paid in taxes, and your after-tax earnings of $50d - 10d = 40d$. As these examples illustrate, sums and differences of dollar flows are again dollar flows. The set of dollar flows is thus a set with addition.

What has just been said about money, measured in dollars, holds also for tuna, measured in cans, as well as for milk, measured in gallons, and for salami, measured in feet. Thus, all tuna flows form a set with addition; all milk flows do too; all salami flows do too.

Examples of sets *without* addition are the group U of units, the set E^2 of locations in the plane, and the set T of instants. It is easy to see why: you can't add 2 feet to 3 gallons; you can't add the location (3,4) to the location (5,1); you can't add 3 P.M. to 2 A.M.

Although the plane E^2 is not equipped with addition, a closely related set is. Picture a man standing at the point $\mathbf{x} \in E^2$, and then moving to the point $\mathbf{x}_1 \in E^2$. His move, or *displacement* as it is called, can be represented by an arrow $\mathbf{v}$ beginning at $\mathbf{x}$ and ending at $\mathbf{x}_1$. One naturally writes $\mathbf{x} + \mathbf{v} = \mathbf{x}_1$. Suppose the man next moves to $\mathbf{x}_2$, a displacement represented by arrow $\mathbf{v}_1$. The sum of his two displacements, $\mathbf{v} + \mathbf{v}_1$, is a move in its own right, from $\mathbf{x}$ to $\mathbf{x}_2$. More formally, the set of displacements in the plane is a set with addition. You know this set—it is R^2.

The set T of instants is related to the set D of *time flows* in the same way that E^2 is related to R^2. If it is $\mathbf{t} = 3$ P.M. now and an hour passes ($\mathbf{d} = 1h$), the time will be $\mathbf{t}_1 = 4$ P.M. The time flow $\mathbf{d}$ is thus a displacement on the time axis, satisfying $\mathbf{t} + \mathbf{d} = \mathbf{t}_1$. If two more hours pass ($\mathbf{d}_1 = 2h$), the time will be $\mathbf{t}_2 = 6$ P.M. The sum of the two time flows, $\mathbf{d} + \mathbf{d}_1$, is a time flow in its own right, from $\mathbf{t}$ to $\mathbf{t}_2$. As this illustrates, D is a set with addition.

MT 4

The third and last algebraic operation is multiplication by a scalar. A set is called a *set with scalar multiplication* if (*a*) each of its elements can be multiplied by any scalar, and (*b*) all thereby obtained scalar multiples also belong to the set. Property (*b*) is usually expressed by saying that the set is closed under scalar multiplication.

The sets of dollar flows, tuna flows, milk flows, and salami flows are all sets with scalar multiplication. For instance, the product of the dollar flow $-2d$ and the scalar 3 is $-6d$, which is again a dollar flow. Another set with scalar multiplication is R^2: the product of the displacement $\mathbf{v}$ and the scalar 2 is $2\mathbf{v}$, which is again a displacement. (As you know, $2\mathbf{v}$ points in the same direction as $\mathbf{v}$ and is twice as long as $\mathbf{v}$.) Still another set with scalar multiplication is D, the set of time flows: if $\mathbf{d}$ represents one hour from now, $-4\mathbf{d}$ represents four hours ago.

Examples of sets *without* scalar multiplication are the set T of instants and the set E^2 of locations in the plane. It is, after all, meaningless to multiply the instant 3 P.M. by 2, and equally meaningless to multiply the location (5,−4) by 3.

MT 5

An *algebraic system* is a set equipped with at least one of the three operations just discussed. There are thus seven main types of algebraic system—three with only one operation, three with two operations, and one with three operations. Since each algebraic operation has several definitions, each of the seven main types has several subtypes.

Some of the seven main types are important enough to have names of their own. A set with multiplication is called a *multiplicative group.* A set with addition is an *additive group.* A set with multiplication and addition is a *ring.* A set with addition and scalar multiplication is a *vector space.* A set with all three operations is an *algebra.*

A set without any of the three operations is often called a *point set,* for emphasis. Its elements are called *points.* Thus, E^2 is a point set, and locations are points; T is a point set, and instants are points.

In economics, the most important algebraic systems are vector spaces. Examples of vector spaces are the set of dollar flows, the set of tuna flows, the set D, and the set R^2. Dollar flows are thus vectors, as are tuna flows, time flows, and displacements in the plane.

MT 6

Because of their importance, vector spaces deserve a more detailed discussion.

In this book, every vector is either a column, of $n \geq 1$ elements, or an arrow. To simplify, arrows will be treated as merely pictures of columns, rather than as vectors in their own right. Effectively then, every vector in this book is a column.

Columns are often written as transposed rows, to save space. An example is $(3f, 2g)'$, which looks like a row but is actually a column.

You know how to add columns: $(3f, 2g, -3h)' + (1f, -3g, 5h)' = (4f, -1g, 2h)'$, for instance. Addition is possible here because the two column-vectors on the left have the same number of elements *and* every two corresponding elements on the left are dimensioned the same way. If either condition is not met, addition is impossible. Thus, the sum of a 2-vector and a 3-vector is undefined, and so is the sum of $(3f, 2g, -3h)'$ and $(1f, -4h, 5g)'$.

Some vector spaces are easy to visualize. Imagine a line, with origin O; all arrows that begin at O and end at some point on the line are pictures of 1-vectors forming a vector space. Imagine a plane, with origin O; all arrows that begin at O and end at some point of the plane are pictures of 2-vectors forming a vector space. Imagine a universe like the one in which we live, with origin O; all arrows that begin at O and end at some point of the universe are pictures of 3-vectors forming a vector space.

The collection of all one-coordinate points is called a line, or the line. The collection of all 1-vectors is also called a line, or the line. Context will have to make clear which interpretation is intended. In the same way, context determines whether a plane is a collection of two-element columns (each pictured as an arrow) or a collection of points. In a world of dimensionless coordinates and elements, there is another way to put this: context determines whether "line" means R^1 or E^1, and whether "plane" means R^2 or E^2.

When a line (or plane, etc.) is viewed as a set of points, it has an *origin*, O. When a line (or plane, etc.) is viewed as a set of vectors, it does not have an origin. Instead it has a *null vector,* written $\mathbf{0}$. It should be added, though, that a null vector is often called an origin.

Is E^1 a subset of E^2? At first glance, the answer seems to be yes. The mind's eye conjures up a picture of E^2, as a plane with an x-axis and a y-axis, and it is natural to think that the x-axis is E^1. But looking at the question algebraically shows otherwise. Every point in E^1 has only one coordinate. Every point in E^2 has two coordinates. (Even the points on the x-axis. They all have a zero second coordinate.) Evidently then, E^1 and E^2 have no points in common, so that E^1 cannot be a subset of E^2. The same reasoning shows that R^1 is not a subset of R^2.

But there is something else. In a picture of R^2, imagine a straight line L going through the origin (strictly: containing the null vector). It is easy to see, and easy to verify algebraically, that L is closed under addition and scalar multiplication. Thus, L is a vector space, like R^1; and L is a line, like R^1. Yet L cannot be R^1, for R^1 consists of 1-vectors whereas L is made up of 2-vectors. One says that the line L is a *subspace* of R^2. Here is the definition: W is a subspace of a vector space V if W is both a subset of V and a vector space.

Every vector space has a *dimension*. (The term has nothing to do with the dimensioning of quantities.) The formal definition is surprisingly intricate, but the following informal description is good enough for our purposes. Every vector space pictured as a line is said to have dimension 1, or to be one-dimensional. Thus, R^1 has dimension 1. So does the subspace L described above. So does any line through the origin of R^5. Every vector space pictured as a plane has dimension 2, or is two-dimensional. Thus, R^2 has dimension 2. So does any plane through the origin of R^3, or of R^{20}. The vector space R^7, which consists of *all* columns of 7 real elements, has dimension 7. A vector space V consisting of *some* columns of 7 real elements is a subspace of R^7; its dimension is less than 7. If, for instance, V is congruent with R^3, its dimension is 3.

A vector space can consist of a single vector, but this is of mostly mathematical interest. In this book, all vector spaces have more than one vector.

As soon as a vector space has more than one vector, it has infinitely many. There is no middle ground; vector spaces with just two or three vectors do not exist. Geometrically this is obvious: there are infinitely many arrows on a line, infinitely many arrows in a plane, and so on. For a less intuitive demonstration, let V be any vector space with at least two vectors. At least one of these two vectors is not 0 dollars, nor 0 cans, nor 0 feet—in short, not null. Denote this vector by $\mathbf{v}$. Next, since V is a vector space, and therefore closed under scalar multiplication, V also contains all scalar multiples of $\mathbf{v}$, like $3\mathbf{v}$ and $-2\mathbf{v}$ and $\frac{1}{2}\mathbf{v}$ and $0\mathbf{v}$ $(= \mathbf{0})$. There are infinitely many such scalar multiples, and they are all different because $\mathbf{v}$ is not null. But then V contains infinitely many vectors. P.O.C.

The preceding paragraph harbors an essential piece of information. It is that *every vector space contains a null vector.* Here is the reasoning again: if V is any vector space and $\mathbf{v}$ is any vector in V, all scalar multiples of $\mathbf{v}$ are also in V; one of those scalar multiples is $0\mathbf{v} = \mathbf{0}$; therefore V contains a null vector. The converse does not hold: a set containing a null vector need not be a vector space. For a proof, take a set consisting of $\mathbf{0}$ and one other object.

Since every vector space contains a null vector, any line in R^2 that does not go through the origin (strictly: does not contain the null vector) cannot possibly be a vector space, let alone a subspace. Similarly, lines and planes in R^3 are subspaces of R^3 if and only if they go through the origin.

Is $5d$ a vector? It depends. The answer is yes if the $5d$ is a dollar flow and no if the $5d$ is a dollar stock. A general point is illustrated here: *Whether any given object is a vector is impossible to tell from its appearance.* The only way to find out if some object is a vector is, first, to determine to what set the object belongs and, next, to determine whether that set is a vector space. The right question is thus not "Is this object a vector?" but "Is this set a vector space?"

MT 7

Algebraic systems and point sets are the theorist's Lego blocks. By combining them in various ways, the model builder erects his theoretical edifice. A particularly potent combination is the *point space.*

Definition. A *point space* is a pair $\{X,V\}$ in which X is a point set, V is a vector space, and the vectors in V are the displacements in X.

The best-known point space is $\{E^2,R^2\}$. Not surprisingly, $\{E^n,R^n\}$ is a point space for every $n \geq 1$. Another point space is $\{T,D\}$, where T is the point set of instants and D is the vector space of time flows.

In the old days, points in X were often called "bound vectors." For contrast, vectors in V were "free vectors." The terminology is no longer widely used.

The heart of Model One is a point space, written $\{X,A\}$. To explain what X and A mean, define E^n_+ to be the nonnegative orthant of E^n (so that E^2_+ is the nonnegative quadrant of E^2). It is easy to see that $\{E^n_+,R^n\}$ is a point space. When measurement units are added, $\{E^n_+,R^n\}$ becomes our $\{X,A\}$. More precisely, points in X, called *endowments*, have dimensioned coordinates (interpretable as commodity stocks) but are otherwise indistinguishable from points in E^n_+; vectors in A, called *actions*, have dimensioned elements (interpretable as commodity flows) but are otherwise indistinguishable from vectors in R^n. Of course, endowment coordinates and action elements must be dimensioned correspondingly. If, for instance, an endowment's third coordinate is measured in gallons, an action's third element must be measured in gallons too.

Being a vector space, A contains a null vector. Since vectors in A are actions, $\mathbf{0} \in A$ is an action, even if by interpretation it represents inactivity.

Endowments, being points, cannot be added. Thus, if John and Joan decide to get married and pool their possessions, we may not regard their combined endowment as the sum of their individual endowments. What we can say is that Joan views the combined endowment as the sum of her endowment (a point in X) and what John contributed (a vector in A). John, of course, may view the couple's endowment as the sum of *his* endowment and *Joan's* contribution.

Sets X and A will be called the *endowment set* and the *action space.* Endowments are written $\mathbf{x}$, $\mathbf{x}_1$, and the like. Actions are written $\mathbf{a}$, $\mathbf{a}_1$, and the like.

The reason that point spaces are the ideal mathematical tool for our purposes lies in their joint emphasis on status quo (X) and change of status quo (V). It matches out joint emphasis on stocks and flows, endowments and actions. Later chapters have further details.

Consider again the man who makes the move $\mathbf{v}$ to get from $\mathbf{x} \in E^2$ to $\mathbf{x}_1 \in E^2$. This was written as $\mathbf{x} + \mathbf{v} = \mathbf{x}_1$. Strikingly, the left side calls for addition across sets: $\mathbf{x}$, which is a point in E^2, is added to $\mathbf{v}$, which is a vector in R^2. What is more, the sum, $\mathbf{x}_1$, is again a point in E^2.

Equivalent to $\mathbf{x} + \mathbf{v} = \mathbf{x}_1$ is $\mathbf{x}_1 - \mathbf{x} = \mathbf{v}$. Subtracting one point from another is thus apparently allowed. This is not to say that E^2 is a set with subtraction. For one thing, E^2 is not closed under subtraction, seeing that the difference of two points is not a point but a vector (in this case, $\mathbf{v}$).

Points are traditionally written as rows. When points are added to vectors, as they are wherever point spaces are found, it is handier to write them as columns, or transposed rows. The point $\mathbf{x} \in E^n$ is then $(x_1,x_2, \ldots ,x_n)'$ rather than $(x_1,x_2, \ldots ,x_n)$. Of course, writing $\mathbf{x}$ as a column does not make it a vector. Whether written as a row or as a column, upside down or in a circle, **x** continues to be a point, continues to belong to E^n. Appearance does not matter. The phrase "**x** belongs to E^n" is the crucial thing.

MT 8

Many vector spaces play a role in this book. Most prominent are R^n, A, A^0, V, and V^0. You know what R^n is. Discussion of the other four follows.

First, A, the action space. Vectors in A, written $\mathbf{a}$, $\mathbf{a}_1$, and the like, are columns of dimensioned elements, each element interpretable as a commodity flow. If good 1 is beer, measured in bottles (b), if good 2 is tuna, measured in cans (c), and if good 3 is money, measured in dollars (d), a typical action would be $(2b, 3c, -7d, \ldots)'$. If you would rather let good 1 be cornflakes, good 2 picture frames, and good 3 umbrellas, fine; but once you have arranged the n goods in the order you prefer, and once you have picked their measurement units, be sure to stick to your choices. Changing either the order or a unit in the middle of the story creates all sorts of confusion and despondency.

Being a vector space, A is closed under addition and scalar multiplication. The sum of any two actions is thus an action, and every scalar multiple of an action is an action too. For an illustration, suppose $\mathbf{a}_1$ is the action "buying a bottle of beer," and $\mathbf{a}_2$ is "buying a can of tuna." Buying two bottles of beer is then $2\mathbf{a}_1$, which is a scalar multiple of $\mathbf{a}_1$ and therefore an action in its own right. Buying three cans of tuna is $3\mathbf{a}_2$, also an action, and for the same reason. Buying two bottles of beer as well as three cans of tuna is the linear combination $2\mathbf{a}_1 + 3\mathbf{a}_2$, which, being the sum of two actions, is itself an action. "Buying beer" is not an action/vector, its length being indeterminate. (Should the need arise, you could identify "buying beer" with "$c\mathbf{a}_1$ for any c." This would make "buying beer" a one-dimensional subspace of A, that is, a line.)

Let the prices of beer, tuna, money, . . . be measured in d/b, d/c, d/d $(= 1)$, ... Obviously, the price vector $\mathbf{p}$ does not belong to A. For one thing, you cannot add $\mathbf{p}$ to any $\mathbf{a} \in A$. What you can do, however, is "multiply $\mathbf{p}$ into $\mathbf{a}$," that is, form $\mathbf{p}'\mathbf{a}$. The outcome, $p_1a_1 + p_2a_2 + \cdots$, is a dollar amount. Consider now all n-element columns whose elements are dimensioned like those of $\mathbf{p}$. It is easy to see that the set of such columns is a vector space. That vector space is called a *dual space* of A.

Another dual space of A is the set of all n-element columns whose elements are measured in g/b, g/c, g/d, ... Any column of this type can be multiplied into any $\mathbf{a} \in A$. The outcome is a certain number of gallons.

You can see where this is going: the action space A has infinitely many dual spaces, one for each unit in the units group U. There is thus a dual space associated with the dollar, another dual space associated with the gallon, and so on.

Since 1 is one of the units in U, there is a dual space associated with 1, as well. This is the *main dual space* of A, denoted A^0. Vectors in A^0 are written $\mathbf{a}^0$, $\mathbf{a}_1{}^0$, and the like. A typical vector in A^0 is $\mathbf{a}^0 = (2/b, -3/c, 5/d, \ldots)'$.

Because of the differences in units, you will never find a picture showing both a vector in A and a vector in A^0.

Remaining to be defined are V and V^0. Whereas R^n, A, and A^0 are specific vector spaces, V is a generic one. A statement concerning V is a statement that holds for all vector spaces consisting of columns. The space V^0 is the main dual space of V. Thus, if $\mathbf{v}$ is any vector in V and $\mathbf{v}^0$ is any vector in V^0, then $\mathbf{v}'\mathbf{v}^0$ is real. Linear–algebraists use a more sophisticated definition, but this one is good enough for our purposes.

It is easy to see that the main dual space of V^0 is V, and that the main dual space of R^n is R^n itself.

Returning to A^0, suppose, for the sake of illustration, that A^0 has dimension 2. A typical vector in A^0 is then $\mathbf{a}^0 = (2/b, -3/c)'$. For another vector in A^0, a more important one this time, let the utility function be $u(\mathbf{x}) = u(x_1,x_2)$, and suppose that u is real-valued, rather than measured in utils. As before, goods 1 and 2 are beer and tuna, measured in bottles (b) and cans (c).

By definition, $\partial u(\mathbf{x})/\partial x_1$ is the limit, as Δx_1 goes to $0b$, of $[u(x_1 + \Delta x_1, x_2) - u(x_1, x_2)]/\Delta x_1$. In this quotient, the numerator is a real number (since it is the difference of two real numbers), and the denominator is measured in b. The marginal utility of beer is thus measured in $1/b$. It goes without arguing that the marginal utility of tuna is measured in $1/c$. The vector of marginal utilities, called the *gradient* of u and written $\nabla u(\mathbf{x})$ or ∇u, is thus a vector in A^0:

$$\nabla u(\mathbf{x}) = \begin{pmatrix} \partial u/\partial x_1 \\ \partial u/\partial x_2 \end{pmatrix} \in A^0.$$

Another way to put it is that $\mathbf{a}'\nabla u$ is real for every $\mathbf{a} \in A$.

MT 9

A *matrix* is by definition a rectangular array of dimensionless quantities. Strictly then, arrays of dimensioned quantities should not be called matrices, although in economics they often are. Take the technology matrix $\mathbf{A}$ of activity analysis. Its columns are vectors in the action space A, so that its elements are dimensioned. But then $\mathbf{A}$ is merely an array, not a matrix.

The same conclusion holds for the Hessian matrix of the utility function u: since the second-order partial derivatives of u are dimensioned, the Hessian matrix of u is actually an array, not a matrix. The same holds again for the observation matrix $\mathbf{X}$ of regression analysis. Arrays like these behave like matrices in some ways, but not in all.

Still, economic and econometric experience convincingly demonstrates that applying matrix algebra to nonmatrix arrays works very well, so long as you keep an eye out for possible existence trouble. With that proviso in mind, this book treats arrays as matrices. It also calls them matrices—usually. When, from time to time, a "matrix" is called an array, it is to stress that its elements are dimensioned.

MT 10

To give some idea of the ways in which arrays do behave like matrices, and also of the ways in which they do not, let $\mathbf{a}_1$, $\mathbf{a}_2$, and $\mathbf{a}_3$ be actions, vectors in A. Form the $n \times 3$ array $\mathbf{A}$ with the three actions as columns: $\mathbf{A} = (\mathbf{a}_1,\mathbf{a}_2,\mathbf{a}_3)$. The linear combination $\mathbf{a}_1c_1 + \mathbf{a}_2c_2 + \mathbf{a}_3c_3$, with the c_i real, can be written as $\mathbf{Ac}$. More generally, *the product of an array (or matrix) and a column of real numbers, in that order, can be viewed as a linear combination of the columns of the array (or matrix).* This is not a deep mathematical fact. It is merely a handy rule to remember.

Setting $\mathbf{Ac}$ equal to some action $\mathbf{b} \in A$ gives $\mathbf{Ac} = \mathbf{b}$, a linear system in $\mathbf{c}$. Regarding the number of solutions of $\mathbf{Ac} = \mathbf{b}$, there are three possibilities: the system has (*i*) one solution, (*ii*) no solution, or (*iii*) infinitely many solutions. In this respect, $\mathbf{Ac} = \mathbf{b}$ is exactly like a linear system in which all quantities are dimensionless.

System $\mathbf{Ac} = \mathbf{b}$ is *consistent* if it has one solution or infinitely many solutions, and *inconsistent* if it has no solution.

System $\mathbf{Ac} = \mathbf{b}$ is *homogeneous* if $\mathbf{b} = \mathbf{0}$ (that is, $\mathbf{0} \in A$, of course, not $\mathbf{0} \in R^n$), and *inhomogeneous* otherwise. A homogeneous system always has *at least* one solution, namely, $\mathbf{c} = \mathbf{0}$. A homogeneous system is thus always consistent.

If $\mathbf{Ac} = \mathbf{0}$ has *exactly* one solution (which must then be $\mathbf{c} = \mathbf{0}$), vectors $\mathbf{a}_1$, $\mathbf{a}_2$, and $\mathbf{a}_3$ are said to be *linearly independent*, and array $\mathbf{A}$ is said to have *full column rank*. If $\mathbf{Ac} = \mathbf{0}$ has infinitely many solutions, the $\mathbf{a}_i$ are *linearly dependent*. Thus, if you are given three numerically specified vectors $\mathbf{a}_1$, $\mathbf{a}_2$, and $\mathbf{a}_3$, columns of $\mathbf{A}$, and you are asked whether they are linearly independent or linearly dependent, you set up the homogeneous system $\mathbf{Ac} = \mathbf{0}$ and find out how many solutions it has. The solutions themselves do not matter. Only their number (1 or ∞) is important.

Ordinarily it takes a good bit of work to solve a linear system. In particular, it ordinarily takes a good bit of work to determine if the columns of a numerically given **A**, whether matrix or array, are linearly dependent or linearly independent. But there is one case in which you know the answer right away. If **A** is "low"—that is, has more columns than rows—the system $\mathbf{Ac} = \mathbf{0}$ *always* has infinitely many solutions. The columns of such an **A** are thus *always* linearly dependent. Or: a low **A** never has full column rank.

MT 11

The next two facts are given without proof. You probably know them.

Let **A** be a matrix, rather than just an array, and suppose its columns are linearly independent. Then:

(i) If **A** is square, $\mathbf{A}^{-1}$ exists.
(ii) If **A** is tall (has more rows than columns), $\mathbf{A}^{-1}$ does not exist, but $(\mathbf{A}'\mathbf{A})^{-1}$ does. Also, the determinant of $\mathbf{A}'\mathbf{A}$ is positive in that case.

If the columns of **A** are linearly dependent, $\mathbf{A}^{-1}$ does not exist, and neither does $(\mathbf{A}'\mathbf{A})^{-1}$.

MT 12

Let V be any vector space, of dimension n. A *basis* for V is a collection $\{\mathbf{v}_1, \mathbf{v}_2, \ldots, \mathbf{v}_n\}$ of n linearly independent vectors in V. For an intuitive explanation, take $n = 2$, so that V is a plane. Think of $\mathbf{v}_1$ and $\mathbf{v}_2$ as arrows. Both arrows can be extended infinitely far, in both directions, to become lines. Because $\mathbf{v}_1$ and $\mathbf{v}_2$ are linearly independent, the two lines do not coincide. They—the lines—can thus be used as coordinate axes for the plane V, which is the whole idea behind the notion of a basis. You might say that a basis is a coordinate system in kit form.

Given any plane, *any* two lines can serve as coordinate axes, so long as they do not coincide. They do not even have to be perpendicular. A two-dimensional vector space thus has infinitely many bases. No basis is mathematically superior to any other. Sometimes you come across a basis that is unusually handy to work with, but that is a practical advantage, not a theoretical one. The way it usually goes is that you pick one basis and ignore the others.

For an example, suppose you live in a world with only two goods, beer and tuna. If you measure beer in bottles and tuna in cans, an obvious basis is the one that consists of the two vectors $(1b,0c)'$ and $(0b,1c)'$. Someone else, working on the same problem as you, could well prefer a different basis. Suppose he regards tuna as the first good, beer as the second; suppose he measures tuna in kilograms (k), beer in gallons (g). To him, it will probably seem most natural to choose $(1k,0g)'$ and $(0k,1g)'$ as basis vectors. The point is that his basis choice is as respectable as yours. After you finish your research and he finishes his, you may find it cumbersome to compare results, but that is as bad as it gets.

Be sure not to confuse vector spaces with their bases. A vector space consists of vectors, and so does a basis; but that does not make them the same. For one thing, the typical vector space has infinitely many vectors, and the typical basis has only a few. Every basis for R^2, for instance, has only two vectors in it, reflecting that if you want to impose order on a plane by putting a coordinate system on it, two coordinate axes are all you need.

MT 13

Back to the action space A. Let A have dimension n, let $\{\mathbf{a}_1, \mathbf{a}_2, \ldots, \mathbf{a}_n\}$ be a basis for A, and let $\mathbf{A}$ be the $n \times n$ matrix with the $\mathbf{a}_i$ as columns. We shall call $\mathbf{A}$ a *basis matrix for A*. You won't find the term in linear-algebra texts, and with good reason: having dimensioned elements, $\mathbf{A}$ is merely an array, not a matrix.

Let $\{\mathbf{a}_1{}^0, \mathbf{a}_2{}^0, \ldots, \mathbf{a}_n{}^0\}$ be a basis for A's main dual space A^0, and let the $\mathbf{a}_i{}^0$ be the columns of a matrix $\mathbf{A}^0$. Then $\mathbf{A}^0$ is a basis matrix for A^0. Also, all elements of $\mathbf{A}^{0\prime}\mathbf{A}$ are real.

If $\mathbf{A}^{0\prime}\mathbf{A} = \mathbf{I}$, the two bases are called *dual bases*, and $\mathbf{A}^0$, $\mathbf{A}$ are *dual-basis matrices*. Had the elements of $\mathbf{A}$ been real, $\mathbf{A}^{0\prime}$ would have been $\mathbf{A}^{-1}$.

MT 14

Nonstandard inner products are next.

The standard inner product of vectors $\mathbf{a}$ and $\mathbf{b}$ is $\mathbf{a}'\mathbf{b}$. It is a definition that works well in some vector spaces, but not in all. For instance, it works well in R^n, but if $\mathbf{a}$ and $\mathbf{b}$ belong to the action space A, $\mathbf{a}'\mathbf{b}$ does not exist. We therefore need a more general definition, a nonstandard definition.

As you will see, the definition below is uncommonly generous: it says that there exist, for every vector space V, infinitely many inner products. And so you will probably want to know, the next time that you tackle a concrete application, which of these infinitely many inner products you should choose.

Mathematics has only a partial answer to that question, but the partial answer is usually good enough. First, many theoretical results hold for every inner product, saving you from the need to choose. Second, when choosing cannot be avoided, there is often one inner product that stands out as the handiest choice, or the most natural choice. On R^n, for example, infinitely many inner products are defined, but the obvious choice is the standard one. It is only when you must choose *and* there is no obvious choice that mathematics tells you you are on your own.

To define nonstandard inner products we must go back, briefly, to R^n and the standard inner product $\mathbf{a}'\mathbf{b}$.

Let $\mathbf{a}$, $\mathbf{b}$, and $\mathbf{c}$ be arbitrary vectors in R^n, and let λ be an arbitrary scalar. Then, as you probably know but can easily verify,

(*a*) $\mathbf{a}'\mathbf{b} = \mathbf{b}'\mathbf{a}$
(*b*) $\mathbf{a}'(\mathbf{b} + \mathbf{c}) = \mathbf{a}'\mathbf{b} + \mathbf{a}'\mathbf{c}$
(*c*) $(\lambda\mathbf{a})'\mathbf{b} = \lambda(\mathbf{a}'\mathbf{b})$ for every scalar λ
(*d*) $\mathbf{a}'\mathbf{a}$ is zero if $\mathbf{a} = \mathbf{0}$, and positive otherwise.

Writing down these four properties is the first step toward the definition sought: mathematics says that you can define "inner product" any way you want, so long as properties (*a*)–(*d*) hold. Formalization follows.

Definition. Let V be any vector space. A function $(\cdot,\cdot): V \times V \to R$ is an *inner product* on V if for all $\mathbf{a}, \mathbf{b}, \mathbf{c} \in V$ and all scalars λ

(*a'*) $(\mathbf{a},\mathbf{b}) = (\mathbf{b},\mathbf{a})$
(*b'*) $(\mathbf{a},\mathbf{b} + \mathbf{c}) = (\mathbf{a},\mathbf{b}) + (\mathbf{a},\mathbf{c})$
(*c'*) $(\lambda\mathbf{a},\mathbf{b}) = \lambda(\mathbf{a},\mathbf{b})$
(*d'*) $(\mathbf{a},\mathbf{a})$ is zero if $\mathbf{a} = \mathbf{0}$, and positive otherwise.

To illustrate, let $\mathbf{H}$ be a symmetric, positive-definite matrix. (Symmetry of $\mathbf{H}$ means $\mathbf{H} = \mathbf{H}'$. Positive definiteness of $\mathbf{H}$ means that $\mathbf{a}'\mathbf{H}\mathbf{a}$ is positive for all nonnull $\mathbf{a}$.) To postpone worries about units, let $V = R^n$ for the moment. Next, define $(\mathbf{a},\mathbf{b}) = \mathbf{a}'\mathbf{H}\mathbf{b}$. We verify that the so-defined $(\mathbf{a},\mathbf{b})$ has the four properties.

(*a'*) To be proved is that $(\mathbf{a},\mathbf{b}) = (\mathbf{b},\mathbf{a})$ or $\mathbf{a}'\mathbf{H}\mathbf{b} = \mathbf{b}'\mathbf{H}\mathbf{a}$. Think of $\mathbf{a}'\mathbf{H}\mathbf{b}$ as a 1×1 matrix. Such a matrix equals its transpose, $\mathbf{b}'\mathbf{H}'\mathbf{a}$. By the symmetry of $\mathbf{H}$, this equals $\mathbf{b}'\mathbf{H}\mathbf{a}$.
(*b'*) To be proved is that $(\mathbf{a},\mathbf{b} + \mathbf{c}) = (\mathbf{a},\mathbf{b}) + (\mathbf{a},\mathbf{c})$, or $\mathbf{a}'\mathbf{H}(\mathbf{b} + \mathbf{c}) = \mathbf{a}'\mathbf{H}\mathbf{b} + \mathbf{a}'\mathbf{H}\mathbf{c}$. This is a familiar matrix-algebraic proposition.
(*c'*) To be proved is that $(\lambda\mathbf{a},\mathbf{b}) = \lambda(\mathbf{a},\mathbf{b})$, or $(\lambda\mathbf{a})'\mathbf{H}\mathbf{b} = \lambda(\mathbf{a}'\mathbf{H}\mathbf{b})$. This too is familiar.
(*d'*) To be proved is that $\mathbf{a}'\mathbf{H}\mathbf{a}$ is zero if $\mathbf{a} = \mathbf{0}$, and positive otherwise. The first part is obvious. The second part follows from the positive definiteness of $\mathbf{H}$.

Shown next is that, with one proviso, *every* inner product $(\mathbf{a},\mathbf{b})$ can be written in the form $\mathbf{a}'\mathbf{H}\mathbf{b}$ for some symmetric, positive-definite $\mathbf{H}$. The proviso is that we must allow the *inner-product matrix* **H** to have dimensioned elements, to be an array rather than a matrix. (Linear algebra does not allow that, and so you won't find the equation $(\mathbf{a},\mathbf{b}) = \mathbf{a}'\mathbf{H}\mathbf{b}$ anywhere in the mathematical literature.) For simplicity, we take V to have dimension $n = 2$, but the proof goes the same way for arbitrary n.

When $n = 2$, any basis for V consists of two vectors. Suppose a basis has been chosen. Let the vectors in this basis be $\mathbf{v}_1$ and $\mathbf{v}_2$, columns of the basis matrix $\mathbf{V}$. Then $\mathbf{a} = \lambda_1\mathbf{v}_1 + \lambda_2\mathbf{v}_2 = \mathbf{V}\boldsymbol{\lambda}$ for some real $\boldsymbol{\lambda} = (\lambda_1, \lambda_2)'$, and $\mathbf{b} = \mu_1\mathbf{v}_1 + \mu_2\mathbf{v}_2 = \mathbf{V}\boldsymbol{\mu}$ for some real $\boldsymbol{\mu} = (\mu_1, \mu_2)'$. Now $(\mathbf{a},\mathbf{b}) = (\mathbf{a},\mu_1\mathbf{v}_1 + \mu_2\mathbf{v}_2)$

$= (\mathbf{a},\mu_1\mathbf{v}_1) + (\mathbf{a},\mu_2\mathbf{v}_2)$ by property (b'),
$= (\mu_1\mathbf{v}_1,\mathbf{a}) + (\mu_2\mathbf{v}_2,\mathbf{a})$ by property (a'),
$= \mu_1(\mathbf{v}_1,\mathbf{a}) + \mu_2(\mathbf{v}_2,\mathbf{a})$ by property (c'),
$= \mu_1(\mathbf{v}_1,\lambda_1\mathbf{v}_1 + \lambda_2\mathbf{v}_2) + \mu_2(\mathbf{v}_2,\lambda_1\mathbf{v}_1 + \lambda_2\mathbf{v}_2)$ by substitution for $\mathbf{a}$,
$= \mu_1(\mathbf{v}_1,\lambda_1\mathbf{v}_1) + \mu_1(\mathbf{v}_1,\lambda_2\mathbf{v}_2) + \mu_2(\mathbf{v}_2,\lambda_1\mathbf{v}_1) + \mu_2(\mathbf{v}_2,\lambda_2\mathbf{v}_2)$
by property (b'),
$= \mu_1(\lambda_1\mathbf{v}_1,\mathbf{v}_1) + \mu_1(\lambda_2\mathbf{v}_2,\mathbf{v}_1) + \mu_2(\lambda_1\mathbf{v}_1,\mathbf{v}_2) + \mu_2(\lambda_2\mathbf{v}_2,\mathbf{v}_2)$
by property (a'),
$= \lambda_1\mu_1(\mathbf{v}_1,\mathbf{v}_1) + \lambda_2\mu_1(\mathbf{v}_2,\mathbf{v}_1) + \lambda_1\mu_2(\mathbf{v}_1,\mathbf{v}_2) + \lambda_2\mu_2(\mathbf{v}_2,\mathbf{v}_2)$
by property (c'),

$$= \boldsymbol{\lambda}'\mathbf{K}\boldsymbol{\mu} \quad \text{with } \mathbf{K} = \begin{pmatrix} (\mathbf{v}_1,\mathbf{v}_1) & (\mathbf{v}_1,\mathbf{v}_2) \\ (\mathbf{v}_2,\mathbf{v}_1) & (\mathbf{v}_2,\mathbf{v}_2) \end{pmatrix}, \tag{1}$$

$= \boldsymbol{\lambda}'(\mathbf{V}'\mathbf{V}^0)\mathbf{K}(\mathbf{V}^{0\prime}\mathbf{V})\boldsymbol{\mu}$, where $\mathbf{V}^0$ is $\mathbf{V}$'s dual-basis matrix
(so that $\mathbf{V}'\mathbf{V}^0 = \mathbf{I}$),
$= (\boldsymbol{\lambda}'\mathbf{V}')(\mathbf{V}^0\mathbf{K}\mathbf{V}^{0\prime})(\mathbf{V}\boldsymbol{\mu})$,
$= \mathbf{a}'\mathbf{H}\mathbf{b}$, say, with

$$\mathbf{H} = \mathbf{V}^0\mathbf{K}\mathbf{V}^{0\prime}. \tag{2}$$

By property (a'), $(\mathbf{v}_1,\mathbf{v}_2) = (\mathbf{v}_2,\mathbf{v}_1)$, so that **K** is symmetric. By (2) then, **H** is symmetric. Finally, by property (d'), $(\mathbf{a},\mathbf{a}) = \mathbf{a}'\mathbf{H}\mathbf{a}$ is positive for all nonnull **a**, and so **H** is positive definite. P.O.C.

The proof gives rise to three remarks.

First, the argument is mathematically legitimate up to and including (1). Only after (1) do arrays enter the story.

Second, because the inner product is real-valued, all elements of **K** are real. Not so the elements of **H**. Seeing that the elements of the columns of $\mathbf{V}^0$ are measured in $1/b$ and $1/c$, you can easily verify that the diagonal elements of **H** are measured in $1/b^2$ and $1/c^2$, and that the off-diagonal elements are measured in $1/bc$.

Third, if in some economic application you find that you need to specify **H**, it may seem that setting $\mathbf{H} = \mathbf{I}$ is the most natural choice. Note, though, that the diagonal elements of this **I** are *dimensioned* 1's (they are $1/b^2$ and $1/c^2$), and the off-diagonal elements are *dimensioned* 0's (both are $0/bc$). Consider now what happens if we change the measurement units from bottles (b) to gallons (g) and from cans (c) to kilograms (k). If $1g = 10.68b$ and $1k = 5.04c$, the diagonal elements change to $(10.68/g)^2$ and $(5.04/k)^2$. The off-diagonal elements remain (dimensioned) zeros, but the harm has been done: the inner-product matrix is no longer **I**. Setting $\mathbf{H} = \mathbf{I}$ is thus not a natural choice after all. (Setting $\mathbf{K} = \mathbf{I}$ is. But that does not specify **H** uniquely.)

On V's main dual space V^0, too, we have infinitely many inner products to choose from. Given, however, that the inner product on V has matrix $\mathbf{H} = \mathbf{V}^0\mathbf{K}\mathbf{V}^{0\prime}$—see (2)—one of those infinitely many choices immediately becomes the most natural one. It is the inner product with matrix $\mathbf{H}^{-1} = \mathbf{V}\mathbf{K}^{-1}\mathbf{V}'$. To see what is so natural about this, let **a** and **b** belong to V. Then $\mathbf{a}'\mathbf{H}\mathbf{b}$ is real, implying $\mathbf{Hb} \in V^0$. Of course, $\mathbf{Ha} \in V^0$ too. With $\mathbf{H}^{-1}$ as the inner-product matrix on V^0, we find the inner product of **Ha** and **Hb** (in V^0) to be $(\mathbf{Ha})'\mathbf{H}^{-1}(\mathbf{Hb}) = \mathbf{a}'\mathbf{H}\mathbf{b}$, the same as the inner product of **a** and **b** (in V).

Characterizing the array $\mathbf{V}\mathbf{K}^{-1}\mathbf{V}'$ as $\mathbf{H}^{-1}$ is a bit dubious. True, the so-defined $\mathbf{H}^{-1}$ satisfies $\mathbf{H}\mathbf{H}^{-1} = \mathbf{I}$; but the **I** on the right has dimensioned elements. It underscores that arrays are tricky and need to be watched.

MT 15

The *standard norm* of vector **v** is $\|\mathbf{v}\| = \sqrt{\mathbf{v}'\mathbf{v}}$. Clearly, if **v** belongs to A, the standard norm is meaningless. We need a nonstandard norm.

Mathematics defines vector norms with great generality, but once an inner-product matrix **H** has been chosen, the generality becomes a matter of indifference. The reason is that the very act of choosing **H** elevates one norm above all others. This anointed norm is $\|\mathbf{v}\| = \sqrt{(\mathbf{v},\mathbf{v})}$, or

$$\|\mathbf{v}\| = \sqrt{\mathbf{v}'\mathbf{H}\mathbf{v}}.$$

MT 16

Picture a triangle OAB. Let its sides have lengths OA $= a$, OB $= b$, and AB $= c$, and abbreviate $\measuredangle$AOB as ϕ. A theorem in elementary geometry says that $c^2 = a^2 + b^2 - 2ab \cos \phi$. (When ϕ is a right angle, so that $\cos \phi$ is zero, the theorem reduces to the Pythagorean theorem.)

We can also construct $\triangle$OAB out of arrows: $\overrightarrow{\mathrm{OA}} = \mathbf{a}$, $\overrightarrow{\mathrm{OB}} = \mathbf{b}$, and $\overrightarrow{\mathrm{AB}} = \mathbf{b} - \mathbf{a}$. The theorem then becomes

$$\|\mathbf{b} - \mathbf{a}\|^2 = \|\mathbf{a}\|^2 + \|\mathbf{b}\|^2 - 2\|\mathbf{a}\| \cdot \|\mathbf{b}\|\cos\phi. \tag{3}$$

If **a** and **b** are vectors in R^n, Eq. (3) can be written as $(\mathbf{b} - \mathbf{a})'(\mathbf{b} - \mathbf{a}) = \mathbf{a}'\mathbf{a} + \mathbf{b}'\mathbf{b} - 2\|\mathbf{a}\| \cdot \|\mathbf{b}\|\cos\phi$. Since the left side equals $\mathbf{a}'\mathbf{a} - 2\mathbf{a}'\mathbf{b} + \mathbf{b}'\mathbf{b}$,

$$\mathbf{a}'\mathbf{b} = \|\mathbf{a}\| \cdot \|\mathbf{b}\|\cos\phi. \tag{4}$$

If **a** and **b** are vectors in a vector space with inner-product matrix **H**, Eq. (3) can be written as $(\mathbf{b} - \mathbf{a})'\mathbf{H}(\mathbf{b} - \mathbf{a}) = \mathbf{a}'\mathbf{H}\mathbf{a} + \mathbf{b}'\mathbf{H}\mathbf{b} - 2\|\mathbf{a}\| \cdot \|\mathbf{b}\|\cos\phi$. Simplifying as before gives

$$\mathbf{a}'\mathbf{H}\mathbf{b} = \|\mathbf{a}\| \cdot \|\mathbf{b}\|\cos\phi. \tag{5}$$

Appearance notwithstanding, the right sides of (4) and (5) are different. In (4), $\|\mathbf{a}\|$ and $\|\mathbf{b}\|$ mean $\sqrt{\mathbf{a}'\mathbf{a}}$ and $\sqrt{\mathbf{b}'\mathbf{b}}$; in (5), $\|\mathbf{a}\|$ and $\|\mathbf{b}\|$ mean $\sqrt{\mathbf{a}'\mathbf{H}\mathbf{a}}$ and $\sqrt{\mathbf{b}'\mathbf{H}\mathbf{b}}$.

MT 17

Equation (4) implies that if $\mathbf{a} \in R^n$ and $\mathbf{b} \in R^n$ are perpendicular or *orthogonal* ($\phi = 90°$), $\mathbf{a}'\mathbf{b}$ is zero. Equation (5) implies that if $\mathbf{a} \in V$ and $\mathbf{b} \in V$ are orthogonal, and the inner product on V has matrix **H**, then $\mathbf{a}'\mathbf{H}\mathbf{b}$ is zero. If, conversely, $\mathbf{a}'\mathbf{b} = 0$ (in R^n) or $\mathbf{a}'\mathbf{H}\mathbf{b} = 0$ (in V), it *could* mean that **a** and **b** are perpendicular; but it could also mean that $\mathbf{a} = \mathbf{0}$ or $\mathbf{b} = \mathbf{0}$ or both. By simplifying convention, mathematics declare **0** to be orthogonal to every vector. With that, we can unambiguously say that **a** and **b** are orthogonal whenever $\mathbf{a}'\mathbf{b} = 0$ (in R^n) or $\mathbf{a}'\mathbf{H}\mathbf{b} = 0$ (in V).

For most matrices **H**, vectors **a** and **b** satisfying $\mathbf{a}'\mathbf{H}\mathbf{b} = 0$ do not look perpendicular when sketched in a diagram. To illustrate, picture a two-dimensional V, and in it two arrows, **a** of length 2 and **b** of length 3, both affixed at **0** and forming a 45° angle ϕ. Or rather, picture **a** and **b** so that $\|\mathbf{a}\|$ would be 2, and $\|\mathbf{b}\|$ would be 3, and ϕ would be 45° if the inner product on V were the standard one. Now use **a** and **b** as basis vectors for V, and specify **K** in (2) as **I**. Setting $\mathbf{K} = \mathbf{I}$ means choosing $(\mathbf{a},\mathbf{a}) = (\mathbf{b},\mathbf{b}) = 1$ and $(\mathbf{a},\mathbf{b}) = 0$. In words, **a** and **b** both have unit length, and they are orthogonal—even if they look anything but.

The moral of the story is that for vector spaces with nonstandard inner products, sketches are no longer quite the useful guides to intuition that they used to be. You will fare better if you put less faith in your eyes and more faith in your formulas.

Let S be any set of vectors in V. One says that $\mathbf{a} \in V$ is orthogonal to S if **a** is orthogonal to every vector in S. To illustrate, picture a three-dimensional coordinate system, with a horizontal x-axis, a horizontal y-axis, and a vertical z-axis. If **a** lies along the z-axis and S is the floor of the diagram, **a** is orthogonal to S.

Vectors belonging to different vector spaces are never orthogonal. In particular, if $\mathbf{a} \in V$, $\mathbf{a}^0 \in V^0$, and $\mathbf{a}'\mathbf{a}^0 = 0$, it does not mean that $\mathbf{a}$ is orthogonal to $\mathbf{a}^0$. One says, rather, that $\mathbf{a}$ and $\mathbf{a}^0$ *annihilate* each other. The connection between annihilation and orthogonality is this: From $\mathbf{a}'\mathbf{a}^0 = 0$ follows $\mathbf{a}'\mathbf{H}(\mathbf{H}^{-1}\mathbf{a}^0) = 0$, which shows that $\mathbf{H}^{-1}\mathbf{a}^0$ belongs to A and is orthogonal to $\mathbf{a}$. From $\mathbf{a}^{0\prime}\mathbf{a} = 0$ also follows $\mathbf{a}^{0\prime}\mathbf{H}^{-1}(\mathbf{H}\mathbf{a}) = 0$, which shows that $\mathbf{H}\mathbf{a}$ belongs to A^0 and is orthogonal to $\mathbf{a}^0$.

MT 18

If $\{X,A\}$ is a point space (see MT 7), vectors in A can be orthogonal to subsets of X. It goes like this.

Let $\mathbf{A}$ be a matrix whose columns are vectors in A, let S be the flat set $\{\mathbf{a}: \mathbf{a} = \mathbf{A}\mathbf{c} \text{ for some } \mathbf{c}\}$, and let $\mathbf{x}_o + S$ be the flat set $\{\mathbf{x}: \mathbf{x} = \mathbf{x}_o + \mathbf{A}\mathbf{c} \text{ for some } \mathbf{c}\}$. There is a big difference between S and $\mathbf{x}_o + S$, in that S is a subspace of the vector space A whereas $\mathbf{x}_o + S$ is a subset of the point set X. Vector $\mathbf{a} \in A$ is said to be orthogonal to $\mathbf{x}_o + S$ if it is orthogonal to S. Note the novelty: so far, orthogonality has been a relation between either two vectors in the same vector space or a vector and a set of vectors, also in the same vector space. We now see that a vector can also be orthogonal to a set of points. Not just any set of points, however. The definition applies only if the point set X containing S and the vector space A containing $\mathbf{a}$ form a point space.

It gets better. Let κ be a curve or (hyper)surface in X, let $\mathbf{x}_o$ be a point on κ, and suppose that κ is smooth enough, near $\mathbf{x}_o$, to ensure existence of a tangent line or (hyper)plane at $\mathbf{x}_o$. Denote that tangent line or (hyper)-plane by $\mathbf{x}_o + S$. Vector $\mathbf{a} \in A$ is said to be orthogonal to κ at $\mathbf{x}_o$ if it is orthogonal to $\mathbf{x}_o + S$. What that means was explained in the preceding paragraph.

MT 19

Orthogonal projection is next. In Figure 1 you see, among other things, a plane S in R^3 and a vector $\mathbf{v}$. The linearly independent vectors $\mathbf{a}_1$ and $\mathbf{a}_2$, columns of $\mathbf{A}$, form a basis for S. Vector $\mathbf{w}$ is the orthogonal projection of $\mathbf{w}$ onto S. Loosely, $\mathbf{w}$ is the shadow that $\mathbf{v}$ would cast if the sun were directly overhead. In this book, all projection is orthogonal projection, and so the adjective "orthogonal" will ordinarily be omitted.

We want to express $\mathbf{w}$ in terms of $\mathbf{a}_1$, $\mathbf{a}_2$, and $\mathbf{v}$. Being a vector in S, $\mathbf{w}$ is a linear combination of $\mathbf{a}_1$ and $\mathbf{a}_2$. Equivalently, $\mathbf{w} = \mathbf{A}\mathbf{c}$ for some column $\mathbf{c}$ consisting of two real numbers.

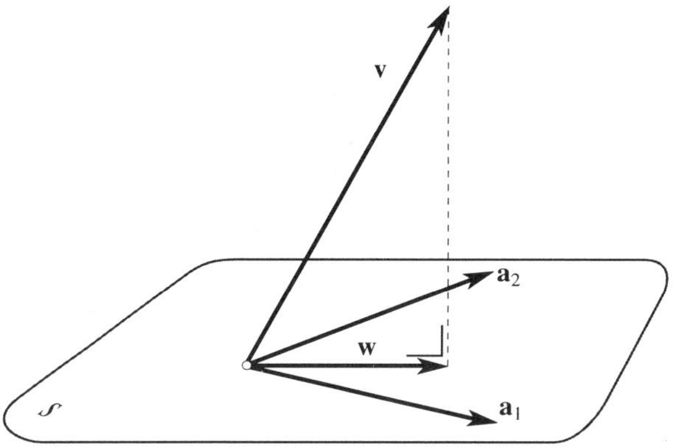

Figure 1. Vector **w** is the projection of **v** onto the plane spanned by $\mathbf{a}_1$, $\mathbf{a}_2$.

Vector $\mathbf{v} - \mathbf{w} = \mathbf{v} - \mathbf{Ac}$ is perpendicular to S, and therefore to both $\mathbf{a}_1$ and $\mathbf{a}_2$. Thus, $\mathbf{a}_1'(\mathbf{v} - \mathbf{Ac}) = 0$ and $\mathbf{a}_2'(\mathbf{v} - \mathbf{Ac}) = 0$. Combining these two equations gives $\mathbf{A}'(\mathbf{v} - \mathbf{Ac}) = \mathbf{0}$, or $\mathbf{A}'\mathbf{v} - \mathbf{A}'\mathbf{Ac} = \mathbf{0}$, or $\mathbf{A}'\mathbf{Ac} = \mathbf{A}'\mathbf{v}$. Premultiplying both sides by $\mathbf{A}(\mathbf{A}'\mathbf{A})^{-1}$ gives $\mathbf{Ac} = \mathbf{w}$ on the left and $\mathbf{A}(\mathbf{A}'\mathbf{A})^{-1}\mathbf{A}'\mathbf{v}$ on the right. Equivalently, $\mathbf{w} = \mathbf{Pv}$, where

$$\mathbf{P} = \mathbf{A}(\mathbf{A}'\mathbf{A})^{-1}\mathbf{A}'.$$

Matrix **P** is a *projection matrix.*

In Figure 1, projecting **w** onto S has no effect on **w**, since **w** is already in S: $\mathbf{Pw} = \mathbf{w}$. Projecting repeatedly is thus equivalent to projecting once: $\mathbf{P} = \mathbf{P}^2 = \mathbf{P}^3 = \cdots$. One says that **P** is *idempotent,* meaning that **P** equals its own second, third, . . . powers.

The definition $\mathbf{P} = \mathbf{A}(\mathbf{A}'\mathbf{A})^{-1}\mathbf{A}'$ holds with far greater generality than is reflected in Figure 1. Let **A** be any $n \times k$ matrix with full column rank, and let S be the set spanned by **A**'s columns. Thus, if $k = 1$, S is a line in R^n; if $k = 2$, S is a plane in R^n; in general, S is a k-dimensional subspace of R^n, with **A** as basis matrix. The orthogonal projection of a vector **v** onto the subspace S is **Pv** with $\mathbf{P} = \mathbf{A}(\mathbf{A}'\mathbf{A})^{-1}\mathbf{A}'$.

If **A** is square (and still with full column rank), $(\mathbf{A}'\mathbf{A})^{-1} = \mathbf{A}^{-1}(\mathbf{A}')^{-1}$. In this case then, $\mathbf{P} = \mathbf{A}(\mathbf{A}'\mathbf{A})^{-1}\mathbf{A}' = \mathbf{A}\mathbf{A}^{-1}(\mathbf{A}')^{-1}\mathbf{A}' = \mathbf{I}$. That stands to reason. If **A** is square, its columns form a basis for the entire R^n; any **v** being projected onto R^n is already in R^n; and so **v** stays the same under projection, meaning $\mathbf{Pv} = \mathbf{Iv} = \mathbf{v}$. Most applications of projection are of course not this trivial. In most applications, **A** is not square but tall, and $\mathbf{P} \neq \mathbf{I}$.

It is easy to verify that $\mathbf{A}'\mathbf{A}$ and $(\mathbf{A}'\mathbf{A})^{-1}$ and **P** are symmetric.

In a vector space V with a nonstandard inner product, the projection matrix looks a little different. Let the inner-product matrix be $\mathbf{H}$; then

$$\mathbf{P} = \mathbf{A}(\mathbf{A}'\mathbf{H}\mathbf{A})^{-1}\mathbf{A}'\mathbf{H},$$

which, incidentally, is not symmetric. The proof follows the same path as before. See Figure 1: $\mathbf{v} - \mathbf{w} = \mathbf{v} - \mathbf{Ac}$ is perpendicular to S, and therefore to both $\mathbf{a}_1$ and $\mathbf{a}_2$. Thus, $\mathbf{a}_1'\mathbf{H}(\mathbf{v} - \mathbf{Ac}) = 0$ and $\mathbf{a}_2'\mathbf{H}(\mathbf{v} - \mathbf{Ac}) = 0$. Combining these two equations gives $\mathbf{A}'\mathbf{H}(\mathbf{v} - \mathbf{Ac}) = \mathbf{0}$, or $\mathbf{A}'\mathbf{Hv} - \mathbf{A}'\mathbf{HAc} = 0$, or $\mathbf{A}'\mathbf{HAc} = \mathbf{A}'\mathbf{Hv}$. Premultiplying both sides by $\mathbf{A}(\mathbf{A}'\mathbf{HA})^{-1}$ gives $\mathbf{Ac} = \mathbf{A}(\mathbf{A}'\mathbf{HA})^{-1}\mathbf{A}'\mathbf{Hv}$, that is, $\mathbf{w} = \mathbf{Pv}$. P.O.C.

The just-found formula remains unchanged if $\mathbf{A}$ is $n \times k$ and has full column rank.

We saw in MT 18 that if $\{X,A\}$ is a point space, vectors in A can be orthogonal to subsets of X. As you then expect, it is possible to project vectors in A onto subsets of X. Figure 2 tells the story. Figure 2 shows a plane $P = \mathbf{x}_o + S$ in $X = E^3$, a point $\mathbf{x}_o$ in that plane, and a vector $\mathbf{v}$ affixed at $\mathbf{x}_o$. It will be clear that S, which is not shown, is a plane in R^3, containing the origin of R^3 and "parallel" to P. Let $\mathbf{a}_1$ and $\mathbf{a}_2$, columns of $\mathbf{A}$, form a basis for S. In Figure 2, $\mathbf{a}_1$ and $\mathbf{a}_2$ are affixed at $\mathbf{x}_o$. The orthogonal projection of $\mathbf{v}$ onto P is the same $\mathbf{w} = \mathbf{Ac} = \mathbf{Pv}$ as the orthogonal projection of $\mathbf{v}$ onto S, except that $\mathbf{w}$ is now affixed at $\mathbf{x}_o$.

Figure 2 could also be said to illustrate that the projection of the *point* $\mathbf{x}_o + \mathbf{v}$ onto P is the *point* $\mathbf{x}_o + \mathbf{w}$. More generally, not just vectors in A but also points in X can be projected onto subsets of X. (The only restriction is that those subsets must be closed in X. MT 27 has further details.)

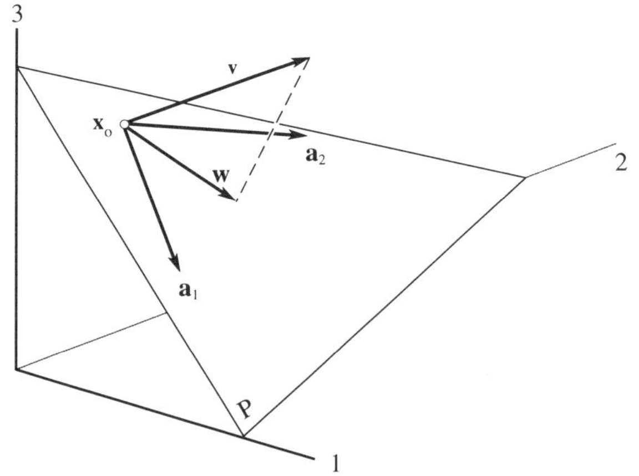

Figure 2. Orthogonal projection of a vector in A onto a plane in X.

The projection of a point onto any subset of X is, if it exists, always a point. The projection of a vector onto any subset of either X or A is, if it exists, always a vector.

MT 20

Let V and W be two vector spaces, and let f be a function from V to W. One says that f is *linear* if for all vectors $\mathbf{a}$ and $\mathbf{a}_o$ in V and for all scalars c,

$$f(\mathbf{a} + \mathbf{a}_o) = f(\mathbf{a}) + f(\mathbf{a}_o) \tag{6}$$

and

$$f(c\mathbf{a}) = cf(\mathbf{a}) \tag{7}$$

both hold.

We show that f, being a linear function, can be represented by a matrix. By this is meant that there exists a matrix $\mathbf{M}$ so that $f(\mathbf{a}) = \mathbf{Ma}$ for all $\mathbf{a}$ in V.

To prove the result, let $\{\mathbf{v}_1,\mathbf{v}_2, \ldots ,\mathbf{v}_n\}$ be a basis for V. Then every $\mathbf{a}$ in V can be written as a linear combination of the $\mathbf{v}_i$. Take $\mathbf{a} = a_1\mathbf{v}_1 + a_2\mathbf{v}_2 + \cdots + \mathbf{a}_n\mathbf{v}_n$. Then

$$\begin{aligned} f(\mathbf{a}) &= f(a_1\mathbf{v}_1 + a_2\mathbf{v}_2 + \cdots + a_n\mathbf{v}_n) \\ &= f(a_1\mathbf{v}_1) + f(a_2\mathbf{v}_2) + \cdots + f(a_n\mathbf{v}_n), \quad \text{by (6)} \\ &= a_1f(\mathbf{v}_1) + a_2f(\mathbf{v}_2) + \cdots + a_nf(\mathbf{v}_n), \quad \text{by (7)} \\ &= \mathbf{m}_1a_1 + \mathbf{m}_2a_2 + \cdots + \mathbf{m}_na_n, \quad \text{where } \mathbf{m}_i \text{ denotes } f(\mathbf{v}_i) \\ &= (\mathbf{m}_1,\mathbf{m}_2, \ldots , \mathbf{m}_n)\mathbf{a}. \end{aligned}$$

Letting $\mathbf{M}$ be the matrix of the $\mathbf{m}_i$ gives $f(\mathbf{a}) = \mathbf{Ma}$. P.O.C.

If f is real-valued, $\mathbf{M}$ consists of a single row. Call that row $\mathbf{m}'$. Then $f(\mathbf{a}) = \mathbf{m}'\mathbf{a}$, just as you have always known a real-valued linear function to be.

MT 21

Topics 21–26 all fall under calculus. We begin with the Taylor expansion of functions of several variables.

Let $\{X,V\}$ be a point space, and let $u{:}X \to E^1$ be a function with partial derivatives of all orders. Think of Figure 3 as depicting a cave, with floor X and thin, transparent roof $u = u(\mathbf{x})$. You are standing at the point $\mathbf{x}_o$. The height of the roof is $u(\mathbf{x}_o)$ there. You now take a small step away from $\mathbf{x}_o$, in the direction of some vector $\mathbf{v} = (v_1,v_2)' \in V$. For concreteness, let $\mathbf{v}$ be a unit vector: $\|\mathbf{v}\| = 1$. Your move is a multiple of $\mathbf{v}$—say, $h\mathbf{v}$. Although h may be as large as you wish, it helps to think of h as fairly small.

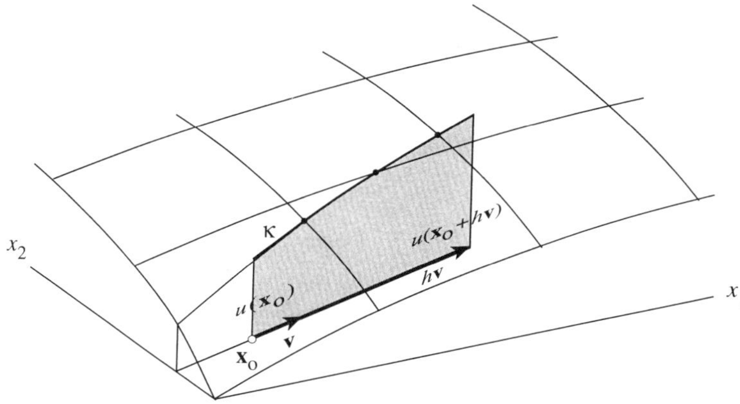

Figure 3. Illustrating the Taylor expansion in the direction of a vector $\mathbf{v}$.

Taking the step $h\mathbf{v}$ brings you to a new point, $\mathbf{x}_o + h\mathbf{v}$. Here the height of the roof is $u(\mathbf{x}_o + h\mathbf{v})$. The Taylor series concerns the difference between this new height and the old. Specifically, the Taylor series says that

$$u(\mathbf{x}_o + h\mathbf{v}) = u(\mathbf{x}_o) + h\sum v_i\frac{\partial u(\mathbf{x}_o)}{\partial x_i} + \frac{1}{2}h^2\sum v_iv_j\frac{\partial^2 u(\mathbf{x}_o)}{\partial x_i\partial x_j} + \cdots. \quad (8)$$

Equation (8) can also be written in vector notation, as

$$u(\mathbf{x}_o + h\mathbf{v}) = u(\mathbf{x}_o) + h \cdot \mathbf{v}'\nabla u(\mathbf{x}_o) + \tfrac{1}{2}\mathrm{h}^2 \cdot \mathbf{v}'\mathbf{U}\mathbf{v} + \cdots, \quad (9)$$

where $\mathbf{U}$ is the matrix of u's second-order partial derivatives, all evaluated at $\mathbf{x}_o$.

For a special case of some interest, let $\mathbf{v} = \mathbf{e}_1$ in (8). (Thus, if $V = R^2$, $\mathbf{e}_1 = (1,0)'$; if $V = A$, $\mathbf{e}_1 = (1b,0c)'$; and so on.) Equation (8) becomes

$$u(\mathbf{x}_o + h\mathbf{e}_1) = u(\mathbf{x}_o) + h\frac{\partial u(\mathbf{x}_o)}{\partial x_1} + \frac{1}{2}h^2\frac{\partial^2 u(\mathbf{x}_o)}{\partial {x_1}^2} + \cdots.$$

As you would expect, this is very nearly the Taylor expansion for a function of one variable, $f(x_o + h) = f(x_o) + h\, df(x_o)/dx + \frac{1}{2}h^2\, d^2f(x_o)/dx^2 + \cdots$.

MT 22

A powerful tool, underused in economics, is the *directional derivative.* See again Figure 3. As you walk away from $\mathbf{x}_o$, in the direction of the unit vector $\mathbf{v}$, the point on the roof directly above your head describes a curve κ. That curve has a slope at every point. At $\mathbf{x}_o$ itself, the slope is

$$\lim_{h \to 0} \frac{u(\mathbf{x}_o + h\mathbf{v}) - u(\mathbf{x}_o)}{h} \qquad (\|\mathbf{v}\| = 1).$$

This limit is denoted $D_{\mathbf{v}}u(\mathbf{x}_o)$ and called the *derivative of* u *in the direction of* **v**, *evaluated at* $\mathbf{x}_o$. By (9), $D_{\mathbf{v}}u(\mathbf{x}_o)$ equals $\mathbf{v}'\nabla u(\mathbf{x}_o)$, as is easy to see. Dropping the emphasis on the specific point $\mathbf{x}_o$ we have, more generally,

$$D_{\mathbf{v}}u(\mathbf{x}) = \mathbf{v}'\nabla u(\mathbf{x}) \qquad (\|\mathbf{v}\| = 1).$$

For a special case of interest, let $V = R^2$, and take $\mathbf{v} = \mathbf{e}_1 = (1, 0)'$. Then $D_{\mathbf{v}}u = D_{\mathbf{e}_1}u = \mathbf{e}_1'\nabla u = \partial u/\partial x_1$. The slope of u in the direction of $\mathbf{e}_1$ (or: in the direction of the positive x_1-axis) is thus the first of u's first-order partial derivatives. By symmetry, $D_{\mathbf{e}_2}u = \mathbf{e}_2'\nabla u = \partial u/\partial x_2$.

MT 23

A surface does not have a slope, but it does have a slope in every direction (if it is smooth enough). See again Figure 3: at $\mathbf{x}_o$, the direction of *steepest ascent* is the direction in which the surface rises fastest. To find that direction, we need to maximize $D_{\mathbf{v}}u(\mathbf{x}_o)$ over all unit vectors **v**; the direction of the maximizing **v** is the direction of steepest ascent (at $\mathbf{x}_o$).

Maximizing $D_{\mathbf{v}}u(\mathbf{x}_o)$ over all unit vectors **v** is surprisingly easy. Suppose first that **v** and $\nabla u(\mathbf{x}_o)$ belong to R^n. Then $D_{\mathbf{v}}u(\mathbf{x}_o) = \mathbf{v}'\nabla u(\mathbf{x}_o)$ is an inner product, and it equals $\|\mathbf{v}\| \cdot \|\nabla u(\mathbf{x}_o)\| \cos \phi$. Since $\|\mathbf{v}\| = 1$ and $\nabla u(\mathbf{x}_o)$ is a fixed vector, maximizing $D_{\mathbf{v}}u(\mathbf{x}_o)$ means maximizing $\cos \phi$. In its turn, this means setting $\phi = 0°$. The maximizing unit vector **v** is thus the one that forms a 0° angle with $\nabla u(\mathbf{x}_o)$. Moreover, the value of $D_{\mathbf{v}}u(\mathbf{x}_o)$ for that **v** is the value of $\|\mathbf{v}\| \cdot \|\nabla u(\mathbf{x}_o)\| \cos \phi$ when $\|\mathbf{v}\| = 1$ and $\phi = 0°$. That value is $\|\nabla u(\mathbf{x}_o)\|$. Seeing that the steepest ascent has both a direction and a norm, it is only natural that we define it as a vector. Summarizing, we have

Definition 1. In R^n, the steepest ascent of $u(\mathbf{x})$ at $\mathbf{x}_o$ is the vector $\nabla u(\mathbf{x}_o)$.

Suppose next that **v** belongs to a vector space V other than R^n, and let the inner product on V have matrix **H**. Vector $\nabla u(\mathbf{x}_o)$ belongs to the main dual space V^0, of course. Now $D_{\mathbf{v}}u(\mathbf{x}_o) = \mathbf{v}'\nabla u(\mathbf{x}_o) = \mathbf{v}'\mathbf{H}\mathbf{H}^{-1}\nabla u(\mathbf{x}_o)$, which is the inner product (in V) of **v** and $\mathbf{H}^{-1}\nabla u(\mathbf{x}_o)$. It therefore equals $\|\mathbf{v}\| \cdot \|\mathbf{H}^{-1}\nabla u(\mathbf{x}_o)\| \cos \phi$. By the reasoning used above, this is largest when **v** forms a 0° angle with $\mathbf{H}^{-1}\nabla u(\mathbf{x}_o)$, in which case it equals $\|\mathbf{H}^{-1}\nabla u(\mathbf{x}_o)\|$. Summarizing, we have

Definition 2. In V, the steepest ascent of $u(\mathbf{x})$ at $\mathbf{x}_o$ is the vector $\mathbf{H}^{-1}\nabla u(\mathbf{x}_o)$.

MT 24

The definition of the steepest ascent allowed **x** to move away from its initial location $\mathbf{x}_o$ in any direction. Suppose now that the direction in which **x**

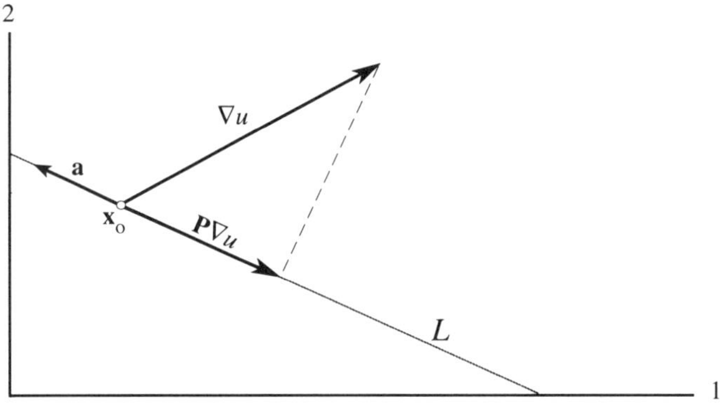

Figure 4. In R^2, the steepest constrained ascent of u at $\mathbf{x}_o$ is $\mathbf{P}\nabla u$.

can move is circumscribed in some (well-defined) way. Given this constraint, what is the steepest ascent of $u(\mathbf{x})$ at $\mathbf{x}_o$?

For an illustration, see Figure 4, which is set in R^2. As $\mathbf{x}$ moves away from $\mathbf{x}_o$, it must stay on the line $L = \{\mathbf{x}\colon \mathbf{x} = \mathbf{x}_o + c\mathbf{a}$ for some $c\}$. It is clear that the direction in which u increases fastest, constraint permitting, is that of the vector labeled $\mathbf{P}\nabla u$. This $\mathbf{P}\nabla u$ is of course the projection of ∇u onto L.

For another illustration, see Figure 5, set in R^3. This time, the moving $\mathbf{x}$ is constrained to remain in the plane $P = \{\mathbf{x}\colon \mathbf{x} = \mathbf{x}_o + c_1\mathbf{a}_1 + c_2\mathbf{a}_2$ for some $c_1, c_2\}$. You can probably guess that the direction in which u increases fastest, constraint permitting, is that of $\mathbf{P}\nabla u$, the projection of ∇u onto P.

Generalizing the problem, let $\mathbf{a}_1, \mathbf{a}_2, \ldots, \mathbf{a}_k$, columns of $\mathbf{A}$, be linearly independent vectors in a vector space V, let S be the subspace spanned by

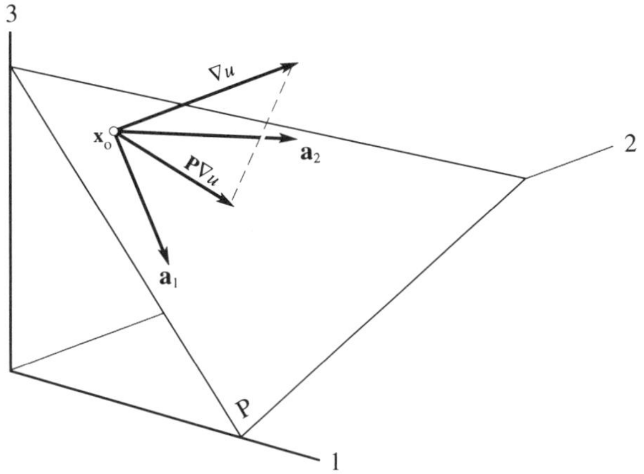

Figure 5. In R^3, the steepest constrained ascent of u at $\mathbf{x}_o$ is $\mathbf{P}\nabla u$.

$\mathbf{A}$'s columns, and let the inner product on V have matrix $\mathbf{H}$. Orthogonal projection onto S is thus represented by $\mathbf{P} = \mathbf{A}(\mathbf{A}'\mathbf{H}\mathbf{A})^{-1}\mathbf{A}'\mathbf{H}$. Suppose the moving $\mathbf{x}$ is constrained to remain in the set $\{\mathbf{x}: \mathbf{x} = \mathbf{x}_o + \mathbf{A}\mathbf{c}$ for some $\mathbf{c}\}$. Define the *steepest constrained ascent* of $u(\mathbf{x})$ *at* $\mathbf{x}_o$ as the vector whose *direction* is that in which $u(\mathbf{x})$ increases fastest at $\mathbf{x}_o$, constraint permitting, and whose *length* is the slope of u in that direction. It will be shown that

The steepest constrained ascent of $\mathrm{u}(\mathbf{x})$ *at* $\mathbf{x}_o$ *is* $\mathbf{PH}^{-1}\nabla\mathrm{u}(\mathbf{x}_o)$.

If V is R^n, and the inner product is standard, the steepest constrained ascent simplifies to $\mathbf{P}\nabla u(\mathbf{x}_o)$, with $\mathbf{P} = \mathbf{A}(\mathbf{A}'\mathbf{A})^{-1}\mathbf{A}'$.

To prove the assertion, we need to maximize $D_\mathbf{v}u(\mathbf{x}_o)$ over all unit vectors $\mathbf{v}$ that can be written as $\mathbf{Ac}$ for some $\mathbf{c}$. As seen in MT 23, $D_\mathbf{v}u(\mathbf{x}_o)$ equals $\|\mathbf{v}\| \cdot \|\mathbf{H}^{-1}\nabla u(\mathbf{x}_o)\|\cos\phi = \|\mathbf{H}^{-1}\nabla u(\mathbf{x}_o)\|\cos\phi$. This is largest when ϕ is smallest, that is, when $\mathbf{v}$ points in the same direction as the projection of $\mathbf{H}^{-1}\nabla u(\mathbf{x}_o)$ onto S. Cos ϕ then equals $\|\mathbf{PH}^{-1}\nabla u(\mathbf{x}_o)\|/\|\mathbf{H}^{-1}\nabla u(\mathbf{x}_o)\|$. The rest is obvious.

MT 25

Near the end of the book we meet the differential-equation system $\dot{\mathbf{y}}(t) + \gamma\mathbf{y}(t) = \mathbf{z}(t)$. Suppose first that $\dot{\mathbf{y}}$, $\mathbf{y}$, and $\mathbf{z}$ are one-element vectors. The system can then be written as $\dot{y}(t) + \gamma y(t) = z(t)$. Multiplying both sides by $e^{\gamma t}$ gives $e^{\gamma t}\dot{y}(t) + \gamma e^{\gamma t}y(t) = e^{\gamma t}z(t)$. The left side is the indefinite integral of $e^{\gamma t}y(t)$, as you can verify by differentiation. Integrating from 0 to t thus gives $e^{\gamma\tau}y(\tau)\big|_0^t = \int_0^t e^{\gamma\tau}z(\tau)d\tau$. The left side equals $e^{\gamma t}y(t) - e^{\gamma\cdot 0}y(0)$, that is, $e^{\gamma t}y(t) - y(0)$, and so we have $e^{\gamma t}y(t) = y(0) + \int_0^t e^{\gamma\tau}z(\tau)d\tau$. Multiplying by $e^{-\gamma t}$ produces the solution,

$$y(t) = e^{-\gamma t}y(0) + e^{-\gamma t}\int_0^t e^{\gamma\tau}z(\tau)d\tau.$$

Sometimes it is handier to go one step further and integrate the last term by parts. The solution is then

$$y(t) = e^{-\gamma t}y(0) + \gamma^{-1}[z(t) - e^{-\gamma t}z(0) - e^{-\gamma t}\int_0^t e^{\gamma\tau}dz(\tau)].$$

If $\dot{\mathbf{y}}$, $\mathbf{y}$, and $\mathbf{z}$ are vectors of $n > 1$ elements, the system $\dot{\mathbf{y}}(t) + \gamma\mathbf{y}(t) = \mathbf{z}(t)$ consists of n differential equations, written underneath each other, and all of the form just solved. Writing the n solutions underneath each other gives, in obvious notation,

$$\mathbf{y}(t) = e^{-\gamma t}\mathbf{y}(0) + e^{-\gamma t}\int_0^t e^{\gamma\tau}\mathbf{z}(\tau)d\tau.$$

When the last vector on the right is integrated by parts, the solution becomes

$$\mathbf{y}(t) = e^{-\gamma t}\mathbf{y}(0) + \gamma^{-1}[\mathbf{z}(t) - e^{-\gamma t}\mathbf{z}(0) - e^{-\gamma t}\int_0^t e^{\gamma\tau}d\mathbf{z}(\tau)]. \qquad (10)$$

MT 26

Delta functions are used to represent events that are sudden, short, and out of the ordinary, like a spike in electrical current, or a photographer's flashbulb going off in front of your eyes, or a phone call notifying you of an inheritance. Let such an event begin at time t_o and end at $t_o + \epsilon$, with ϵ positive and very small. Figure 6 illustrates the corresponding delta function, written as $\delta(t_o)$. For t between t_o and $t_o + \epsilon$, the value of the function is $1/\epsilon$; for all other t, the value of the function is zero.

Actually, the definition just given is somewhat unauthorized. Mathematicians define $\delta(t_o)$ as *the limit of* our $\delta(t_o)$ as ϵ goes to zero. Since that limit does not exist in the usual sense, the mathematicians' definition of $\delta(t_o)$ calls for an excursion outside the bounds of traditional calculus. As it turns out, however, we do not need to go there. We do not need to go there because our use of $\delta(t_o)$ is confined to integrals of the form

$$\int_{-\infty}^{+\infty} \delta(t_o - \tau)f(\tau)d\tau$$

(any integrable f); and no problems arise if we *first* evaluate this integral using our own definition of $\delta(t_o)$ and *afterward* let ϵ go to zero. Here is how it goes.

Since δ is zero everywhere except between t_o and $t_o + \epsilon$,

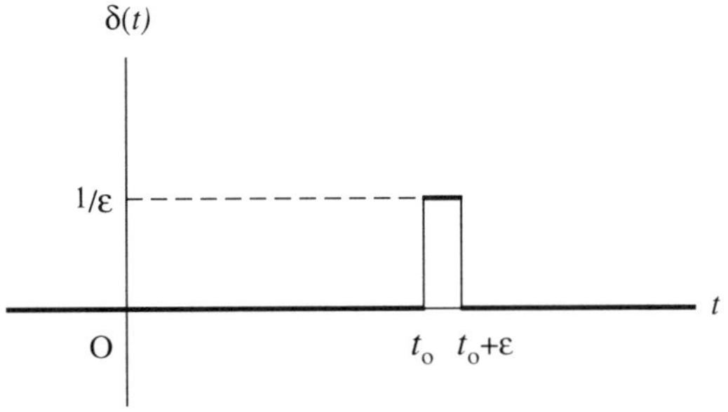

Figure 6. A delta function.

$$\int_{-\infty}^{+\infty} \delta(t_o - \tau)f(\tau)d\tau = \int_{t_o}^{t_o+\epsilon} \delta(t_o - \tau)f(\tau)d\tau.$$

Now $\delta = 1/\epsilon$ between t_o and $t_o + \epsilon$, and so the integral becomes

$$\epsilon^{-1} \int_{t_o}^{t_o+\epsilon} f(\tau)d\tau.$$

By the mean-value theorem, this equals $\epsilon^{-1}[\epsilon f(\tau^*)]$ for some τ^* between t_o and $t_o + \epsilon$. Letting ϵ go to zero gives $f(t_o)$. In all then,

$$\int_{-\infty}^{+\infty} \delta(t_o - \tau)f(\tau)d\tau = f(t_o). \tag{11}$$

MT 27

Finally, a bit of real analysis. The treatment is casual.

Let $\{X,A\}$ be any point space.

A subset S of X is *convex* if for every two points $\mathbf{x}_0$ and $\mathbf{x}_1$ belonging to S, every point between $\mathbf{x}_0$ and $\mathbf{x}_1$ also belongs to S.

What "between $\mathbf{x}_0$ and $\mathbf{x}_1$" means is obvious geometrically, but it is not obvious analytically. To explore, let $\mathbf{x}_0$ be a point in X and $\mathbf{a}$ a nonnull vector in A. Then $\mathbf{x}_0 + c\mathbf{a}$ is for every real c a point in X. It is easy to see that the set of those points, $\{\mathbf{x}: \mathbf{x} = \mathbf{x}_0 + c\mathbf{a}$ for some c$\}$, is a line. The line—call it L—goes through $\mathbf{x}_0$ and is parallel to $\mathbf{a}$. One of the points of L is $\mathbf{x}_0 + \mathbf{a}$. Call it $\mathbf{x}_1$. Then L can also be described as the set $\{\mathbf{x}: \mathbf{x} = \mathbf{x}_0 + c(\mathbf{x}_1 - \mathbf{x}_0)$ for some $c\}$. It is geometrically clear that if c is any number between 0 and 1, then the point

$$\mathbf{x}_0 + c(\mathbf{x}_1 - \mathbf{x}_0)$$

lies between $\mathbf{x}_0$ and $\mathbf{x}_1$. Conversely, every point between $\mathbf{x}_0$ and $\mathbf{x}_1$ can be written in the form $\mathbf{x}_0 + c(\mathbf{x}_1 - \mathbf{x}_0)$, for some c between 0 and 1. This is the analytical version of "between" that we were looking for.

A subset S of X is *closed* if it contains its entire boundary. For an example, let X be the plane E^2, and let S be the set of all points (x,y) with $x^2 + y^2 \leq 1$. Its boundary is the circle $x^2 + y^2 = 1$. Since the boundary is part of the set, S is closed. For an example of a set that is not closed, strip S of its boundary. That leaves the set of all points (x,y) with $x^2 + y^2 < 1$, and this set is not closed.

A subset S of X is *bounded* if there is some distance ρ, possibly very large, so that every $\mathbf{x}$ in S is less than ρ away from the origin of X. To illustrate, let $X = E^2$. For an example of a bounded set, think of any rectangle. For an example of an unbounded set, take the graph of $y = e^{-x}$.

To see why this set is not bounded, pick a number ρ as big as you like. Now consider the point $(x, y) = (\rho + 1, e^{-(\rho+1)})$. On the one hand, the point lies on the graph of $y = e^{-x}$. On the other, its distance to the origin of X exceeds ρ, as is easy to see.

A subset S of X is *compact* if it is both closed and bounded.

Proof of the following theorem can be found in most—maybe all—texts on real analysis.

THEOREM 1. *Let the set* S $\subset$ X *be closed, and let* $\mathbf{p} \in$ X *be some point outside* S. *There then exists a point* $\mathbf{q}$ *in* S *that is closest to* $\mathbf{p}$.

The distance between $\mathbf{p}$ and $\mathbf{q}$ is also called the distance between $\mathbf{p}$ and S.

If S is not closed, Theorem 1 does not hold. For an example, let $X = E^2$, let $\mathbf{p}$ be the origin, and let S be the set $\{(x,y): x > 1\}$. This S is not closed, for it does not contain its boundary (the line $x = 1$). It is easy to see that there is no point $\mathbf{q}$ in S that is closest to the origin $\mathbf{p}$. On the other hand, if we define S as the set $\{(x,y): x \geq 1\}$, which is closed, the theorem does apply. In that case, $\mathbf{q} = (1, 0)$, as you can verify from a diagram.

Theorem 1 does not guarantee that $\mathbf{q}$ is unique. Indeed it need not be. For an illustration, take $X = E^2$, let S be the V-shaped graph of $y = |x|$, and let $\mathbf{p} = (0, 2)$. If you make a picture, you will see that there is one $\mathbf{q}$ at $(1, 1)$ and another at $(-1, 1)$. The distance minimum is unique, but the distance minimizer is not.

In some cases, the minimizing $\mathbf{q}$ *is* unique. One of those cases is particularly relevant for Models One and Two. Theorem 2 describes it.

THEOREM 2. *If the set* S *of Theorem 1 is not only closed but also convex,* $\mathbf{q}$ *is unique.*

Proof. Suppose the theorem is false—suppose there are *two* points in S with minimum distance to $\mathbf{p}$. Call them $\mathbf{q}_1$ and $\mathbf{q}_2$. The triangle with vertices $\mathbf{p}$, $\mathbf{q}_1$, and $\mathbf{q}_2$ is then isosceles. It is easy to see that the point $\mathbf{q} = \frac{1}{2}(\mathbf{q}_1 + \mathbf{q}_2)$, which lies midway between $\mathbf{q}_1$ and $\mathbf{q}_2$, is closer to $\mathbf{p}$ than is either $\mathbf{q}_1$ or $\mathbf{q}_2$. Since S contains $\mathbf{q}_1$ and $\mathbf{q}_2$ and is convex, S contains $\mathbf{q}$ as well. But then $\mathbf{q}_1$ and $\mathbf{q}_2$ cannot be the distance minimizers we took them to be. The contradiction proves the theorem. P.O.C.

Questions

1. If $f(t) = e^{at}$, and t is measured in hours, in which unit is a measured?
2. (Continuation) Expand e^{at} in a Taylor series around $t_o = 0$. Does your answer to Question 1 still hold?
3. If $y_t = 3y_{t-1}$ for $t = 1, 2, 3, \ldots$, and $y_0 = 1$, it is easy to see that $y_t = 3^t$. In which unit is t measured?

4. Let S be the set of all functions of the form

$$(Ap^2 + Bp + C)/(3p^2 + 2p + 1),$$

with A, B, and C real. In which unit is p measured? Is S a set with multiplication? Addition? Scalar multiplication? Is S a vector space?

5. The set of columns of the form (x lbs., y gal.)′, with x, y real, is a vector space. So is the set of columns of the form (x gal., y lbs.)′. Are the two vector spaces the same?

6. As said, every vector space contains a null vector. How many null vectors can a vector space have, at most?

7. If a vector space consists of a single vector, which vector is that?

8. Let $\mathbf{A}$ and $\mathbf{B}$ be arrays, both 3×3. In both, the elements of the first row are measured in b, the elements of the second row are measured in c, and the elements of the third row are measured in d. Is $\mathbf{A} + \mathbf{B}$ defined? $\mathbf{A} + \mathbf{B}'$? $\mathbf{AB}$? $\mathbf{A}'\mathbf{B}$? $\mathbf{AB}'$?

9. Does a 2×3 matrix *always* have infinitely many solutions?

10. Remember the definition of a point space. What can you say about $\mathbf{x}_1$ and $\mathbf{x}_2$ if $\mathbf{x}_1 + c(\mathbf{x}_2 - \mathbf{x}_1) = (1 - c)\mathbf{x}_1 + c\mathbf{x}_2$?

11. The proof of Theorem 2, in MT 27, defines $\mathbf{q}$ as $\frac{1}{2}(\mathbf{q}_1 + \mathbf{q}_2)$. Strictly, this is meaningless, since $\mathbf{q}_1$ and $\mathbf{q}_2$ are points. Rewrite $\frac{1}{2}(\mathbf{q}_1 + \mathbf{q}_2)$ in a way that does not require addition of points or multiplication of points by scalars.

12. Let $\mathbf{x}_1, \mathbf{x}_2, \ldots, \mathbf{x}_n$ be points, in a point set S. The *average* of the $\mathbf{x}_i$ is $(1/n)\Sigma\mathbf{x}_i$. Since addition and scalar multiplication have not been defined on S, the average of the $\mathbf{x}_i$ is, strictly, a meaningless quantity. Rewrite $(1/n)\Sigma\mathbf{x}_i$ in a way that does not require addition of points or multiplication of points by scalars.

13. Write $\mathbf{a}_1c_1 + \mathbf{a}_2c_2 + \mathbf{a}_3c_3$ as $\mathbf{Ac}$. Vectors $\mathbf{a}_1, \mathbf{a}_2, \mathbf{a}_3$ are linearly independent if $\mathbf{Ac} = \mathbf{0}$. True or false?

14. (Continuation) If $\mathbf{Ac} = \mathbf{0}$ has one solution, the $\mathbf{a}_i$ are linearly independent; if $\mathbf{Ac} = \mathbf{0}$ has infinitely many solutions, the $\mathbf{a}_i$ are linearly dependent; if $\mathbf{Ac} = \mathbf{0}$ has no solution, the $\mathbf{a}_i$ are neither linearly independent nor linearly dependent. True or false?

15. Are the columns of

$$\mathbf{A} = \begin{pmatrix} 2 & 3 & 5 \\ 1 & 4 & 7 \end{pmatrix}$$

linearly dependent or linearly independent? Does $\mathbf{A}^{-1}$ exist? Does $(\mathbf{A}'\mathbf{A})^{-1}$ exist? Does $(\mathbf{AA}')^{-1}$ exist? Find $\det(\mathbf{A}'\mathbf{A})$.

16. (Continuation) Do the columns of $\mathbf{A}$ form a basis for R^2 or for R^3? Do the columns of $\mathbf{A}'$ form a basis for R^2 or for R^3?
17. Let $(1b, 0c)'$ and $(0b, 1c)'$ form a basis for the action space A. What does the basis matrix look like in this case? Find the dual-basis matrix.
18. What is the transpose of $\mathbf{ABC}$? Of $\mathbf{a}'\mathbf{Bc}$? Is $\mathbf{a}'\mathbf{Bc}$ symmetric when $\mathbf{B}$ is? Is $\mathbf{a}'\mathbf{Bc}$ symmetric when $\mathbf{B}$ is not?
19. Prove that $\mathbf{V}^0\mathbf{K}\mathbf{V}^{0\prime}$ is symmetric if $\mathbf{K}$ is.
20. Let $\mathbf{V}^0$ and $\mathbf{H}$ have the meaning in the text. The elements of the first row of $\mathbf{V}^0$ are measured in $1/b$; the elements of the second row are measured in $1/c$. Verify that the diagonal elements of $\mathbf{H}$ are measured in $1/b^2$ and $1/c^2$, and that the off-diagonal elements are measured in $1/bc$, as the text says. How are the elements of $\mathbf{HH}^{-1} = \mathbf{I}$ dimensioned?
21. In V^0, the inner product of $\mathbf{Ha}$ and $\mathbf{Hb}$ is $(\mathbf{Ha})'\mathbf{H}^{-1}(\mathbf{Hb})$. What is it in V?
22. In the utility function $u(x_1,x_2)$, x_1 is measured in b and x_2 is measured in c. How are the elements of the Hessian matrix of u dimensioned? Can the Hessian matrix serve as an inner-product matrix?
23. Are $(2b, 3c)'$ and $(3/b, -2/c)'$ orthogonal?
24. Let $\mathbf{H}$ and $\mathbf{H}^{-1}$ be the inner-product matrices on V and V^0. Suppose $\mathbf{a} \in V$ annihilates $\mathbf{b} \in V^0$ if and only if $\mathbf{a}$ is orthogonal to $\mathbf{x}$. What is $\mathbf{x}$?
25. Vectors $\mathbf{a}_1$, $\mathbf{a}_2$, and $\mathbf{a}_3$ are the columns of $\mathbf{A}$. The *linear span* of $\mathbf{a}_1$, $\mathbf{a}_2$, and $\mathbf{a}_3$ is the set of all linear combinations of the three $\mathbf{a}_i$, that is, the set of all vectors $\mathbf{Ac}$ (any $\mathbf{c}$). Prove that, if $\mathbf{c}_1$, $\mathbf{c}_2$, and $\mathbf{c}_3$ are linearly independent, the linear span of $\mathbf{Ac}_1$, $\mathbf{Ac}_2$, and $\mathbf{Ac}_3$ is the same as the linear span of $\mathbf{a}_1$, $\mathbf{a}_2$, and $\mathbf{a}_3$. (Hint: let $\mathbf{C}$ be the matrix with the three $\mathbf{c}_i$ as columns. What is the connection between $\mathbf{C}$ and the matrix whose columns are the $\mathbf{Ac}_i$?)
26. Prove that if $\mathbf{Pv} = \mathbf{A}(\mathbf{A}'\mathbf{A})^{-1}\mathbf{A}'\mathbf{v}$ for all $\mathbf{v}$ in R^3, then $\mathbf{P} = \mathbf{A}(\mathbf{A}'\mathbf{A})^{-1}\mathbf{A}'$. (MT 19 implicitly assumed this result.)
27. Compute $\mathbf{A}(\mathbf{A}'\mathbf{A})^{-1}\mathbf{A}'$ if $\mathbf{A}$ is the 3×2 matrix with columns $\mathbf{a}_1 = (1, 2, 3)'$ and $\mathbf{a}_2 = (0, 2, 3)'$. (Hint: use Question 25.)
28. Let $\mathbf{a}_1 = (1, -1, 2)'$, $\mathbf{a}_2 = (0, 1, 3)'$, and $\mathbf{a}_3 = (0, 0, 5)'$ be the columns of $\mathbf{A}$. Compute $\mathbf{A}(\mathbf{A}'\mathbf{A})^{-1}\mathbf{A}'$.
29. Find the gradient of $e^{1-x^2-y^2}$.
30. Find the derivative of $e^{1-x^2-y^2}$ in the direction of $\mathbf{v} = (3/5, 4/5)'$. Evaluate at the point $(x, y) = (2, 1)$.
31. Define the derivative of $f(\mathbf{x})$ in the direction of $\mathbf{v}$ if it is known that $\mathbf{v}$ is nonnull but it is not known whether $\mathbf{v}$ is a unit vector.
32. Write the Taylor expansion of $f(\mathbf{x})$ in the direction of a unit vector $\mathbf{v}$.

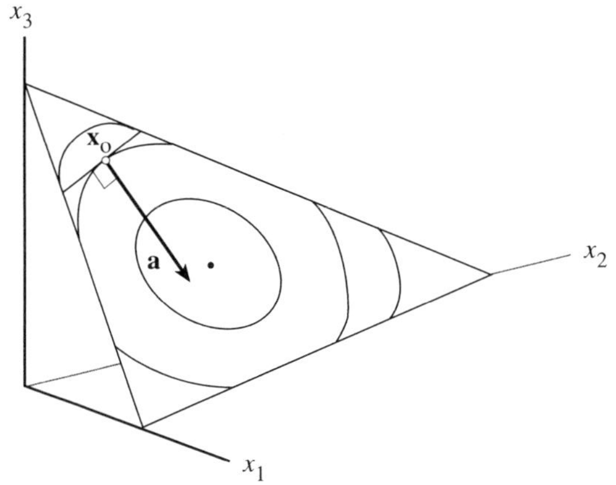

Figure 7. The steepest constrained ascent is orthogonal to the "constrained contour line."

33. Find the steepest ascent of $e^{1-x^2-y^2}$ at the point $(x, y) = (2, 1)$.
34. Find the steepest constrained ascent of $e^{1-x^2-y^2}$ at the point $(x, y) = (2, 1)$, if (x, y) is constrained to remain on the line $y = 3x + b$. (Find b first.) Make a sketch, preferably three-dimensional.
35. Let $\{X, V\}$ be a three-dimensional point space, and let $u(\mathbf{x})$ be a real-valued, differentiable function on X. Prove that, if $\mathbf{x}$ is constrained to remain in the plane $\mathbf{x} = \mathbf{x}_o + \mathbf{a}_1 c_1 + \mathbf{a}_2 c_2$, the steepest constrained ascent at $\mathbf{x}_o$ is orthogonal, at $\mathbf{x}_o$, to the intersection κ of the constraining plane and the contour surface $u(\mathbf{x}) = u(\mathbf{x}_o)$. See Figure 7, where $\mathbf{a}$ represents the steepest constrained ascent. Vectors $\mathbf{a}_1$ and $\mathbf{a}_2$, which span the plane, are not shown.
36. Verify that $e^{-\gamma t}\int_0^t e^{\gamma\tau}z(\tau)d\tau = \gamma^{-1}[z(t) - e^{-\gamma t}z(0) - e^{-\gamma t}\int_0^t e^{\gamma\tau}dz(\tau)]$, as MT 25 implies.
37. The origin of E^2 has distance 1 to every point on the circle $x^2 + y^2 = 1$. Does this not contradict Theorem 2 in MT 27, seeing that a circle is a convex set?

3

Methodological Preliminaries

Building a model is sometimes likened to doing a jigsaw puzzle. Inaccurate though it may be, the simile is worth examining.

The puzzle pieces needed for a model do not come out of a box. They are scattered throughout Reality, and it is up to the model builder to gather them. There are no edge pieces to reveal where the puzzle ends; there is no guarantee that the finished puzzle will have a pleasantly regular shape; the model builder cannot be sure that all the necessary pieces are on the table, nor that all pieces on the table are necessary.

Some puzzle pieces are big and bright and colorful. They represent things that are important in everyday life. In economics, for example, Money and Price are bright pieces. So are Consumer, Producer, Market, Buying, Selling, Demand, Supply, Income, Expenditures, Profit, Taxes.

It is natural to think that the brighter the piece, the more central it must be to the picture. It is also a fallacy. Importance in real life is a bad predictor of importance in theory. Almost all of the bright pieces will be shown to be peripheral, in that their disappearance would affect the picture barely or not at all.

And some dull pieces are essential. Foremost among them are Stock, Flow, Endowment, and Action. What makes these four notions important is, in small part, their generality and, in much larger part, their mathematical nature.

Model building is governed by several principles. Five, in particular, steer this book. The first is by far the most important; the other four are arranged in no particular order.

FIRST PRINCIPLE: DEFINE MATHEMATICALLY

The first principle, a variant of the universally accepted recommendation that every model define its concepts, is that every mathematical model should define its concepts mathematically. A model will be designated "pure theory" if all its concepts are mathematically defined.

According to the first principle, a mathematical model is a good deal more than just a theory with mathematics in it. For an example, take a statement from verbal economics: "People spend part of their incomes, and the rest they save." When rewritten as $Y = C + S$, the statement *still* belongs to verbal economics. The symbols Y, C, and S are mere abbreviations, not definitions, of "income," "consumption," and "savings."

To see the first principle at work, we accompany an aspiring mathematical-model builder. Call him the Scientist. Having observed the real world, especially the part he wishes to model, the Scientist retires to his place of work, the Ivory Tower. He closes the door, locking out Reality, and begins.

First he defines the necessary concepts, in mathematical terms.

Foundation laid, he starts to build on top of it. The superstructure consists of *statements*. Some may be called theorems, or lemmas, or assertions, but that is only for variety or emphasis; they are still statements.

The Scientist deduces all his statements from the definitions. In so doing, he is guided solely by the rules of logic, which we trust him to apply flawlessly. His model is thus logically coherent. Whether it is also realistic is, at this point, of no concern.

And this is all there is. A model consists of definitions and statements, and nothing else. There is no room for axioms, for postulates, for assumptions. Or rather, all axioms, and postulates, and assumptions are definitions in disguise. It is widely recognized, for example, that Kolmogorov's *axioms* are nothing but a definition of probability; the *postulate* that the consumer maximizes utility is actually a definition of final bundle ("The final bundle is the bundle that maximizes utility"); the *assumption* that all commodities are perfectly divisible amounts to a definition of commodity quantity ("A commodity quantity is the product of a real number—rather than an integer—and a measurement unit").

A qualification should be made here. There are two kinds of assumptions. Those of the first kind—assumptions of *substance*—affect the theory itself. They are definitions in disguise. Assumptions of the second kind—assumptions of *convenience*—affect only the presentation of the theory. An example is, "All commodity quantities are assumed positive rather than nonnegative." This is merely an attempt to streamline the exposition, its message being, "Corner solutions are ignored, to keep things simple." Assumptions of convenience are housekeeping rules, not definitions in disguise.

A comment in passing. A widely recommended goal for model builders is the *axiomatization* of their theories. If, as was argued above, mathematical models have no room for axioms, *mathematization* seems a better word.

After the Scientist has been working on his model for a while, a friend drops in. The friend, to be called the Visitor, collects everything the Scientist has written and returns to the real world. There he interprets the model, by translating its (mathematical) statements into everyday language. Next he compares his interpretation with reality. Comparison completed, the Visitor pronounces on the model's realism. His judgment is subjective; it cannot be backed by proof, nor vitiated by disproof. Gauging the correspondence between model and reality is thus not a science. It is an art.

In actuality, the typical model builder is both Scientist and Visitor, in that he keeps one eye on logic and one eye on realism. It is nevertheless useful to separate the two personae, for it underscores that model and reality are different worlds.

Suppose the Visitor considers the model falsified, in that he finds it unrealistic. He goes back to the Scientist and makes his objections known. The Scientist has two possible responses.

First, he can disregard the Visitor's criticism. Lightning will not strike, and incarceration will not follow. But there is a penalty: the Visitor, finding his objections ignored, leaves in a huff and does not return. The Scientist thus loses his audience. He brings isolation on himself. His theory is still logically perfect, but it is unpopular.

The Scientist's other response is to meet the Visitor's objections and change the model. "Changing the model," incidentally, does not mean patching up. Since the Scientist's logic is presumably flawless, every model change inevitably begins with the definitions—an addition here, a deletion there, a modification elsewhere. After making those definitional changes, the Scientist rebuilds the entire theoretical edifice. He then hands his revised model to the Visitor, who takes it back to reality for further comparison, returns with comments, and so on.

According to this picture, a theory cannot be falsified, in the sense of being *proved* wrong. (But the Visitor can *regard* a theory as falsified.) By the same token, a theory cannot be proved right, cannot be proved unrealistic, cannot be experimentally tested or confirmed or refuted. (When Chapter 1 announced nine testable results, it was the Visitor speaking.) From this view also follows that a theory neither explains nor predicts. A theory can be used for explanation and prediction, but that is the Visitor's province. As far as the Scientist is concerned, his model is a purely mathematical world, parallel to and separate from the real world.

Actually, a complete separation of model and reality is impossible, at least if the Scientist values his friendship with the Visitor. Were there no Visitor, the Scientist would be free to put together a theory consisting of statements like *brgl!tt@*. But there is a Visitor, and his visit awakens in the Scientist a desire to communicate. This is where reality comes in. Put differently, the only theories the world gets to see are the intelligible ones—

the ones with a link to reality. The Model Builder's Canon merely asks that the link be as simple and basic as possible.

It may be useful to illustrate the near separation of model and reality with actual cases. The social sciences do not appear to offer any, but the more rugged sciences do. Two examples follow.

The first example is plane geometry. The original geometers were Egyptian priests charged with measuring the area of peasants' lands along the Nile. (Geometry's preoccupation with triangles comes from the serpentine course of the Nile: lands inside a bight had to be triangular to have enough riverine frontage. Lands on the other side were trapezoids, or at any rate quadrilaterals). Over time, geometry gradually distanced itself from its concrete beginnings, until Euclid attenuated the link to the point where for twenty centuries further improvement was believed impossible.

The second example is probability theory. For many years, statisticians sought a mathematical definition of probability—just the sort of thing that the Scientist does after he enters the Ivory Tower. But unlike the Scientist, the statisticians left the door open. Keeping one foot in the real world, they tried to construct their mathematical definition out of nonmathematical notions like "coin" and "toss" and "repeated trials." The impossible quest ended in 1933, when Kolmogorov closed the door and defined probability in purely mathematical terms, unrelated to actual experiments or other real-life events.

Obeying the first principle can be difficult. Saying that all concepts should be mathematically defined is one thing; doing it is another. What if the Scientist is unable to formulate a definition he needs? Can he expect better luck tomorrow? Can he be sure that the necessary mathematics has already been invented? Can he be sure that the concept he wants to define is "mathematical enough" to have a definition at all?

Faced with uncertainties like these, the Scientist has to cut some knots. He first of all decides which notions are probably "not mathematical enough"—will probably never find a definition—and he leaves those notions out of his model. This is precisely the reason that Models One and Two avoid anthropic terms like consumer, producer, and agent; cognitive terms like free will, choice, decision, preference, rationality, and uncertainty; and institutional terms like property, ownership, contract, law, and government. Although some of these notions may someday acquire mathematical definitions, this book, for one, gambles that it will not happen and keeps them out.

Once the Scientist has discarded all concepts he believes mathematically undefinable, there may still be, among the remaining ones, some that he needs but does not know how to define. Presumably he will go ahead anyway, building his model and hoping for the best. It is at this point, when the Scientist begins to work with an incomplete collection of definitions, that gremlins get their chance to creep into the model. The most common gremlins are the Bright Puzzle Piece Fallacy—the belief that importance in practice implies importance in theory—and its offspring, the *false dichotomy.* This brings us to the second principle.

SECOND PRINCIPLE: BEWARE DICHOTOMIES

Any set with two or more elements can be partitioned into two or more nonempty subsets. The set of economic agents, for example, can be partitioned into consumers and producers; the set of human beings can be partitioned into females and males, or into men, women, and children; and so on.

A partitioning of a set into two subsets becomes a *dichotomy* once the subsets receive different theoretical treatment. Absent such different treatment, there is no dichotomy. For example, economics does not have separate theories for the behavior of women and the behavior of men, and so the male–female distinction, when made at all, defines only a partitioning, not a dichotomy. The consumer–producer partitioning, on the other hand, is a dichotomy, at least in neoclassical economics (not in Model One), for neoclassical economics has one theory for the consumer and another for the producer.

A dichotomy is either valid or false. If both subsets of a dichotomized set are mathematically defined, and the definitions differ, the dichotomy is valid, and it will remain valid so long as those definitions are left in force. If the two subsets are not well defined, the dichotomy stands a good chance of being false, no matter how plausible it may look.

To model builders, the greatest strength of mathematics is the poverty of its vocabulary. Correspondingly, the greatest weakness of literary models is the opulence of the English language. A model builder who believes two concepts to be essentially different needs different terms to name them, and the Oxford English Dictionary stands ready to accommodate him with a flood of words. English thus facilitates, perhaps even promotes, specious dichotomization. Mathematics does the opposite. The very paucity of mathematical terms forces the model builder to tighten and unify his theories, to cut superfluities, to turn away from the specific and toward the general.

Turning away from the general and toward the specific, we examine some familiar dichotomies. A few pertain to social rather than individual behavior and so do not directly affect the theories in this book.

It was submitted that "consumer" and "producer" are not definable. If this is indeed so, if it is impossible to make a (mathematical) distinction between consumers and producers, then it is also impossible to distinguish consumer goods from producer goods, consumption activities from production activities, market behavior from nonmarket behavior, the household sector from the industrial sector, a pure-exchange economy from a productive economy, demand from derived demand. Expectedly then, Models One and Two do not make any of these distinctions.

Another familiar dichotomy is that between money and commodities. It has already been noted that money and monetary notions, being institutional concepts, have no place in theories of behavior. The same conclusion can be reached by the definitional route. In Chapter 4, "money" and "commodity" are (mathematically) defined, and the definitions prove to be the same. According to those definitions then, the money/commodity dichotomy is false: money is merely a commodity, no more different from tea than tea is from salt.

The implications, some obvious and some not, are as momentous as they are underrated. An obvious implication is that if money is a commodity, barter is indistinguishable from monetary exchange. A not so obvious implication is that if money is a commodity, monetary concepts are indistinguishable from nonmonetary ones and so lose their status of fundamental notions. Words like profit, cost, revenue, income, and money prices are then dropped from the vocabulary of pure theory. And of course, if *profit* is no longer a theoretical term, profit maximization is not either. The neoclassical theory of the firm thus loses its footing. (Details are discussed in Chapter 4.) As for *income,* its demise as a theoretical concept pulls the rug out from under all income-related notions, among them the Slutsky equation and the consumer's budget constraint $\mathbf{p}'\mathbf{q} = y$. Some of the very things commonly taken to form the essence of economics thus turn out to be nothing but Bright Puzzle Pieces, either peripheral or irrelevant.

Abandoning the money–commodities dichotomy is only the beginning. This book does not dichotomize the set of goods in any other way, either. No distinction is thus made between edible and inedible goods, perfectly divisible and imperfectly divisible goods, durable and nondurable goods, private and public goods, primary and nonprimary goods, intermediate and final goods, capital and other goods, human capital and other goods, financial instruments and other goods. Of course, dropping all these distinctions may some day turn out to be a mistake. Perhaps some day a mathematical definition will be found for, say, private goods, and a different mathematical definition for public goods, and that will prove the distinction between public goods and private goods to be a legitimate dichotomy. But it is assumed here that this will not happen.

Leaving the set of goods adichotomous has some surprising implications. For an example, we temporarily return to neoclassical utility theory and show that *the neoclassical demand curve cannot be a straight line.* Assume there is indeed only one type of commodity. Any theoretically derived demand function is then necessarily unique (it being understood that the function will have some unspecified parameters whose values vary from commodity to commodity and from consumer to consumer). Because the unique demand function must fit normal goods as well as Giffen goods, its graph must be capable of bending back. But then the demand function cannot be linear.

A comment in passing. Some authors define *goods* as *commodities* plus *money*. This presumes that money is not one of the commodities. But in this book it is. Accordingly, "goods" and "commodities" are used interchangeably throughout.

Whatever a theorist has to say about an element of an undichotomized set, he says about all elements of that set. Conversely, when a theorist fails to treat all elements of a set the same way, the very asymmetry is evidence that at some point he has dichotomized the set, wittingly or unwittingly. Illustrations follow.

The neoclassical theory of the firm does not dichotomize the set of inputs. It therefore must treat all inputs the same way. Suppose there are three inputs, and let the production function be $f(x_1,x_2,x_3)$. Then f must be *symmetric in its indices,* meaning that every permutation of the subscripts 1, 2, and 3 leaves the function unchanged (except for appearance, which is immaterial). For example, an acceptable production function is $f(x_1,x_2,x_3) = \lambda x_1^{\alpha_1}x_2^{\alpha_2}x_3^{\alpha_3}$: if the order of the subscripts is changed from 1–2–3 to 2–3–1, the function becomes $\lambda x_2^{\alpha_2}x_3^{\alpha_3}x_1^{\alpha_1}$, which is effectively the same as the original. Even $f(K,L) = \lambda K^{\alpha}L^{\beta}$ is symmetric, although not in its indices. (There are none.) Rather, $\lambda K^{\alpha}L^{\beta}$ is symmetric because interchanging K and α with L and β, in that order, leaves the function unchanged except for appearance. Another way to put it is this: If capital and labor are the only inputs, all conclusions of the theory of the firm must remain the same if you interpret K as labor and L as capital.

Suppose, on the other hand, that the Scientist says he has deduced from his definitions that, in a world with only two inputs, the production function is $f(K,L) = K/L$. You then know, without any further information, that the Scientist must have begun by dichotomizing the set of inputs, one subset containing capital alone and the other subset containing labor alone. Had he not introduced that dichotomy, it would have been impossible for him to deduce an asymmetric production function. Even a magician cannot pull a rabbit out of a hat without putting it in first.

For the next example, imagine a Hicksian consumer in a world with only three goods, bread, milk, and money. The budget constraint is $p_1q_1 + p_2q_2 = y$, where y is income. Whether good 1 is bread and good 2 is milk or the other way around is impossible to tell, for the constraint is symmetric in the indices 1 and 2. But the constraint does not treat all three goods symmetrically—just the first two. The asymmetry of the constraint is evidence that the set of goods has been dichotomized, with one subset containing bread and milk and the other subset containing money only. Without such a dichotomy, the budget constraint would be symmetric in all three goods. It would be, say, $p_1q_1 + p_2q_2 + p_3q_3 = 0d$. (Recall that d stands for dollar.)

Continuing the illustration, suppose that the three prices p_1, p_2, p_3 were doubled or tripled. The left side of $p_1q_1 + p_2q_2 + p_3q_3 = 0d$ would then double or triple; but the equation would still represent the same plane. The plane is thus unique but the prices are not. To make the prices unique we set one of them, p_3 say, identically equal to 1. Doubling or tripling all three prices is thus now no longer possible. The equation

$$p_1q_1 + p_2q_2 + p_3q_3 = 0d$$

becomes

$$p_1q_1 + p_2q_2 + q_3 = 0d, \text{ or } p_1q_1 + p_2q_2 = -q_3.$$

Even though symmetry in indices is now destroyed, symmetry in interpretation remains preserved, for it has been left open whether good 3 is bread or milk or money. It is only when good 3 is specified as money, and $-q_3$ relabeled as y, that symmetry of interpretation, too, is lost, and a dichotomy is introduced.

One more example. Consider a perfectly competitive industry, with a large number of identical firms all earning zero profit. Economic theory says that if a demand shift causes profits to fall below zero, some firms will drop out. That sounds plausible; in a real industry, something like that may indeed happen. But it won't happen in a theoretical industry consisting of identical firms. Identical firms behave identically. If one drops out, all drop out. And of course, after dropping out they all notice immediately that there is now a great deal of unsatisfied demand, and therefore a chance to make a great deal of profit. They therefore all enter the industry again. And drop out. And come back. And drop out. And come back. Evidently, the assumption that all firms in the industry are identical is untenable.

This concludes the discussion of the second principle. A few more dichotomies are examined later in this chapter.

THIRD PRINCIPLE: SMALL IS NOT ZERO

A rich source of false dichotomies is the practice of equating "small" with "zero." Some fictitious quotes serve as examples.

Quote 1: "The difference between 777.01 and 777 is so small that we might as well declare it to be zero, for simplicity." This is reasonable.

Rounding 777.01 to 777 is a practical step, the kind of thing the Visitor might do.

Quote 2: "Earth attracts the apple, and the apple attracts Earth. But the force with which the apple attracts Earth has so little effect that we might as well declare it to be zero, for simplicity." Unlike the first quote, this one concerns theory, the Scientist's domain. This time, equating "small" with "zero" does not simplify anything. It complicates. It dichotomizes the set of all objects into "large" ones, like Earth, and "small" ones, like the apple; and in so doing it destroys an essential part of Newton's theory of gravitation, namely, the symmetry with which that theory treats all objects.

Quote 3: "Fluctuations in the U.S. economy greatly affect the Liechtenstein economy—much more so than the other way around. Indeed, the influence of events in Liechtenstein on the U.S. economy is so small that we might as well declare it to be zero, for simplicity." This is like Quote 2. Equating "small" with "zero" simplifies nothing if it destroys symmetry.

Quote 4: "Capital flows easily across a nation's borders. For labor this is less true. So much less, in fact, that we might as well declare the cross-border labor flow to be zero, for simplicity." Again, symmetry is destroyed. The goal may be simplicity, but the outcome is complexity.

Quote 5: "Many industries have a dominant firm, called the Leader; all other firms are Followers. The Followers use the Leader's actions as a given when they make their decisions. Perhaps the Followers influence the Leader, too, but if they do, their influence is so small that we might as well declare it to be zero." Here too, essential symmetry is thrown away in the mistaken name of simplicity. The destruction of symmetry marks the leader–follower partitioning as a false dichotomy.

Quote 6: "In theory, every producer of widgets can influence the price of widgets. If, however, the number of firms in the widget industry is very large, each firm's influence is so small that we might as well declare it to be zero." This is the idea behind perfect competition.

Consider one of those widget manufacturers, and suppose he produces under conditions of constant returns to scale. A doubling of all inputs will thus double the firm's output. Suppose further that there is perfect competition in the input markets as well. It means that input prices, too, are fixed. Suppose, finally, that the producer is making a profit of $1 per week.

Would it pay the producer to double his inputs and thereby his outputs? Doubling the output will double revenue, for the output price is by assumption fixed. Doubling all inputs will double cost, for input prices are by assumption fixed. And since profit equals revenue minus cost, doubling both revenue and cost will double profit, to $2. The answer is thus, yes, doubling inputs and output is a good idea.

But if doubling is a good idea when profit is $1, it must be a good idea also when profit is $2, or $4, or $8, or $16. More to the point, there is no limit to the amount of profit the producer can make; all he has to do is expand and expand and expand. We have an example here of a producer who, while searching for a profit maximum, is delighted to discover that none exists. No one else is happy, though. Nonexistence of a profit maximum is disconcerting to the Scientist, absurd to the Visitor.

We go through the argument again, but this time without equating "small" with "zero." There is thus now no fixed-price assumption, no perfect competition.

Regardless of how insignificant his firm may seem initially, once the producer has doubled and redoubled his inputs and output twenty or thirty times, the insignificance is a thing of the past. Now the world is running out of workers he can hire, machines he can buy, and consumers he can sell his millions of widgets to. If he is to keep expanding, he will have to lower the widget price, pay more for what little capital is still available, offer higher wages to the few workers not yet in his employ. It means that the next time the producer doubles all inputs (and thereby output), he will find that cost more than doubles and revenue less than doubles. Profit, squeezed from both sides, thus stops expanding. And if the producer continues his doubling, profit will eventually contract. Somewhere along the way, profit must reach a maximum. It is an outcome of both realism and simplicity. Worth stressing is that the simplicity is the result of rejecting perfect competition, of *not* equating "small" with "zero."

FOURTH PRINCIPLE: AVOID ARBITRARINESS

Among physicists, the fourth principle is known as the Principle of Least Astonishment. Some illustrations follow.

The first illustration comes from the life insurance business. Trying to construct mortality tables, two actuaries discover that they need to specify the maximum age of a human being. Smith thinks the maximum is 130 years. Jones asks if it might be one second more. Smith concedes that it might. Jones asks if perhaps it could be *two* seconds more. Smith concedes that too.

But Smith now sees that Jones will continue to propose increases of the maximum age until he, Smith, finally stops conceding. At that point, he, Smith, will have committed himself to a maximum age specified in seconds, which is sure to raise the eyebrows of his fellow actuaries everywhere. Rethinking the question, Smith decides that astonishment will be least if he chooses a nonarbitrary specification of the maximum age.

That leaves only two possibilities, zero and infinity. Ruling out zero for obvious reasons, Smith declares infinity to be the maximum age. With that comes the understanding that the probability of living past 130 is very small, like 0.0000000001; but at least the probability is not zero, as Smith held originally.

The preceding story is not entirely fictitious. Actual mortality tables use infinity as the maximum human age.

For the second illustration, suppose there are 5000 palm trees on Robinson Crusoe's island. If Crusoe chops down all of them, the effects will be large and inescapable—no more coconuts for dessert, for one thing. If, on the other hand, Crusoe chops down only one or two trees, the consequences will be barely noticeable; his action will have little or no echo, so to speak. The question is, what is the critical number m, between 0 and 5000, so that cutting more than m trees has an echo and cutting m or fewer does not? Perhaps $m = 100$ sounds about right. But if $m = 100$ is plausible, it is difficult to defend that m cannot be 101. And if we make $m = 101$ our definitive choice, some skeptic is bound to ask why it cannot be $m = 102$.

The Principle of Least Astonishment says that the only way to keep the skeptics quiet is to choose m nonarbitrarily. That leaves two possibilities, $m = 0$ and $m = 5000$. Of these two, $m = 0$ is the more plausible choice. Choosing $m = 0$ expresses the belief that felling even just one tree will have an echo—will change the environment enough to make Crusoe notice and respond. Of course, the change in the environment will be very small. But small is not zero.

The third illustration concerns *individual behavior,* the topic of this book. A brief introduction is needed.

Individual behavior can be defined as consisting of all actions without a perceptible echo. Other agents may respond to such actions, or Nature may; but the absence of a "perceptible echo" means that the original agent either does not notice those responses or finds them too insignificant to warrant a reaction.

Social or *interactive behavior* consists of all actions with an echo, or, equivalently, all actions that are not classifiable as individual behavior. It is social behavior if Crusoe chops down all the trees, for Nature's response will noticeably affect his life from then on.

Introduction completed, we ask, how many actions have echos? By the fourth principle, the answer is either all or none. The latter is implausible. We therefore take it that every action has an echo. All behavior is thus social behavior.

Still, some actions have very faint echos—so faint as to be, for *practical* purposes, nonexistent. Those are the actions investigated in this book. They constitute "individual behavior." Individual behavior and social behavior are thus not at all the separate dominions that their names suggest. Rather, individual behavior is a province of social behavior—a province with a very vague border.

But if individual behavior is a subfield of social behavior, why bother with it? Why not build a model of social behavior and be done? The reason is practical: even if its boundaries are imprecisely defined, individual behavior is easier to model than behavior in general. By studying individual behavior first, we confront the modeling problems in stages instead of all at once.

A note in passing. Although "the theory of the firm" and "the theory of the producer" are generally used synonymously, the theory of the firm is by interpretation a theory of social behavior, whereas the theory of the producer is, also by interpretation, a theory of individual behavior. To emphasize the difference, "the firm" is from here on replaced with "the producer" whenever the demands of clarity permit.

The fourth illustration concerns a particular form of social behavior. If all consumers in the United States double their bread consumption from today forward, the price of bread will go up. If, instead, only one consumer doubles his bread consumption, does the price of bread go up too? Suppose not. There must then be some critical number m, between 0 and 260 million, so that the bread price will go up if more than m people double their consumption and stay the same if m or fewer do. By the Principle of Least Astonishment, m must be either 0 to 260 million, with $m = 0$ the more plausible choice. That is to say, as soon as even one consumer doubles his bread consumption, the bread price is affected. Naturally, the effect will be very small. But small is not zero.

The last paragraph implies that, in theories of *social* behavior, all economic agents are price makers. And since all behavior is, strictly speaking, social behavior, there is no such thing as a price taker. The partitioning of the set of agents into price makers and price takers is thus yet another false dichotomy.

Price takers do appear in theories of *individual* behavior, like Model One. But as pointed out a moment ago, individual behavior does not really exist. What we call individual behavior is nothing but an imperfect approximation to social behavior. And the price taker is one of its imperfections.

The fifth and last illustration concerns the duration of the economic period. Period-analytical models typically leave that duration indeterminate. They thereby deprive their assertions of empirical content. A statement like "the consumer demands one loaf of bread per period," for instance, has no operational meaning when the period length is unspecified.

Suppose then that we specify the length of the period, as one week, say. Right away Jones will ask if it cannot be a second longer, and you know where that leads. By the principle of least astonishment, the period length can only be zero or infinity. Logic expresses no preference, but a zero period length is a bit easier for the intuition to accept. Models One and Two treat time as a continuous variable, which is another way of saying that the period length is zero.

Worth noting is that if the period length is zero, there is no "next period," for the same reason that there is no smallest number greater than 3. Of course, if the period length is infinite, there is no next period either.

FIFTH PRINCIPLE: AVOID CIRCULARITY

Perhaps the best-known principle of model building is that definitions must never be circular. So long as the Scientist sticks to mathematical definitions, circularities are unlikely to appear. But they may show up when the Scientist cannot think of a mathematical definition and settles for a literary one. Some examples follow.

The formulation of the neoclassical budget constraint implies that every good has exactly one price. Yet two Shell gas stations will often charge different prices for a gallon of Regular Unleaded, and two supermarkets will often charge different prices for a jar of Taster's Choice instant coffee. In fact, it is not unusual for a single supermarket to sell one product at two prices; when the price of a jar of coffee goes up, alert shoppers will sometimes find, way back on the shelf, a few dusty jars with the old price tags still attached. How can these occurrences be reconciled with the one-good–one-price doctrine?

The traditional solution declares that any good found to have two prices is actually two goods. *Price* thus becomes a defining characteristic of *good,* implying that *price* must be defined before *good.* On the other hand, a price is always the price of a good, and so we must define *good* before we can define *price.* The argument is clearly circular. But then the neoclassical budget constraint is untenable. (Model One ties prices to actions, not goods, and so avoids circularity. Of course this also means that the budget constraint cannot be part of Model One.)

Our next example concerns *bads.* Typically, a bad is defined as something with negative marginal utility. Bads thus belong in the domain of the utility function. But the domain of the utility function should be defined first, before utility. The definition of bads in terms of utility is therefore circular. (In this book, marginal utilities are not required to be positive, and "bad" is left undefined.)

The third and last example concerns *money.* Money is often said to differ from (other) commodities in that it is the preferred medium of exchange. But to know what "exchange" means, one must first know what commodities are, and what money is. Defining money in terms of exchange thus brings circularity. The same objection can be made against the assertion that money is wanted not for its own sake but for what it can buy: the definition of money logically comes before the definition of "buy."

SUMMARY

According to the first principle, Define Mathematically, a mathematical model consists of mathematical definitions and statements derived from those definitions—nothing else. Tests and experiments can show a model to be plausible or implausible, persuasive or unpersuasive; but they cannot prove it right or wrong.

The second principle, Beware Dichotomies, cautions against false dichotomies, of which economics has many. Most consequential, and therefore most damaging, is the money–commodities dichotomy; were it abolished, all monetary notions—profit, money prices, income, and the like—would have to be banned from pure theory. Only slightly less injurious is the consumer–producer dichotomy.

The third principle, Small Is Not Zero, holds that equating small with zero is a mistake if it destroys symmetry.

The fourth principle, Avoid Arbitrariness, implies among other things that the period length should be either zero or infinity, and also that, strictly speaking, individual behavior does not exist.

The fifth principle, Avoid Circularity, points out that some economic notions are vitiated by definitional circularities. An example is the budget constraint.

Questions

1. Parmenides (ca. 500 B.C.) held that Earth is at the center of the universe. What mistake did Parmenides make, assuming that he made one?
2. If a profit-maximizing producer discovers that he can make a bigger profit by doubling output, can he make a still bigger profit by tripling his output?
3. Utility theory generally assumes that the consumer's tastes are constant. What does that mean?
4. Farmer Bob refuses to grow anything other than wheat and corn. He owns one acre, on which he grows wheat. He will be able to sell the wheat for \$800. Had he planted corn instead, he would have been able to sell the harvest for \$700. According to traditional economic theory, what is his opportunity cost?
5. The neoclassical consumer returns to the market at regular intervals, of duration τ, say. Why does he not return one second sooner?
6. The neoclassical consumer is a utility maximizer. The bundle he buys every Monday is thus exactly what he wants, given his budget con-

straint. Last Monday he bought a quart of milk and nothing else. Since his budget would have allowed him to buy one sip less than a quart, he has revealed, through his purchase, that he prefers a quart of milk to a quart of milk minus one sip. It follows that he will not drink even one sip of the milk he bought. But then why will he go back to the market next Monday, and all the Mondays afterward?

7. Polykeynesia has 2000 utility-maximizing inhabitants. Of these, n_1 live in Big City, and the remaining $n_2 = 2000 - n_1$ live in Fat City. Goods are so plentiful that no one has a budget constraint. Everyone's utility function has the form $u(\mathbf{x}) = e^{-n_i}$, with $i = 1$ for those who live in Big City and $i = 2$ for those who live in Fat City. The utility function thus measures congestion: the greater the number of people living in your city, the smaller the value of your utility function. It follows that if you migrate you improve the lot of those you leave behind, but you make everyone in your new city worse off. Suppose migration is instantaneous and costless. Is there an equilibrium, that is, a situation in which no one migrates? If there is no such equilibrium, why not? If there is, will it be attained?

4

Economic Preliminaries

In this chapter we begin by formulating mathematical definitions of *time, commodity,* and *money,* and drawing some conclusions. By the light of those conclusions—which, incidentally, are a good deal more consequential than the definitions themselves—we then examine five mainstream models of individual behavior. From that examination flow most of the features of Model One. The chapter concludes with a few remarks about demand and supply.

Of the five mainstream models to be examined, three are based on utility maximization, two on profit maximization. The utility-driven models are Pareto's utility theory, Hicks's utility theory (often thought to be the same as Pareto's, but actually quite different), and the theory of labor supply. The profit-driven models are the neoclassical theory of the producer and the activity-analytical theory of the producer.

Recall that the time axis T is the set of instants, and D is the one-dimensional vector space of time flows.

DEFINITION 1. *Time* is the one-dimensional point space $\{T,D\}$.

(See Chapter 2, MT 7.) Definition 1 says that time is a collection of instants and time flows, and has no other defining characteristics.

Next to be defined are "commodity" and its synonym, "good."

The endowment set X, a collection of n-coordinate points, can be written as the Cartesian product $X_1 \times X_2 \times \cdots \times X_n$. Here, X_1 is the set of stocks of good 1, X_2 is the set of stocks of good 2, and so on.

The action space A, a collection of n-vectors, can be written as the Cartesian product $A_1 \times A_2 \times \cdots \times A_n$. Here, A_1 is the set of flows of good 1, A_2 is the set of flows of good 2, and so on.

Like $\{T,D\}$, the pairs $\{X_1,A_1\}$, $\{X_2,A_2\}$, . . . are one-dimensional point spaces. But there is a difference: whereas points in T (instants) can be of any sign, points in X_1, X_2, . . . (stocks) must be nonnegative. To emphasize the difference, the $\{X_i,A_i\}$ will be called *nonnegative point spaces.*

Definition 2. The ith *commodity* or *good* is the one-dimensional nonnegative point space $\{X_i, A_i\}$.

Stripped of its intimidating verbiage, this merely says that every commodity quantity is either a stock or a flow, and that this defines "commodity" completely. Nothing else plays a role. Weight, size, price, importance in everyday life—none of these is a defining characteristic. Nor is location. Nor is time (or age). An apple leaving New York City at 10 A.M. is still the same apple when it arrives in Chicago at 2 P.M., and a rose at dawn is a rose at noon is a rose at dusk.

Comparing Definitions 1 and 2, you see that *time is not a good.* "I have lots of time" is thus essentially different from "I have lots of oranges," and "production processes use up time" is essentially different from "production processes use up inputs." Put another way, of the n flows that make up an action, none is a time flow.

Going a small step further, we shall say that *no good is measured in units of time.* That concerns, in particular, two goods traditionally measured in hours, *labor power* and *leisure.* Labor power is from here on measured not in hours but in some unit of energy, like the erg, and renamed *energy,* to avoid confusion. Leisure plays no role in what follows, so that it needs neither another measurement unit nor another name.

Money is next.

Definition 3. *Money* is a one-dimensional nonnegative point space.

This says that every quantity of money is either a stock or a flow, and that there are no other defining characteristics.

Putting Definitions 2 and 3 side by side shows that money is a commodity—is one of the $\{X_i, A_i\}$. Thus, although money is arguably the most important good in everyday life, and the brightest puzzle piece on the table, in the world of theory it is as insignificant as sausage. Its rightful place is with the other commodities, far from the center of the puzzle. Its contribution to the picture is the same as that of any other (specific) good: nil.

The main consequence of treating money as a commodity was noted earlier but bears repeating: *when money is an ordinary commodity, "money" cannot be a theoretical term, anymore than "tea" and "salt" and "strawberry jam" are theoretical terms.* And of course, if money does not belong in the theoretical dictionary, then neither do monetary concepts: *when money is an ordinary commodity, monetary notions like profit, revenue, cost, expenditure, income, consumption, savings, investment, taxes, imports, and exports have no place in pure theory.* Where they do belong is in normative theory and in applications of pure theory. By implication, any theory in which monetary concepts appear is a normative theory, or an application of a (perhaps still unwritten) positive theory, or a bit of both.

Whether money is a commodity is widely held to be a trivial issue. But then, the meaning of "money is a commodity" is generally misunderstood. The usual interpretation is that if money comes to be regarded as a commodity, nothing changes except that money "enters the utility function." It would be more accurate to say that the utility function is not noticeably affected but almost everything else is. That the utility function is not noticeably affected is because it is written $u(\mathbf{x})$ either way. That almost everything else changes is because all monetary concepts—like income, profit, money prices, and money itself—cease to be theoretical terms when money is a commodity. The language of economic theory thus changes beyond recognition.

So it turns out that what seems a trivial issue is actually of overriding importance. It raises the question of what the literature has to say on the subject.

What the literature has to say on the subject is little. Mathematical definitions of money and commodity are altogether nonexistent. But there are some nonmathematical descriptions, all aiming to prove that money is essentially different from commodities. Five are examined below. Several others appear in the questions at the end of the chapter.

1. *Money is different from commodities in that it is used but not used up.* By that criterion, ashtrays, mirrors, and jewelry would not be commodities either.

2. *Money is different from commodities in that it is wanted not for its own sake but for what it can buy.* When a pharmacist stocks a large supply of aspirin, he does not do so because he expects a headache. He does so because selling aspirin enables him to buy other things. Put differently, he enjoys having the aspirin not for its own sake but for what it can buy. Nor is this true just for money and aspirin. *Every* good offered in exchange for something else is a good that its owner enjoys having not for its own sake but for what it can buy. Statement 2 thus fails to separate money from commodities. It separates supplied goods from demanded goods.

If statement 2 sounds plausible, it may well be because elementary utility theory tends to portray money as the only supplied good. The dividing line between supplied goods and demanded goods is then also the dividing line between money and commodities.

Statement 2 is wrong for yet another reason, mentioned in the preceding chapter: it is circular. Its use of the word "buy" makes it so.

3. *Money is different from commodities in that it is the unit of account, a store of value, and the preferred medium of exchange.* Although this argument is meant to prove that money is a noncommodity, it cannot possibly do so. Presenting a list of properties that money has and other goods do not have, or have only in part, serves to identify money as a

separate good, different from tea, say. But salt, too, is different from tea, and yet salt is a commodity. More generally, whether or not *any* thing is a commodity cannot be decided by a list of properties identifying that thing.

Another weakness of statement 3 is the circularity implied in the use of "exchange," commented on before.

4. *Money is different from commodities in that money buys commodities whereas commodities do not buy money.* The appearance of the word "buy" marks this statement, too, as circular. Further, the assertion is false; as every store owner can attest, goods do buy money. Perhaps Webster disagrees, but economics need not take its cues from lexicographers.

5. *Money is different from commodities in that it can be exchanged directly (that is, without intermediation by another good) for all other goods. Commodities may be directly exchangeable for* some *other goods, but never for* all *other goods.* If a commodity were directly exchangeable for all goods, it would be money, or a money.

Like its predecessors, assertion 5 is circular, since it refers to exchange. Also, it fails to furnish a proof that the set of commodities is nonempty, a proof that there indeed exist commodities that cannot possibly be directly exchanged for each other. Never mind that no one has ever acquired a submarine in exchange for geraniums; never mind that, absent a substantial grant, no one ever will. What is needed here is an example of two commodities that are *logically* unexchangeable. Until two such commodities are found, we are forced to conclude that the set of commodities—in the sense of statement 5—is empty. Every good is then a money. Or what amounts to the same thing, money is one of the commodities.

Of course, the money/commodities dichotomy may well be valid. But a demonstration of its validity would take considerably more than arguments of the type just discussed. Specifically, one would need mathematical definitions of commodity and money, and those definitions would have to be different. Until such a two-step demonstration is found, there are no reasons to view the dichotomy as valid, and good reasons to view it as false.

MAINSTREAM MODELS OF INDIVIDUAL BEHAVIOR

Pareto's Utility Theory

Pareto's utility theory presents the consumer as maximizing utility, u, subject to a budget constraint. Utility—Pareto called it *ophélimité,* but that name never caught on—is defined over the endowment set X. Pareto does not specify the length of the period, but talks about it as if it were positive and finite.

The budget constraint is $\mathbf{p}'\mathbf{x} = \mathbf{p}'\mathbf{x}_0$ or

$$p_1x_1 + p_2x_2 + \cdot \cdot \cdot + p_nx_n = p_1x_{10} + p_2x_{20} + \cdot \cdot \cdot + p_nx_{n0},$$

in which $\mathbf{x}_0 = (x_{10}, x_{20}, \ldots, x_{n0})'$ is the initial endowment and $\mathbf{x}$ generically represents all attainable endowments. All n prices p_i are positive. Both $\mathbf{p}$ and $\mathbf{x}_0$ are assumed given, making the budget constraint an equation in $\mathbf{x}$. Pareto regards (nominal) money as one of the commodities, at least in his utility theory. For concreteness and specificity, he takes money to be good 1, so that $p_1 \equiv 1$.

Discussion

It will become clear later, in the discussion of Hicksian utility theory, that Pareto's finest contribution is his choice of the endowment set X as the domain of u. After examining whether u should be a function of quantities consumed or a function of quantities "at the individual's disposal," Pareto decides that the latter is the right choice (1971, Sect. 4, p. 182). At times his arguments are baffling ("If a woman has ten dresses, she need not wear them all at once . . ."), and in the conversational parts of his book he often confuses utility with usefulness, talking about utility as if it were a function of quantities ingested or otherwise consumed. When he turns to mathematics, however, he invariably assigns utility to endowments.

Some of Pareto's critics say that defining utility over endowments is the wrong thing to do. They argue that "utility" connotes satisfaction, and that there is more satisfaction in acquiring than in possessing. They conclude that utility should be a function of demanded bundles.

This argument has its priorities wrong. Pareto defined utility over X, rather than over the set of demanded bundles, because he found that it led to a more powerful theory. Next to this, connotations stand irrelevant. Their irrelevance is particularly easy to demonstrate in the case at hand: the critics' argument instantly evaporates when "utility" is replaced with the connotation-free "objective function."

Since Pareto's constraint is formulated in terms of endowments, the consumer chooses an $\mathbf{x} \in X$. On the other hand, to turn his initial endowment $\mathbf{x}_0$ into the chosen one, the consumer must undertake an action. Translated into our terminology, it means that he must choose an $\mathbf{a} \in A$. If the chosen $\mathbf{x}$ is the utility-maximizing $\mathbf{x}$, is not the chosen $\mathbf{a}$ the utility-maximizing $\mathbf{a}$? The answer has to be no, since a function of endowments can be maximized only by endowments. Still, a "utility-maximizing $\mathbf{a}$" sounds intuitively plausible. Some probing is in order.

Undertaking $\mathbf{a}$ will change the endowment from $\mathbf{x}_0$ to $\mathbf{x}_0 + \mathbf{a}$. As a result, the value of the utility function increases, from $u(\mathbf{x}_0)$ to $u(\mathbf{x}_0 + \mathbf{a})$. The increase, $u(\mathbf{x}_0 + \mathbf{a}) - u(\mathbf{x}_0)$, is a function of $\mathbf{x}_0$ and $\mathbf{a}$. If $\mathbf{x}_0$ is regarded as fixed, the increase is a function of $\mathbf{a}$ alone. Call it $v(\mathbf{a})$. It is this $v(\mathbf{a})$ that the chosen $\mathbf{a}$ maximizes. But $v(\mathbf{a})$ is not the utility function. It would therefore be wrong to say that the chosen $\mathbf{a}$ is the utility-maximizing action.

That Pareto regards nominal money as a commodity, and treats it the same as all other goods, there can be no doubt (Sect. 37, p. 411; Sect. 52, p. 421). Since he makes money good 1, the first coordinate of $\mathbf{x}_0$ is the amount of money that the consumer has at the beginning of the period, and the first coordinate of the $\mathbf{x}$ appearing in the utility function is a money stock.

The two p_1's in Pareto's constraint could be suppressed without harm, since they are identically equal to 1. But the equation looks nicer if they are left in.

It is sometimes held that if money appears in the utility function, it ought to appear as real money. According to this opinion, Pareto's utility function must be changed from $u(x_1,x_2, \ldots, x_n)$ to $u(x_1/P, x_2, \ldots, x_n)$, where P is a price index. This would be an important change: $u(x_1/P, x_2, \ldots, x_n)$ is asymmetric in its indices, implying that money is not a commodity. Besides, the introduction of P would mean that money prices, which like all other monetary notions were so recently sent to the edge of the puzzle, belong in the center after all. A step that big requires strong justification indeed.

The justification offered in the literature is that the consumer needs to determine whether he has enough money to meet future expenses, and, to do so, must let himself be guided by the *real* value of his money balances. This is a normative ideal. It has no place in positive theory. Utility theory declares the consumer to be a utility maximizer; utility theory therefore cannot declare the consumer to be, as well, an optimizer of spending patterns, or a rationer of cash, or a bookkeeper.

For another look at the issue of nominal vs. real balances, let the utility function have its original, Paretian form, with nominal money as its first variable, and let all marginal utilities be positive. Suppose that the price of tea goes up. The tea-drinking consumer then sees his budget constraint tighten. It follows that the old utility-maximizing endowment is no longer affordable. It also follows that the new utility-maximizing endowment is less attractive than the old one. The consumer is thus worse off, *even though the utility function is unchanged.* But this means that, if the money stock appearing in the utility function were changed from nominal to real, from x_1 to x_1/P, the increase in the price of tea would hurt the consumer *twice:* his new utility-maximizing endowment would (*i*) carry less utility than the old one and (*ii*) carry less utility than it used to. Putting real rather than nominal balances into the utility function thus leads to double counting.

Nor is this all. The real-balance approach completely distorts the picture when the price of a good goes up and the consumer is a *seller* of that good. For an example, suppose the increased price is the wage, and the consumer is a seller of energy. To the consumer, the wage increase is a good thing. But the real-balance approach says it is a bad thing.

Linear-algebraically speaking, the two sides of Pareto's budget constraint, $\mathbf{p}'\mathbf{x}$ and $\mathbf{p}'\mathbf{x}_0$, are undefined, since $\mathbf{x}$ and $\mathbf{x}_0$ are points. But $\mathbf{x} - \mathbf{x}_0$ is a vector, in *A*, and so $\mathbf{p}'(\mathbf{x} - \mathbf{x}_0) = 0d$—the *d* stands for dollar—is well defined. From here on, $\mathbf{p}'\mathbf{x} = \mathbf{p}'\mathbf{x}_0$ is understood to mean $\mathbf{p}'(\mathbf{x} - \mathbf{x}_0) = 0d$ or, equivalently, $d^{-1}\mathbf{p}'(\mathbf{x} - \mathbf{x}_0) = 0$.

Since $\mathbf{x}$ and $\mathbf{x}_0$ are *points,* their *coordinates* must be positive or zero. By contrast, $\mathbf{x} - \mathbf{x}_0$ is a *vector*; its *elements* may be negative. Because of this, Pareto's model has no difficulty in dealing with supply. Whenever and whatever the consumer supplies—energy to his employer, money to his creditors, his old car as part payment for a new one—the model captures it effortlessly.

Pareto's budget constraint makes it impossible for the consumer to add as little as one penny to his wealth, even if he trades all day long, every day of his life. A more realistic constraint would be $\mathbf{p}'\mathbf{x} \geq \mathbf{p}'\mathbf{x}_0$; but conventionally defined utility does not attain a maximum over the set of endowments $\mathbf{x}$ satisfying that inequality. One way out of the dilemma is to replace utility maximization with another behavioral principle. Model One chooses this exit.

In conclusion, an intriguing remark of Pareto's. At one point Pareto says that prices are "auxiliary unknowns . . . which must in the end be eliminated" (Sect. 152, p. 152). Thus, rather than merely banishing prices to the edge of the puzzle, Pareto actually pushes them off the table. Since he does not amplify, and since his theory is not noticeably free of prices, it is impossible to tell what sort of price-free theory he had in mind. Model One is formulated without reference to prices—maybe he was thinking of something like Model One.

Hicks's Utility Theory

Like Pareto, Hicks presents the consumer as maximizing utility subject to a budget constraint. Unlike Pareto, Hicks defines utility over the set of *demanded bundles.* A demanded bundle is a collection of flows. That makes it an action, a vector in the action space *A*. More precisely, a demanded bundle is a *nonnegative* action. The domain of *u* is thus a rather limited subset of *A*, quite different from the domain *X* of Pareto's utility function.

Like Pareto, Hicks does not specify the length of the period, but talks about it as if it were positive and finite. Hicks does depict the consumer as going to the market once a week, but stresses that "week" should not be taken literally.

How should demanded bundles be denoted? Hicks uses $\mathbf{x}$, which risks confusion with endowments. (On one occasion, it trips up even Hicks himself. See the Discussion below.) Use of $\mathbf{a}$ would risk confusion too:

everywhere else in this book, **a** stands for *any* action, rather than just a *nonnegative* action. Probably safest is to use the textbooks' favorite, **q**. A **q** is thus a nonnegative **a**.

The Hicksian budget constraint is $\mathbf{p}'\mathbf{q} = y$.

Discussion

Why did Hicks decide to define utility over demanded bundles? A plausible guess is that it was not a deliberate choice; perhaps he viewed acquisition as more satisfying than possession and gave the matter no thought beyond that. Reading *Value and Capital* (Hicks, 1946), one comes away with the impression that Hicks thought his model to be fundamentally the same as Pareto's. Hicks does criticize Pareto, but only on the implications of ordinality, a small point.

Hicks's practice of denoting demanded bundles by **x** rather than **q** makes it easy to overlook the difference between his theory and Pareto's. Contributing to the confusion is the resemblance between a demanded bundle and an endowment: both the elements (flows) of a demanded bundle and the coordinates (stocks) of an endowment are nonnegative quantities.

For a graphical illustration of the difference between the two models, Pareto's and Hicks's, suppose the only goods are beer, tuna, and money. Figure 1, which illustrates Pareto's model, shows three axes—one for each good—and a budget plane. Points on the axes represent stocks. The budget plane contains all endowments **x** that satisfy $\mathbf{p}'\mathbf{x} = \mathbf{p}'\mathbf{x}_0$, including the initial endowment $\mathbf{x}_0$ and the utility-maximizing endowment $\mathbf{x}^*$. No indifference surfaces are shown, but some indifference surfaces intersect the budget

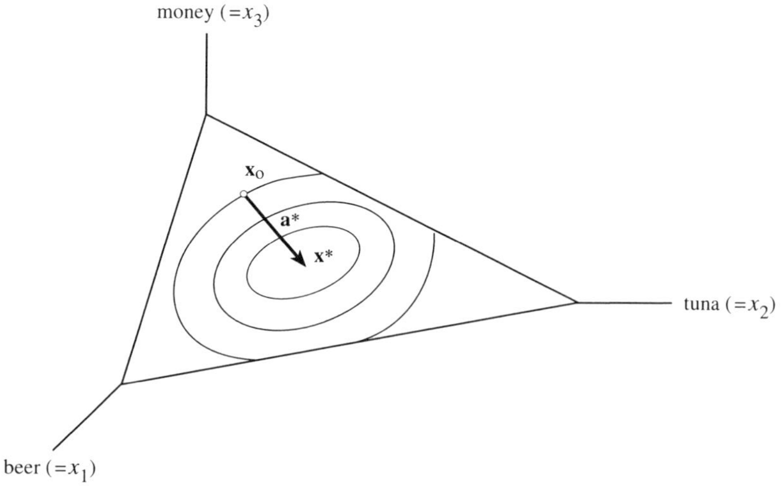

Figure 1. When money is a good: Pareto's model.

plane, and a few of those intersections, which may be called *constrained indifference curves,* do appear in the picture. Arrow **a*** represents the action undertaken by the consumer.

Figure 2 illustrates the Hicksian model. Points on the axes represent flows. Because Hicks views money as a nongood, there are only two goods here. The indifference contours are thus not surfaces but curves on the floor (that is, in the beer–tuna coordinate plane). The money axis, not strictly needed, is included to ease comparison with Figure 1. Also shown is a slanted plane whose intersection with the floor is the budget line. The plane itself has no name. Arrow **a*** represents the action undertaken by the consumer. Arrow **q*** represents a demanded bundle—in fact, the utility-maximizing one.

Suppose a Paretian consumer inherits a million cans of tuna from an eccentric uncle. That changes $\mathbf{x}_0$, and thereby $u(\mathbf{x}_0)$, and induces the consumer to buy no more tuna for the next few centuries. It is a realistic outcome. Now suppose a Hicksian consumer inherits a million cans of tuna. Since Hicks assigns utility to demanded bundles, the change of $\mathbf{x}_0$ has no effect on the consumer's conception of optimality: any **q*** that maximized utility before the inheritance will still maximize utility afterward. If, for instance, the Hicksian consumer used to buy two cans of tuna per week before his uncle died, he will continue to do so now that he has a basement full of tuna. It is an unrealistic and implausible conclusion.

And this is only the beginning. A far more crippling feature of the Hicksian model is that it knows only positive and zero flows. It is therefore

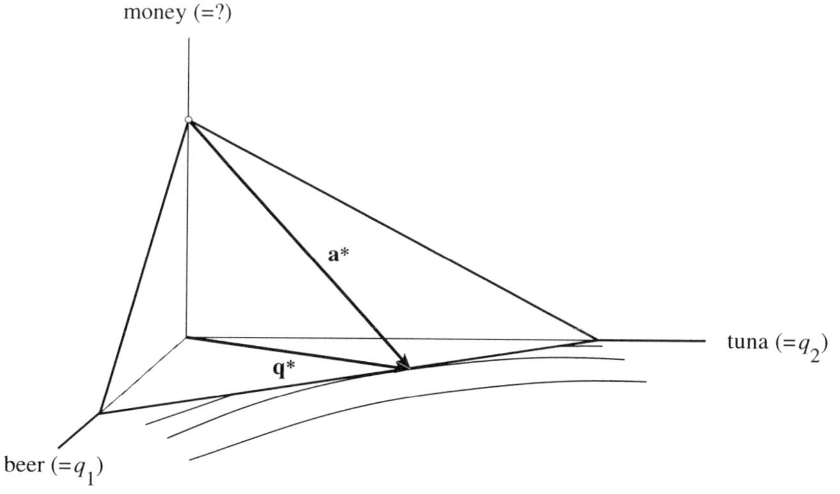

Figure 2. When money is not a good: Hicks's model.

unable to deal with negative flows. That is to say, it lacks the theoretical apparatus to deal with supplying by the consumer.

But does the consumer supply? Yes, he does, and quite a lot of it. He supplies money when he pays for his purchases. He supplies energy when he works. He supplies a sixpack when he accepts the barbecue invitation. And when his neighbor supplies him with apples, he, in exchange, supplies the neighbor with pears. Pareto would describe each of these events by saying that some coordinate in the final endowment is smaller than the corresponding coordinate in the initial endowment, but Hicks does not have that option. "Endowment" is not in the Hicksian dictionary.

Noting his model's inability to deal with the supplying of *money,* Hicks declares money to be a nongood. This implies that there is no money in the Hicksian world—or rather, that is what it ought to imply. But at one point, Hicks puts money on one of the axes of an indifference map (p. 39), and money remains firmly present in the budget constraint, as y. How Hicks sees the role of money is thus unclear.

The supplying of *energy* or labor power is traditionally handled by viewing it as the demanding of leisure. More on that in a moment, when the third model is discussed.

To deal with the supplying of *goods other than money and energy*—the sixpack, the apples, the pears—Hicks offers this proposal: If the consumer "comes to the market not only as a buyer but also as a seller . . . [w]e may suppose, if we like, that he exchanges [the stock he wishes to sell] into money . . . when he will find himself in exactly the same position as our consumer . . ." (p. 36). A flesh-and-blood supplier might act this way, but the model consumer will not. Since Hicks has declared money a nongood, his consumer is not going to accept any. Apart from that, it is illegitimate to assume that the consumer starts by selling all he has. Selling is behavior, and behavior must be modeled, not assumed.

Perhaps aware of the inadequacy of his proposal, Hicks advances another one. To deal with supply, he says, all one has to do is replace the budget constraint with $\mathbf{p}'\mathbf{x} = \mathbf{p}'\mathbf{x}_0$. It is "the only alteration which has to be made to the system" (p. 313). This is where Hicks trips over his own notation. The constraint $\mathbf{p}'\mathbf{x} = \mathbf{p}'\mathbf{x}_0$ is Pareto's, and the $\mathbf{x}$ in it is an endowment, a point in X; in the rest of the Hicksian model, $\mathbf{x}$ (our $\mathbf{q}$) is a demanded bundle, a vector in A. Replacing $\mathbf{p}'\mathbf{q} = y$ with $\mathbf{p}'\mathbf{x} = \mathbf{p}'\mathbf{x}_0$ thus cannot be "the only alteration." *Everything* changes. Utility, in particular, must change from $u(\mathbf{q})$ to $u(\mathbf{x})$, for Pareto's constraint will not grow in Hicks's utility domain. And of course, once the constraint is $\mathbf{p}'\mathbf{x} = \mathbf{p}'\mathbf{x}_0$ and the utility function is $u(\mathbf{x})$, Hicks's theory ceases to exist as a separate entity. It becomes Pareto's.

In the light cast by these observations, Hicks's proposal to change $\mathbf{p}'\mathbf{q} = y$ to $\mathbf{p}'\mathbf{x} = \mathbf{p}'\mathbf{x}_0$ is probably best ignored. Of course, the return to

$\mathbf{p}'\mathbf{q} = y$ leaves the Hicksian model unable to deal with supply—any kind of supply—but at least the model's identity is preserved.

The constraints $\mathbf{p}'\mathbf{q} = y$ and $\mathbf{p}'\mathbf{x} = \mathbf{p}'\mathbf{x}_0$ have one thing in common: both keep the consumer from increasing his wealth by even a fraction of a cent. Unrealistic though such constancy of riches may be, it is nearly impossible to avoid so long as utility maximization remains the consumer's goal.

In conclusion, some remarks about the marginal utility of money and about money illusion.

To Pareto, the marginal utility of good i is $\partial u(\mathbf{x})/\partial x_i$, and, since he regards money as good 1, the marginal utility of money is $\partial u(\mathbf{x})/\partial x_1$. To Hicks, who takes money to be a nongood, the marginal utility of good i is $\partial u(\mathbf{q})/\partial q_i$, and the marginal utility of money is undefined.

But there does exist, in Hicksian utility theory, a "marginal utility of income." Judging by the sound of the term, you would expect it to be $\partial u(\mathbf{q})/\partial y$, but that is not it; u is not a function of y. The actual definition of "marginal utility of income" is $\partial u(\mathbf{q}^*)/\partial y$, where $\mathbf{q}^*$ is the utility-maximizing bundle. Evidently this is not a marginal utility in the usual sense.

Turning next to money illusion, suppose all prices and income are doubled, in the Hicksian model. That changes the constraint from $\mathbf{p}'\mathbf{q} = y$ to $(2\mathbf{p})'\mathbf{q} = 2y$. Actually, this is no change at all. Since the two equations are equivalent they have the same solutions $\mathbf{q}$. The model consumer thus necessarily chooses the same utility-maximizing bundle $\mathbf{q}^*$ as before. One expresses this by saying that the Hicksian model consumer "does not suffer from money illusion."

A flesh-and-blood consumer need not behave like the model consumer. When *his* income is doubled, and all prices are too, he may very well choose a bundle different from his customary one. If he does, he is said to "suffer from money illusion." It sounds as if he is castigated for being less sensible than the model consumer, but it is of course the other way around. The living consumer is free to behave any way he wants to, and it is up to the model consumer to do the imitating. In other words, that the model consumer is incapable of money illusion is a weakness of the Hicksian model, not a strength. "Money illusion" is merely a badly chosen term.

What happens to Pareto's budget constraint,

$$p_1x_1 + p_2x_2 + \cdots + p_nx_n = p_1x_{10} + p_2x_{20} + \cdots + p_nx_{n0}, \qquad (1)$$

when income and all prices are doubled? The question needs some rewording. First, what Hicks calls income is the amount of money initially held; Pareto calls that x_{10}. Second, doubling *all* prices is, to Pareto, impossible, for p_1 will always be 1. The question thus becomes, What happens to Pareto's budget constraint if we double x_{10} and all prices other than p_1? A look at (1) gives the answer: all terms except p_1x_1 $(= x_1)$ will be doubled. Since x_1 is a variable and cannot be manipulated, the postchange (1) is not equivalent to the prechange (1). It follows that in all but the most unusual circumstances, the utility-maximizing endowment will change. Pareto's consumer is thus capable of money illusion. It makes him more flexible than the Hicksian consumer.

Theory of Labor Supply and Leisure Demand

In the theory of labor supply and leisure demand, leisure is measured in hours, as is labor (meaning labor power). Our version of labor power—energy, measured in ergs—is put on hold.

In the simplest and most common form of the theory, utility is a function of demanded bundles of the form (L,y). Here, L is the number of hours of leisure demanded during the period, and y is income, the number of dollars demanded during the period.

The period length τ is positive and finite, and otherwise unspecified. (There is a temptation to set $\tau = 24$, that being the number of hours in a day. But then we could equally well take $\tau = 12$, that being the number of hours in a dozen.)

Utility is maximized subject to the constraint $y = w(\tau - L)$, where w is the wage rate.

Discussion

The first thing to note about the labor-supply model is that it lists income y among the arguments of the utility function. It makes money a commodity, a utility carrier. The labor-supply model is thus inconsistent with Hicksian utility theory, which declares money a nongood. There is some irony in this—the theory of labor supply, designed to cure a weakness of Hicksian utility theory, winds up contradicting that theory.

What makes the labor-supply model interesting is its approach to this modeling question: If a theory declares utility to be a function of demanded bundles, how can it possibly deal with supply? The straightforward answer is that it cannot, and that therefore utility should be assigned to endowments, not to demanded bundles; but the labor-supply model takes another route. It introduces the good "leisure," declares it to be the opposite of labor power, and so translates the theoretically vexatious "supplying of labor" into the theoretically manageable "demanding of leisure."

It is a clever trick, clearly applicable to all forms of supply, rather than just the supplying of labor. Take a consumer who is paying for something he just bought. To avoid modeling difficulties we must not say that he is supplying money. We must say that he is demanding poverty. It should be no deterrent if the phrase sounds strange at first. If "demanding leisure" is acceptable, "demanding poverty" is too.

But now another problem emerges. Money is not only supplied, it is also demanded. It is demanded when the consumer sells his labor power to an employer, or his old refrigerator to a neighbor. The "clever trick" thus does not work for money. More generally, it does not work for any good that is *both* supplied *and* demanded. It works only for goods that are just supplied, never demanded. Apparently, labor power is such a good.

But it is not. The consumer who supplies labor power demands it as well. He has to; if he is to go back to work tomorrow, he must replenish his stock of labor power today. And he does. He replenishes his stock of labor power by *eating*. It is at this point that a remarkable controversy arises.

Economic behavior is plausibly regarded as behavior that affects the stock of at least one good. By that informal standard, economic behavior includes more than just market-related, price-governed activities like buying and selling. It also includes manufacturing, destroying, borrowing, lending, stealing. And it includes eating.

Not everyone regards eating as economic behavior. Economics, it is sometimes said, has no business in the dining room. Why this should be persuasive is not clear, seeing that economics has always been quite nosy in the pantry. Besides, there is this weightier argument: eating is the only action that produces labor power. Thus, if theory declares that eating is not an action, theory is bound to conclude, first, that labor power is not produced and, next, that labor power must be a "primary good," magically springing from nowhere. Procrustes invented more elegant fits. A much simpler solution is to admit economics to the dining room. Eating thereby becomes economic behavior. More precisely, eating becomes a collection of actions, each with one or more negative elements pertaining to foods, and each with a positive element pertaining to labor power. It will be clear that this approach works only if we follow Pareto and assign utility to endowments. And of course, once we adopt Pareto's version of utility theory, supplying by consumers is easy to model. Leisure instantaneously becomes superfluous, and the need to regard money as a nongood disappears. Whatever the theory of labor supply does, Pareto's utility theory does it better.

A parenthetical note. Labor, short for *labor power,* is reasonably considered a good. But it is sometimes confused with *laboring,* and then is called a bad. Laboring—giving up labor power—is painful, of course, but that does not make labor a bad, anymore than money becomes a bad when you discover that it is painful to pay for the groceries. Every transaction has a painful side; bads have nothing to do with it.

We now bring back *energy,* our temporarily shelved substitute for labor power. Unlike labor power, energy is measured in energy units.

Neoclassical Theory of the Producer

In the neoclassical theory of the producer, the objective function is profit, π. During each period, of unspecified duration, the producer seeks to maximize profit by undertaking some action $\mathbf{a} \in A$. The domain of π is thus a subset of A. To the domain belong manufacturing activities, like "making widgets," and some transactions, like "hiring a worker" and "selling a unit of output." But the domain does not contain transactions undertaken by supermarket shoppers, like "buying a can of tuna." This is an unattractive state of affairs, considering that "buying a can of tuna" is mathematically indistinguishable from "making widgets." In effect it means that the domain of π is a very fuzzy set, its boundaries determined not by mathematics but by connotations.

Unlike utility, profit is a precisely specified function of its arguments. Let $\mathbf{a}$ be any vector in the domain of π, and let $\mathbf{w}$ be a vector of prices. Then $\pi = \pi(\mathbf{a}) = \mathbf{w}'\mathbf{a}$, a dollar amount. If $\mathbf{a}$ is interpretable as a production process, its positive elements are outputs, and its negative elements inputs. In that case, adding all positive terms in $\mathbf{w}'\mathbf{a} = w_1a_1 + \cdot \cdot \cdot + w_na_n$ gives the market value of the output or outputs, and adding all negative terms gives explicit cost, except for sign. A traditional assumption is that the producer sells everything he makes and uses up everything he buys as inputs. Given that assumption, the market value of the output or outputs identically equals the producer's revenue. Without that assumption, $\mathbf{w}'\mathbf{a}$ would merely be value added.

Profit is maximized subject to at least one constraint, a technologically determined relation between inputs and outputs. That relation is represented here by $g(\mathbf{a}) = 0$, with the function g regarded as unknown. If the producer manufactures only one product (in quantity a_1, say), and if the constraint can be solved for that quantity, to give $a_1 = f(a_2,a_3, \ . \ . \ .)$, then f is the producer's production function. The producer has no production function if he makes more than one output.

When f does exist, its form is unknown (since g is unknown). Theorists often improvise, however, by specifying f in one of several ways widely considered plausible. Best known among these specifications are the Cobb–Douglas and CES (Constant Elasticity of Substitution) production functions.

Discussion

As several authors have pointed out, producers rarely maximize profit, and often do not even try. But then the neoclassical theory of the producer should be considered a *normative* theory, a manual for those who wish to maximize profit. (Its dependence on a monetary notion—namely, profit—points to the same conclusion.) It means there exists no *positive* theory of producer behavior. Model One seeks to fill the void, but that is still a chapter away.

Its focus on flows leaves the theory of the producer little to say about stocks. By assumption, the producer's customers snap up every widget as soon as it comes off the production line, so that the widget stock is always zero; but the theory understandably plays down this unrealistic implication.

For all its popularity, the production function f is an implausible construct. Suppose that it is technically possible to make a 3-lb. boffle out of 3 lbs. of carrots and a certain quantity of energy. According to neoclassical theory, the producer can make a 3-lb. boffle also out of 2 lbs. of carrots, provided he uses enough extra energy. This is less than believable.

Another drawback of the production function is that it concerns manufacturing activities only. Many putative profit maximizers do not manufacture anything. Wholesalers and retailers, for instance, typically confine their activities to trading. As for profit maximizers who do manufacture, an important part of their business consists of nonmanufacturing activities. Buying inputs and selling outputs are obvious examples. The neoclassical theory of the producer does recognize the existence of these activities, but only indirectly, through its assumption that all inputs bought are also used up and all output produced is also sold.

The Activity-Analytical Theory of the Producer

The activity-analytical theory of the producer also presents the producer as a profit maximizer. It too should therefore be considered a normative theory. But it has something we need: a superior constraint. With only slight changes, the activity-analytical constraint is adopted as one of the core ingredients of Model One. An outline follows.

By interpretation, an *activity* is a production process. By definition, an activity is an n-vector of flows, indistinguishable from vectors in the action space A. Suppose, for example, that a producer knows how to make widgets out of plastic and green ink. Let $\mathbf{a} \in A$ represent "making one widget"; then $\mathbf{a}$ has a negative plastic element, a negative green ink element, a negative energy element, and a widget element equal to $+1$. The other $n - 4$ elements are all zero. "Making two widgets" is $2\mathbf{a}$.

Activities can have two or more positive elements. Activity analysis is thus well suited to describe the behavior of producers who make two or more products.

An activity is either *feasible* or *infeasible.* By interpretation, an activity is feasible if it can actually be undertaken, or at any rate could be undertaken by a producer with large enough stocks. By interpretation, an activity is infeasible if it is impossible.

Given enough time, the widget producer can make any number of widgets he wants. He can undertake $7\mathbf{a}$, or $33\mathbf{a}$, or $5000\mathbf{a}$. All those scalar multiples of $\mathbf{a}$ are thus feasible also.

Activities are assumed *irreversible,* that is, impossible to undo. Once the producer has turned quantities of plastic and green ink into widgets, he cannot turn widgets into quantities of plastic and green ink. Formally: if $\mathbf{a}$ is feasible, $-\mathbf{a}$ is not.

If making widgets is the only thing the producer knows how to do, his *feasible set* consists of just the vectors $c\mathbf{a}$ with $c \geq 0$. Those vectors form a halfline or ray.

Figure 3 illustrates this. Shown there is the producer's endowment set X, his initial endowment $\mathbf{x}_0$, and the feasible set affixed at $\mathbf{x}_0$. It looks like the producer can make only about four widgets before he runs out of plastic, but that means nothing. What matters is that he could make any number of widgets if only his stocks were large enough. In other words, $c\mathbf{a}$ is feasible for all nonnegative c, no matter how large.

Suppose there were another way to make widgets. To distinguish the two production processes, relabel $\mathbf{a}$ as $\mathbf{a}_1$, and let the other activity be $\mathbf{a}_2$. The producer can now undertake any nonnegative multiple of either activity. He can also do a bit of both. His feasible set thus contains not just $c_1\mathbf{a}_1$ for all $c_1 \geq 0$, nor just $c_2\mathbf{a}_2$ for all $c_2 \geq 0$, but $c_1\mathbf{a}_1 + c_2\mathbf{a}_2$ for all $c_1 \geq 0$ and all $c_2 \geq 0$. Letting $\mathbf{A}$ be the matrix with columns $\mathbf{a}_1$ and $\mathbf{a}_2$, you can also say that the feasible set consists of all vectors $\mathbf{Ac}$ with $\mathbf{c} \geq \mathbf{0}$. (See Chapter 2, MT 10.) Figure 4 illustrates this.

If there are three ways to make widgets, you get a picture like Figure 5. This time, $\mathbf{A}$ has three columns. The feasible set again consist of all vectors $\mathbf{Ac}$ with $\mathbf{c} \geq \mathbf{0}$.

Not counting $\mathbf{0}$, every feasible activity in Figures 3, 4, and 5 "points downward," that is, has at least one negative element. This is no accident; it is part of how activity analysis defines its constraint. To see why, suppose there were a feasible activity with at least one positive element and no negative elements. The feasible set would then be unbounded, rendering a constrained profit maximum nonexistent.

An activity with at least one positive element and no negative elements represents "production *ex nihilo*" or, as it will be called in this book, *free*

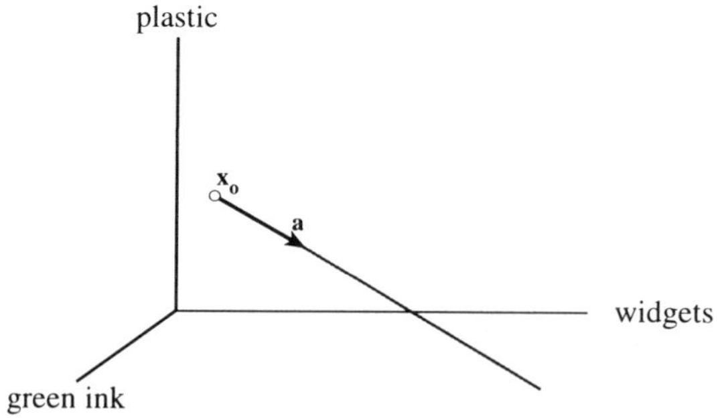

Figure 3. A feasible set with one basic activity.

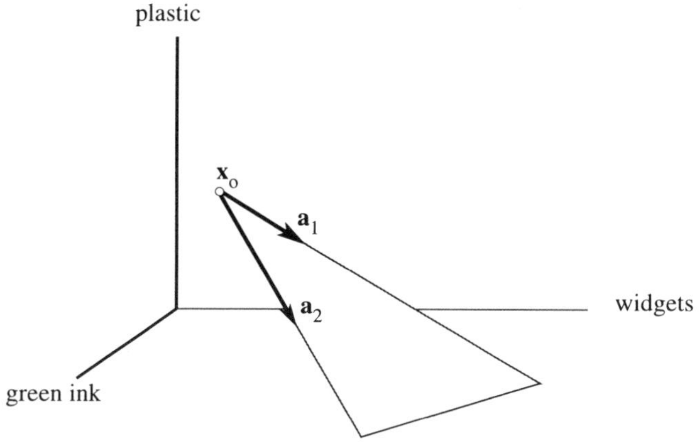

Figure 4. A feasible set with two basic activities.

access. Its opposite, an activity with at least one negative element and no positive elements, represents *free disposal.* Activity analysis rules out free access but allows free disposal.

Activity analysis captures all this and more in a few definitions, as follows.

Given is a matrix **A**, the *technology matrix* or *technology.* Its columns are the *basic activities.* Their nonnegative linear combinations, that is, the vectors **Ac** with $\mathbf{c} \geq \mathbf{0}$, are the *feasible activities.* They form the *feasible set.* Free access is impossible, meaning that every feasible activity, except **0**, has at least one negative element. (This constitutes a restriction on the technology matrix **A**.) Finally, and expectedly, the activity-analytical *constraint* says that when the producer chooses an activity, it must be a feasible one.

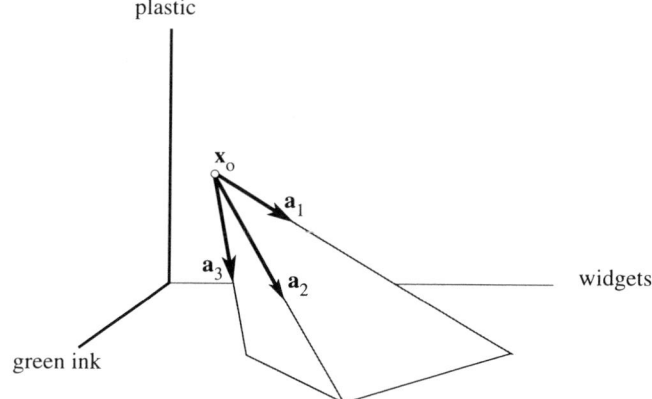

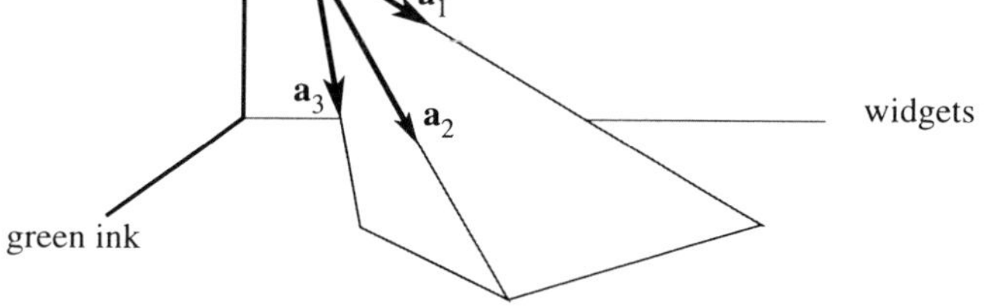

Figure 5. A feasible set with three basic activities.

In Figure 5, the three basic activities are linearly independent. The same is true for the two basic activities in Figure 4, and even for the single basic activity in Figure 3. You might think that this is a general rule, but activity analysis is not quite that strict. Activity analysis allows the $\mathbf{a}_i$ to be linearly dependent. It means that many feasible activities, maybe even all feasible activities, can be written as linear combinations of the $\mathbf{a}_i$ in infinitely many ways. Thus, when the producer chooses a particular feasible $\mathbf{a}^*$, there are likely to be many $\mathbf{c}$'s for which $\mathbf{a}^* = \mathbf{Ac}$; and so he has to choose one of those $\mathbf{c}$'s as well. It is a case of multiple equilibria. How the producer finds the best $\mathbf{c}$ does not matter here.

The prism-like feasible set of Figure 5 is an example of a *pointed, convex, polyhedral cone.* The feasible set of Figure 4 is a pointed, convex, polyhedral cone too. Even the ray in Figure 3 is one. Here is the definition: a pointed, convex, polyhedral cone is any set of vectors $\mathbf{a}$ that can be written as $\mathbf{Ac}$ for some $\mathbf{c} \geq \mathbf{0}$.

Discussion

Model One adopts the activity-analytical constraint, except for two features (and some inessential terminological differences). The excepted features follow.

First, Model One requires $\mathbf{A}$'s columns to be linearly independent. You already know why: were the $\mathbf{a}_i$ linearly dependent, there would be multiple equilibria, and the endowment would then have to choose among them. Since endowments do not know how to choose, Model One is forced to rule out linear dependence of the $\mathbf{a}_i$. It goes to show that positive theories, like Model One, cannot be quite as liberal as normative theories, like activity analysis.

Second, Model One permits free access, unlike activity analysis. In this respect then, Model One is the liberal theory.

When free access is allowed, the feasible set is unbounded. Effectively this means that infinite wealth is attainable. It is not as unrealistic as it sounds. For as will be seen in the next chapter, Model One is set up so that the endowment always travels with finite speed. Given that, attainment of infinite wealth takes an infinitely long time. And that is not unrealistic at all.

The discussion of the five traditional theories of individual behavior is now over. We conclude the chapter with a few remarks about demand and supply.

An agent's demand for good i is sometimes defined as the sum of a stock and a flow, the stock being the agent's holdings of good i at the beginning of the period, and the flow being what the agent buys, or is willing to buy, during the period. The flow part is then called "excess demand." Demand itself is a stock according to this definition, for the sum of a stock and a flow is always a stock.

Staying closer to custom, this book takes "the demand for a good" to mean the demand *rate* for that good—the rate at which the commodity is demanded at a particular instant. Demand is thus a *flow rate,* that is, the time derivative of a flow. If some flow is measured in bottles, cans, or dollars, the corresponding flow rate is measured in bottles per hour, cans per hour, or dollars per hour.

For more detail, consider the Marshallian price-quantity diagram, with its vertical p-axis, its downward-sloping demand curve, and its upward-sloping supply curve. Let $E = (\dot{q}_E, p_E)$ be the point at which the curves intersect. If $(\dot{q}, p)$ is a point on the demand curve other than E, then $\dot{q}$ is the rate at which the demander would be *willing* to buy if the price were p. The demander is also *unable* to buy, at that rate and at that price, not because he lacks money but because the supplier refuses to accommodate him. A similar interpretation fits any point $(\dot{q}, p)$ on the supply curve except E. With the exception of $\dot{q}_E$ then, every $\dot{q}$ is a rate at which the demander offers to buy but does not buy, and the seller offers to sell but does not sell.

Only some of this affects us here, not all of it. After all, the Marshallian model concerns social or interactive behavior, whereas our concern lies with individual behavior. We are thus not bound by the Marshallian interpretation of demand and supply. In particular, we are free to view the demand curve as measuring the rate at which the agent *actually* buys, at various values of the price. And we are free, by symmetry, to view the supply curve as measuring the rate at which the agent *actually* sells, at various values of the price. With these interpretations, followed from here on, not only demand curves but also supply curves will customarily slope downward. The higher the price, the more slowly you buy; the higher the price, the more slowly you sell.

A small point should be made here. Although supply rates are negative, we tend to think of them as positive. That is to say, the supply rates of ordinary conversation are not really supply rates. They are the *absolute values* of supply rates. It is only when supply rates are interpreted in this way, as absolute values, that the supply curve slopes downward.

SUMMARY

The chapter began with definitions of time, commodity, and money. From these definitions follows that money is a commodity and time is not. Armed with these conclusions, the chapter discussed the highlights of five mainstream theories: Pareto's utility theory, Hicks's utility theory, the theory of labor supply, the neoclassical theory of the producer, and the activity-analytical theory of the producer.

Pareto's model almost completely dominates the other two utility-based theories. Its dominance is the result of its practice (which Model One adopts) of assigning utility to endowments rather than to demanded bundles.

The activity-analytical model almost completely dominates neoclassical producer theory. The reason is its superior constraint (which, with small variations, Model One adopts).

References

Hicks, J. R. (1946). *Value and Capital,* 2nd ed. Oxford Univ. Press, London. The first edition was published in 1938.

Pareto, V. (1971). *Manual of Political Economy,* A. S. Schwier (transl.), A. S. Schwier and A. N. Page (eds.). Kelly, New York. The translation is from the French edition of 1927.

Questions

1. Someone says that, to him, the utility of two steaks is 1.3 times the utility of one steak. Is it possible to verify this statement (*i*) in practice? (*ii*) in theory?
2. "If the Hicksian consumer wants a \$15 CD and a \$15 book but has only \$15, he will buy the CD now and the book later, or vice versa." Discuss.
3. "Most people get sick if they eat too much ice cream. It illustrates that the marginal utility of ice cream diminishes." Discuss.
4. "The Paretian consumer's final endowment maximizes utility. Presumably then, any endowment he has *before* he reaches the final endowment does *not* maximize utility. And that violates the utility-maximization postulate." Discuss.
5. At the utility-maximizing endowment (Pareto) or at the utility-maximizing demanded bundle (Hicks), the gradient of u points in the same direction as the price vector: $\nabla u = \lambda \mathbf{p}$. Equating corresponding elements shows that the marginal utility of good i equals λp_i, for all i. When written in the form $\text{MU}_1/p_1 = \text{MU}_2/p_2 = \ldots$, this is known as the Equimarginal Principle. Now for the question. The Equimarginal Principle is sometimes said to express that *marginal utilities per dollar* are equal. Check units to find out if this is an accurate description.

6. Theorists customarily assume marginal utilities to be positive. What do you think is their reason?
7. "Consider a world with just two goods, money and beer, As the consumer buys beer, which he loves, his endowment slides down the budget line toward the point at which utility is maximized. The fact that trading then comes to a halt is evidence that the marginal utility of beer diminishes." Discuss.
8. Figure 6 purports to illustrate the Hicksian consumer's actions in a world with more than two goods. The quantity of beer demanded per week is measured along the horizontal axis; the quantity of money spent on all goods other than beer is measured along the vertical axis. Utility is maximized, subject to constraint, at M. If you write the budget constraint as $p_1 q_1 + \Sigma p_i q_i = y$, the summation being over all $i > 1$, you will have no trouble verifying that OA represents income y, that weekly beer demand is OB, and that weekly expenditure for all goods other than beer is OC. Apparently, CA represents weekly expenditure for beer. Does the picture do what it is meant to do?
9. "That Hicksian utility theory cannot deal with supply is of no consequence. After all, the consumer is ultimately a demander; everything he does serves but one purpose: consumption." Discuss.
10. "The distinction between consumers and producers is not quite the dichotomy that this chapter makes it out to be. True, economics has different theories for consumers and producers. But there is, on the

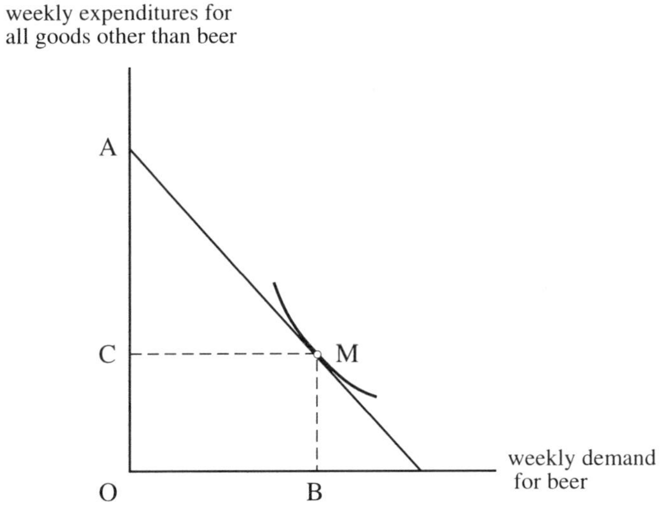

Figure 6. What is wrong with this picture?

other hand, nothing in traditional economic theory to prevent firms from being wholly owned by a single household. Traditional theory thus includes as a special case the setting in which there is no formal distinction between producers and consumers." Discuss.

11. "Contrary to what traditional theory says, consumers get their utility not from goods but from the characteristics of those goods—the coffeeness of coffee, the breadness of bread, the vinyl-slipcoverness of vinyl slipcovers." Discuss.
12. Is money an input? If yes, does that imply an asymmetry in the behavior of the profit-maximizing producer? If no, then what is the role of money in a business firm?
13. "The utility embodied in a dollar is the utility of the commodities we can buy for that dollar. Putting both money and commodities into the utility function is thus a form of double counting." Discuss.
14. "Putting money into the utility function is unacceptable if utility theory does not at the same time offer an explanation of why people hold cash balances." Discuss.
15. "One of the functions of money is to serve as a medium of exchange. Pareto's theory completely ignores that intermediary function when it introduces money directly into the utility function and treats it the same way as tea and salt. As a result, Pareto's theory is useless when it comes to explaining such things as the properties of the demand for money and the process of monetization of an economy." Discuss.
16. "A satisfactory analysis of the role of money, and therefore the right theoretical treatment of money, requires explicit consideration of the technology and network of exchange." Discuss.
17. "If the nominal money stock were suddenly doubled, the real money stock (measured in commodity units) would less than double. This sort of thing is not true for, say, cars. It follows that money *is* different from commodities." Discuss.
18. "Imagine an economy in which information is costless. Such an economy has no justifiable use for money; but it does have as much use for commodities as the kind of economy in which we live. It follows that money is different from commodities." Discuss.
19. "Barter transactions, in which commodities are exchanged for commodities, involve substantially higher costs than do trades in which commodities are exchanged for money. It follows that money is different from commodities." Discuss.
20. "The selection of a numeraire cannot be treated as a mere formality; the numeraire should have a certain moneyness. Because commodi-

ties like tea and salt lack that property, they are unsuitable as numeraires. In fact, only money has that property to the required degree, and so money is the logical numeraire." Discuss.

21. "Money differs from commodities in that it is the only good whose value is fixed in terms of the unit of account." Discuss.
22. "Of course money is an ordinary commodity. Most people hold positive money balances; this in itself proves that money is a utility-yielding good." Discuss.
23. "Economics is not mathematics." Discuss.

Part II

MODEL ONE

5

Introduction

Part II consists of three chapters. The starting point is Pareto's utility theory. Utility is thus a function of endowments, $u = u(\mathbf{x})$, and the budget constraint is $\mathbf{p}'\mathbf{x} = \mathbf{p}'\mathbf{x}_0$. In the course of this chapter, which uses as little mathematics as possible, Pareto's theory is gradually molded and bent and shaped into an outline of Model One. Chapter 6 adds mathematical details, polishes rough spots, and presents the complete theory. Chapter 7 derives the nine testable results mentioned in the beginning of the book.

The road to Model One takes the form of five elementary questions concerning the neoclassical consumer. The questions are these:

1. How does the consumer maximize utility?
2. Once the consumer arrives at the market, how long does it take him to maximize utility?
3. Once the consumer has done his shopping, what does he do the rest of the week?
4. How is the consumer constrained between trips to the market?
5. Every producer becomes a consumer now and then, and goes back to being a producer a while later; when does he make these changes?

QUESTION 1. *How does the consumer maximize utility?*

To maximize utility, must the consumer know "his" utility function? Or is it enough if he knows "his" indifference map? Does he use advanced calculus to buy lettuce?

None of the above. Consumers no more maximize utility than a schoolboy, doing his algebra homework, maximizes functions. A function of $\mathbf{x}$ can be maximized only by a value of $\mathbf{x}$; utility, a function of endowments, can be maximized only by an endowment. The protagonist of Pareto's utility theory is thus not a consumer at all. It is, rather, an endowment, a moving point. In the same way, the protagonist of Hicksian theory is a demanded bundle $\mathbf{q} \in A$; that of the theory of labor supply is the pair (L,y); that of producer theory is an action $\mathbf{a} \in A$; and so on.

We briefly discuss the nature of the endowment's motion.

Commodities are customarily assumed perfectly divisible, meaning that every commodity quantity is the product of a measurement unit and a real number, rather than an integer. This might be called *weak divisibility.* Model One calls for *strong divisibility.* By this is meant that the endowment's path is differentiable with respect to time.

In the everyday world, actions are undertaken either sequentially or simultaneously. When you drive to the market and, once there, buy an apple, you undertake two actions sequentially. When you eat the apple while driving home, you undertake two actions simultaneously.

The world of theory is different, or at least Model One is. Whereas a living consumer can do first this and then that, the consumer of Model One undertakes his activities both simultaneously and all the time. A living consumer can buy an apple and be done; the model consumer buys a thin trickle of apple every second, pays for his purchase with a thin trickle of money every second, eats a thin trickle of apple every second, drives a few feet every second, and so on. Absurdities like these are hard on the intuition, but they are the price of admission to the House of Calculus. One way to salvage a semblance of normality is to monitor the consumer's doings intermittently, rather than continually. Integrated over one week, for instance, those unrealistic trickles of fruit and money become a realistic apple and a realistic dollar.

Figure 1 illustrates the time path of someone's (gradually rising) stock of milk. The thin line, showing the actual path, reflects the unremitting pulse of household life; you can almost hear the opening and closing of the refrigerator door. The thick line shows Model One's version of the actual path.

When time is a continuous variable, as it is in Model One, the length of the economic period is zero. Words like *velocity* and *speed* then enter the

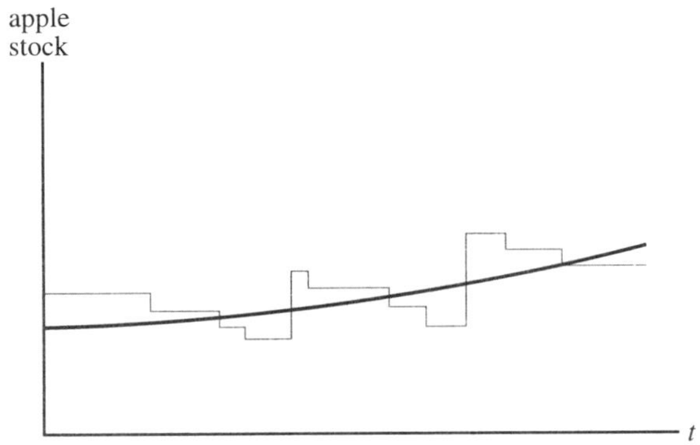

Figure 1. Smoothing the time path of a stock.

theoretical vocabulary. For an example, suppose apples are a normal good and the price of apples goes down. The neoclassical consumer then buys more apples per period. Not so the consumer of Model One: when the period length is zero, "buying more apples per period" is a meaningless phrase. But it is quite acceptable to say that the reduction of the apple price swells the trickle of apple that the consumer is in the habit of acquiring. In other words, the consumer responds to the price reduction by buying apples *faster*.

To sum up, utility can be maximized only by an endowment, not by a consumer. And: over time, the endowment travels along a smooth path.

QUESTION 2. *Once the consumer arrives at the market, how long does it take him to maximize utility?*

It takes him—or rather, his endowment—less than an instant. Neoclassical theory says that the consumer maximizes utility; by definition then, there never is a moment at which utility is not maximized. Even when there is a change in a price or some other parameter, the consumer adjusts his endowment instantaneously. If he were to take as little as one second to make the adjustment, the utility-maximization postulate would be violated during that second.

Actually, it is only the mathematical version of neoclassical theory that is this strict. The literary version, less formal, inhabits a more believable world. In that world, the consumer is not said to maximize utility. More accurate would be to say that he is presented as *trying* to maximize utility. He enters the market with a bundle of submaximum utility, which he then transforms, in the course of the day, into the utility-maximizing bundle.

Unfortunately, "the consumer tries to maximize utility" is not suitable as a guiding principle. A theory that has the consumer try, without saying whether he succeeds or fails, is too indeterminate to be useful. Apart from that, the behavior of the consumer does not matter. What matters is the behavior of the endowment, and endowments do not try.

But if "trying to maximize utility" is a phrase without a future, there is promise in its implication that utility can be, at times, less than the maximum. The following informal discussion builds on this idea. Out of it comes, eventually, the *motion law* for Model One. The motion law is a rule dictating how the endowment moves. Unlike the postulate of utility maximization, the motion law allows the endowment to carry submaximum utility. Implicitly then, the motion law gives the consumer time to adjust to changes.

For the time being, all quantities are assumed dimensionless.

Figure 2 illustrates the case $n = 2$, with beer as good 1 and money as good 2. The constraint shown is the traditional budget line. The price vector is $\mathbf{p} = (p, 1)'$, with p the price of beer. Figure 2 also shows the gradient ∇u (Chapter 2, MT 8) and its projection $\mathbf{P}\nabla u$ onto the budget line (Chapter

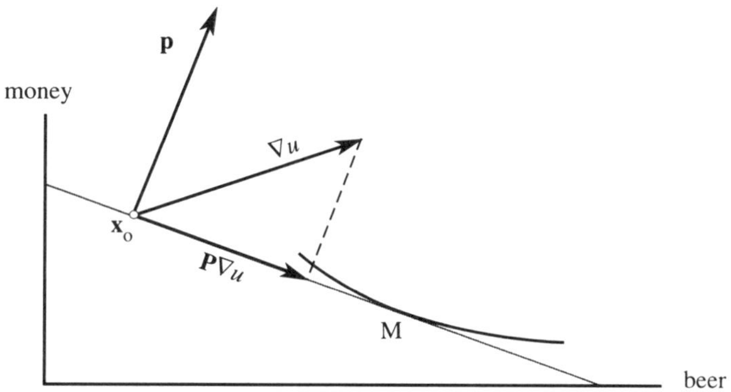

Figure 2. In R^2, the steepest constrained ascent of u at $\mathbf{x}_o$ is $\mathbf{P}\nabla u$.

2, MT 19). For clarity, both **p** and ∇u have been affixed at the endowment $\mathbf{x}_0$. Utility reaches its constrained maximum at M.

As was shown in Chapter 2, MT 24, the vector $\mathbf{P}\nabla u$ is the steepest constrained ascent of u at $\mathbf{x}_0$. That is to say, the direction of $\mathbf{P}\nabla u$ is that in which u increases fastest, constraint permitting, and the norm of $\mathbf{P}\nabla u$ is the slope of the utility surface in that direction.

We now discard the postulate of utility maximization. In its place comes, temporarily, a definition of the endowment's velocity. According to this definition, which is only a first and very provisional step toward the motion law for Model One, the endowment's velocity is $\gamma\mathbf{P}\nabla u$, where γ is a positive constant. Thus, as the endowment **x** moves away from its current location $\mathbf{x}_0$, it travels in the *direction* in which utility increases fastest, constraint permitting, and with a *speed* proportional to the slope of u in that direction. The steeper the utility surface (in the chosen direction), the faster **x** moves. It is as if the endowment perceives that when a small step along the budget line will earn a large utility increase, it pays to take that step quickly. If u is shallow (in the chosen direction), so that the same small step will bring only a small utility increase, the endowment acts blasé.

What has just been described is obviously unrelated to utility maximization. "Utility slope maximization" is closer to the mark.

Figure 2 can serve as an illustration, if you are willing to pretend, temporarily, that $\gamma = 1$. Vector $\gamma\mathbf{P}\nabla u$, then the same as $\mathbf{P}\nabla u$, is a vector with two elements. Its first element, which is positive, measures how fast **x** moves east. Its second element, which is negative, measures how fast **x** moves south. The first element of $\gamma\mathbf{P}\nabla u$ is thus the demand rate for beer, and the second element is the supply rate of money—the rate at which the consumer gives up money in exchange for the beer he buys. That the supply rate is negative could lead to misunderstanding, since it is customary to talk about supply rates as if they were positive, as if they were their own absolute values. In the few places below where this kind of confusion threatens, the text will sound an alert.

Time to take stock. We started with Pareto's utility theory, took out the utility-maximization postulate, and put in the provisional definition of the endowment's velocity, as $\gamma \mathbf{P}\nabla u$. The resulting model is still close to the Paretian original, still nearly neoclassical. It is all the more striking, therefore, that some of the testable results promised earlier can already be derived at this point, and by very elementary reasoning at that. Examples follow. Chapter 7 derives the results again, but in a more general way.

We return to Figure 2. Suppose that the price p of beer goes up. The budget line then rotates, with $\mathbf{x}_0$ as the pivot, to become steeper. The gradient, ∇u, stays the same. Vector $\gamma \mathbf{P}\nabla u$ does not. Its first element becomes smaller, in Figure 2. As is easy to verify graphically, its second element becomes larger, in absolute value, provided the price increase is not too great. The smaller first element means that the consumer buys beer more slowly now. The larger absolute value of the second element means that the consumer increases his expenditure rate for beer. His demand rate for beer is apparently inelastic.

Exactly how do the beer-demand rate and the money-supply rate depend on p? There are two ways to find out, one direct and one indirect. We do the direct way first. Recall that, by simplifying and temporary assumption, all quantities are real.

Writing the constraint as $\mathbf{p}'(\mathbf{x} - \mathbf{x}_0) = 0$ shows that $\mathbf{p}$ is perpendicular to the budget line. Abbreviate $\mathbf{x} - \mathbf{x}_0$ to $\mathbf{a}$. Then $\mathbf{p}'\mathbf{a} = 0$. To reduce clutter, $\mathbf{a}$ has been omitted from Figure 2. It will be obvious that $\mathbf{a}$ is parallel to the budget line, and would lie on the budget line if it were affixed at $\mathbf{x}_0$.

From $\mathbf{p}'\mathbf{a} = 0$ follows, since $\mathbf{p} = (p, 1)'$, that $\mathbf{a}$ can be any scalar multiple of $(1, -p)'$. Taking the simplest possibility, we choose $\mathbf{a} = (1, -p)'$.

Shorten $\partial u/\partial x_i$ to u_i. Since $\mathbf{a}$ is parallel to the budget line, $\mathbf{P} = \mathbf{a}(\mathbf{a}'\mathbf{a})^{-1}\mathbf{a}'$ (Chapter 2, MT 19). The endowment's velocity is thus $\gamma \mathbf{P}\nabla u = \gamma \mathbf{a}(\mathbf{a}'\mathbf{a})^{-1}\mathbf{a}'\nabla u$. Now $\mathbf{a} = (1, -p)'$, and so $\gamma \mathbf{P}\nabla u = \gamma(1, -p)'(p^2 + 1)^{-1}(u_1 - pu_2)$. The first element of $\gamma \mathbf{P}\nabla u$, the demand rate for beer, is $\gamma(u_1 - pu^2)/(p^2 + 1) = (Bp + C)/(p^2 + 1)$, with $B = -\gamma u_2$ and $C = \gamma u_1$. Multiplying by $-p$ gives the second element, which is the supply rate of money. (If you would rather view supply rates as positive, take the absolute value instead.)

Since u has not been specified, B and C are neither known nor computable. If, in some application, their values are needed, they will have to be found through estimation.

Next, the indirect route. In Figure 2, imagine a line drawn through $\mathbf{p}$. Projecting ∇u onto this line gives $\mathbf{p}(\mathbf{p}'\mathbf{p})^{-1}\mathbf{p}'\nabla u$. But then the projection of ∇u onto the budget line must equal $\nabla u - \mathbf{p}(\mathbf{p}'\mathbf{p})^{-1}\mathbf{p}'\nabla u$, that is,

$(\mathbf{p}'\mathbf{p})^{-1}[\mathbf{p}'\mathbf{p}\nabla u - \mathbf{p}\mathbf{p}'\nabla u]$. The projection of ∇u onto the budget line is also $\mathbf{P}\nabla u$. Equating the two expressions easily leads to the conclusion that the demand rate for beer is $(Bp + C)/(p^2 + 1)$ and the supply rate of money is $-p$ times that (or $+p$ times, if you prefer to interpret supply rates as their own absolute values). Reassuringly then, the indirect route ends in the same spot as the direct one.

Early in the book it was said that the demand function is $(Bp + C)/(Dp^2 + Ep + 1)$. What we just found, $(Bp + C)/(p^2 + 1)$, is thus too specific. The reason sits in the too-specific assumption that all quantities are real numbers. So we go through the argument again, but this time with measurement units taken into account, and with A replacing R^2. Let the matrix of the inner product on A be $\mathbf{H}$ (Chapter 2, MT 14).

Since $\nabla u \in A^0$ and $\mathbf{a} \in A$ cannot appear in the same picture, Figure 2 is no longer right. To make it almost right, change $\mathbf{p}$ and ∇u to $\mathbf{H}^{-1}\mathbf{p}$ and $\mathbf{H}^{-1}\nabla u$. To make it completely right, divide all prices by one dollar. This changes $\mathbf{H}^{-1}\mathbf{p}$ to $d^{-1}\mathbf{H}^{-1}\mathbf{p}$, which is a vector in A.

We use the direct route. The steepest constrained ascent, formerly $\mathbf{P}\nabla u$, is now $\mathbf{P}\mathbf{H}^{-1}\nabla u$ (Chapter 2, MT 24). The endowment's velocity, formerly $\gamma\mathbf{P}\nabla u$, is now $\gamma\mathbf{P}\mathbf{H}^{-1}\nabla u$. A unit check will verify that if time is measured in hours h, the parameter γ is measured in $1/h$.

Since $\mathbf{P}$ is now $\mathbf{a}(\mathbf{a}'\mathbf{H}\mathbf{a})^{-1}\mathbf{a}'\mathbf{H}$ (Chapter 2, MT 19), the endowment's velocity, $\gamma\mathbf{P}\mathbf{H}^{-1}\nabla u$, equals $\gamma\mathbf{a}(\mathbf{a}'\mathbf{H}\mathbf{a})^{-1}\mathbf{a}'\nabla u$. Arguing as before gives almost the same beer-demand function and money-supply function. The only salient difference lies in their common denominator. Before, that denominator was $\mathbf{a}'\mathbf{a} = p^2 + 1$. This time it is $\mathbf{a}'\mathbf{H}\mathbf{a} = Dp^2 + Ep + F$, with D, E, F unspecified constants. Since $\mathbf{a}'\mathbf{H}\mathbf{a}$ is positive definite, F is not zero. We may therefore, in both the beer-demand function and the money-supply function, divide the numerator and denominator by F. Equivalently, F may be set equal to 1. With that, the demand function for beer takes on its promised appearance.

For three goods, the reasoning is the same but the harvest is bigger, and the indirect route is quicker. Let the goods be beer, tuna, and money, in that order. The price vector is $\mathbf{p} = (p_1,p_2,1)'$. Suppose that p_1, the price of beer, is the only variable price. For simplicity and emphasis, p_1 is shortened to p. The following results will be proved, if somewhat sketchily:

(*a*) The demand rate for beer as a function of p (own-price demand function) is the quotient of a linear numerator, $Bp + C$, and a quadratic denominator, $Dp^2 + Ep + 1$

(*b*) The demand rate for tuna as a function of p (cross-price demand function) is the quotient of a quadratic numerator and a quadratic denominator

(*c*) The supply rate of money as a function of p is the quotient of a quadratic numerator and a quadratic denominator

(*d*) The quadratic denominators in (*a*), (*b*), and (*c*) are the same.

Rather than going through the argument twice, once without units and once with, we right away assume that all quantities are dimensioned. To see how the argument would run if all quantities were dimensionless, all you have to do is set $\mathbf{H} = \mathbf{I}$.

Recall that d stands for dollar. Writing the budget constraint as $d^{-1}\mathbf{p}'\mathbf{H}^{-1}\mathbf{H}(\mathbf{x} - \mathbf{x}_0) = 0$ shows that $d^{-1}\mathbf{H}^{-1}\mathbf{p}$ is orthogonal to the budget plane (Chapter 2, MT 17). Imagine a line L drawn so that $d^{-1}\mathbf{H}^{-1}\mathbf{p}$ lies on it.

Vector $\mathbf{H}^{-1}\nabla u$ is the sum of two orthogonal projections. One is its projection onto the budget plane; this is $\mathbf{PH}^{-1}\nabla u$. The other is its projection onto L; this is $\mathbf{H}^{-1}\mathbf{p}(\mathbf{p}'\mathbf{H}^{-1}\mathbf{p})^{-1}\mathbf{p}'\mathbf{H}^{-1}\nabla u$. (The factor d^{-1} drops out). In all then, $\mathbf{H}^{-1}\nabla u = \mathbf{PH}^{-1}\nabla u + \mathbf{H}^{-1}\mathbf{p}(\mathbf{p}'\mathbf{H}^{-1}\mathbf{p})^{-1}\mathbf{p}'\mathbf{H}^{-1}\nabla u$. Rearranging gives $\mathbf{PH}^{-1}\nabla u = [\mathbf{I} - \mathbf{H}^{-1}\mathbf{p}(\mathbf{p}'\mathbf{H}^{-1}\mathbf{p})^{-1}\mathbf{p}']\mathbf{H}^{-1}\nabla u$. The endowment's velocity is γ times that, i.e.,

$$\gamma(\mathbf{p}'\mathbf{H}^{-1}\mathbf{p})^{-1}[\mathbf{p}'\mathbf{H}^{-1}\mathbf{p}\mathbf{H}^{-1}\nabla u - \mathbf{H}^{-1}\mathbf{p}\mathbf{p}'\mathbf{H}^{-1}\nabla u].$$

Shorten the 3-vector in brackets to $\mathbf{v}$, with elements v_1, v_2, v_3. Shown first is that v_1 is linear in p and v_2, v_3 are quadratic in p.

Premultiplying $\mathbf{v}$ by $\mathbf{e}_1' = (1, 0, 0)$ gives $v_1 = \mathbf{p}'\mathbf{H}^{-1}\mathbf{p}(\mathbf{e}_1'\mathbf{H}^{-1}\nabla u) - \mathbf{e}_1'\mathbf{H}^{-1}\mathbf{p}(\mathbf{p}'\mathbf{H}^{-1}\nabla u)$. This appears to be a quadratic form in p, but it is not: the coefficient of p^2 is $\mathbf{e}_1'\mathbf{H}^{-1}\mathbf{e}_1(\mathbf{e}_1'\mathbf{H}^{-1}\nabla u) - \mathbf{e}_1'\mathbf{H}^{-1}\mathbf{e}_1(\mathbf{e}_1'\mathbf{H}^{-1}\nabla u) = 0$. It follows that v_1 is linear in p. Next, premultiplying $\mathbf{v}$ by $\mathbf{e}_2'$ and $\mathbf{e}_3'$ gives v_2 and v_3, both appearing to be quadratic forms. In both, the coefficient of p^2 is easily seen to be nonzero, or at least not necessarily zero. It follows that v_2 and v_3 are indeed quadratic in p. Assertions (a), (b), and (c) now follow right away, seeing that $\mathbf{p}'\mathbf{H}^{-1}\mathbf{p}$ is quadratic in p. P.O.C.

To summarize, an examination of Question 2—"Once the consumer has arrived at the market, how long does it take him to maximize utility?"—made it clear that the implications of utility maximization are unacceptably unrealistic. A substitute (roughly, utility slope maximization) was proposed. Although the complete motion law has not yet been formulated, the illustrations above have already shown its promise, in the form of some testable consequences.

QUESTION 3. *Once the consumer has done his shopping, what does he do the rest of the week?*

If the consumer were a person, he would do the commonsensical thing and use up, during the week, all or part of what he bought on Monday. But he is not a person, and he is not guided by common sense. He is a robot, guided by the utility-maximizing urge that neoclassical theory has built into him. And just as a windup doll, programmed to maximize altitude, will climb to the top of Mount Everest *and stay there,* so will the neoclassical consumer, programmed to maximize utility, acquire his utility-maximizing endowment *and keep it.*

The implications of utility maximization thus prove even worse than the discussion of Question 2 found them to be. After his initial visit to the market, the neoclassical consumer goes back only when a change in a price or some other parameter forces him to adjust his endowment (which he does instantaneously, yet). At all other times he stays home, contentedly guarding his utility-maximizing bundle and constitutionally incapable of changing it. If that seems irrational behavior, it should again be remembered that the consumer is a robot, a creature of theory; whenever the consumer happens to behave in unacceptable ways, theory deserves the blame. And if that still seems unconvincing, it should be further remembered that the robot-consumer is merely an expository device. It is the endowment that does the behaving.

Does utility slope maximization perform better? Barely. For an illustration, consider again Figure 2. Utility slope maximization makes the endowment gradually move toward the point M at which utility takes on its constrained maximum. It is easy to see that the endowment will never quite reach M, although it comes arbitrarily close, given enough time. By contrast, a model based on utility maximization puts the endowment at M right away. Under utility slope maximization, therefore, the consumer is never wholly inactive, as he would be under utility maximization; but he gradually becomes inactive, which is almost as bad. It should perhaps be stressed that "the consumer gradually becomes inactive" does not mean that his transacting slows to a crawl near the period's end: there are no periods in Model One. It means that as the years go by, the quantities the consumer buys and sells dwindle to zero. Apparently, the motion law is not yet complete.

To get an idea of what kind of modeling feature might solve the problem, picture a flesh-and-blood consumer sitting on the porch, doing nothing. If he expects his endowment to remain constant, he is in for a surprise. As he sits and daydreams, the tomato plants in the backyard keep increasing his stock of tomatoes, the oil well in the front yard keeps increasing his stock of oil, the mice in the pantry keep reducing his stock of cheese, and the very act of living keeps draining his stock of energy ("labor power"). In short, even though the man does nothing, his endowment is changing left and right.

Of particular interest is the autonomous energy drain. It makes the consumer hungry, thus forcing him to eat. Eating depletes his food stocks, and so he must buy food. Since that reduces his money stock, he must sell some of his oil, sell some of his tomatoes, get a job, or all three. In short, he must work. Since that diminishes his energy stock, he must eat. In fact, he must eat enough to make up for the exogenous energy loss caused by living *and* the endogenous energy loss caused by working. With good luck, the entire cycle leaves him with a surplus of money, a surplus of food, a surplus of energy (in the form of increased ventricular convexity), or all three. With bad luck, he comes out of the cycle with an energy deficit, eventually to die of hunger. In between is the break-even case characteristic of stagnant societies. A perfect model of individual behavior should cover all of this.

Model One is not perfect, and it does not cover all. But it covers most. In fact, it covers everything except the sequentiality of the cycle. (According to Model One, whatever the consumer does—eating, buying, working, and the like—he does simultaneously rather than sequentially.) Model One captures, in particular, the *exogenous influences* affecting the consumer's stocks—like the autonomous energy drain. The exogenous influences are represented by a vector to be called the *driver*. It is the driver that keeps the consumer from lapsing into inactivity.

You could think of the endowment as a rowboat on a river, its motion determined jointly by the force of the current (the driver) and the oarsman's efforts (the consumer's actions). Even if the rower wants merely to stay stationary with respect to the riverbanks, he will still have to row, to offset the pull of the current. Or in economic terms: even if the consumer wants merely to keep his endowment constant, he will still have to keep busy. Just like his living counterpart.

The motion law for Model One is beginning to take shape. From here on, the velocity of the endowment $\mathbf{x}$ is the sum of two vectors, one representing the effect of the exogenous influences and the other representing the effect of what the consumer himself does. Further, what the consumer does is defined this way: if there were no exogenous influences, the velocity of $\mathbf{x}$—then due to the consumer's actions alone—would be $\gamma\mathbf{P}\mathbf{H}^{-1}\nabla u$. All of this does not yet quite add up to the motion law, but it is getting close.

Figures 3 and 4 serve as illustrations. In Figure 3, the consumer's action, **a**, exactly offsets the exogenous influences, **b**. The endowment is thus for the moment stationary and will continue to stay where it is so long as **b** changes neither its direction nor its length. In Figure 4, the consumer does not quite manage to offset the exogenous influences. As a result, the endowment drifts away. If both marginal utilities are positive, the direction in which the endowment drifts away (in Figure 4) is unattractive. Since the endowment always lies on the budget line, the budget line, too, drifts away, parallel to itself.

Introduction of a driver is less of a novelty than it may seem. True, Pareto's and Hicks's utility theories have none, and neither does the theory of labor supply and leisure demand; but some other economic models do. An example is the theory of the monopolistic firm. In that theory, the driver takes the form of exogenously given consumer demand. It is through

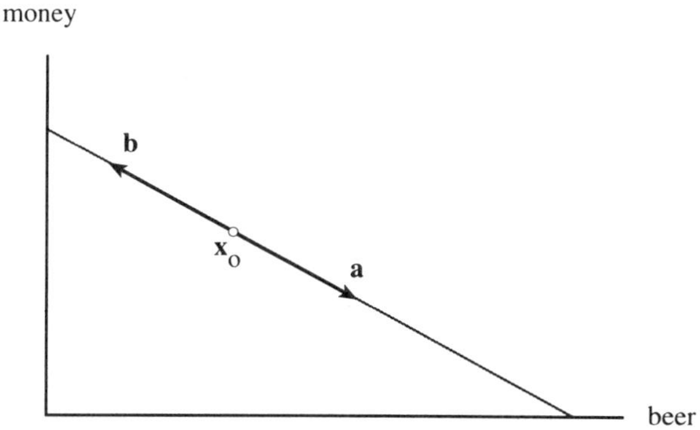

Figure 3. Since the action offsets the exogenous influences, the endowment is stationary.

this demand that the producer is kept on his toes: unless he produces ceaselessly, his stock of finished product will soon be depleted.

Worth noting is that, thanks to the presence of a driver, the theory of the monopolistic firm is very nearly dynamic. To make it fully dynamic, all one has to do is choose the period length zero. That may not be customary, but it does not contradict any part of the theory, either.

Exogenously given consumer demand is also the driver in the open input–output model. Comparison with the closed input–output model is illuminating. The closed model has no driver. As a result, it has infinitely many solutions, each representing an equilibrium. Those infinitely many equilibria leave the closed model with little usefulness.

A striking feature of the motion law is that the future plays no role in it. According to the motion law, the endowment behaves like a sightless bug, scampering about in unfamiliar territory, its every move dictated by

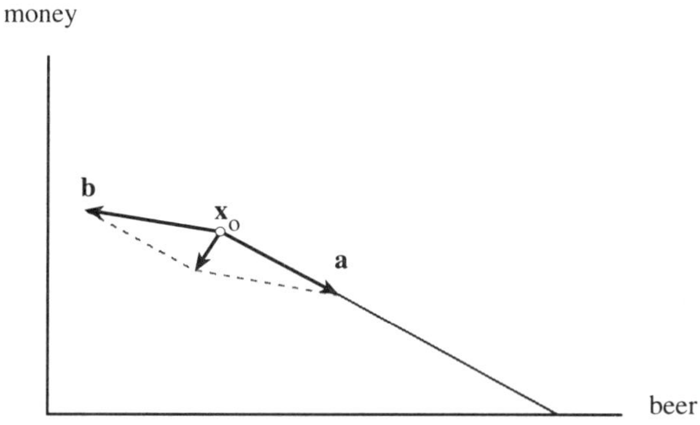

Figure 4. Since the action does not quite offset the exogenous influences, the endowment drifts.

the shape of the ground under its feet. Of course, this is precisely how a choiceless, planless point can be expected to behave. But is it realistic? Do endowments found in the real world act this way too? One would not think so. Since a real-life endowment is under the control of its real-life owner, and since the future affects the owner's behavior, the future indirectly affects the behavior of the owner's endowment. Realism thus demands that Model One take account of future pleasures, suitably discounted.

Or so its seems. But the argument is wrong. *The future cannot possibly affect today's behavior, for the simple reason that it is not here yet.* What the (living) consumer acts on is not the future but his *perception* of the future; and that perception is itself a thing of the present. The consumer thus gets his marching orders from his immediate environment, from the here and now. A happy implication is that there is nothing wrong with keeping the future out of the motion law. There is, in particular, no need to encumber the objective function with a discount factor. The idea that present utility is nicer than future utility may be appealing, but only if one identifies utility with usefulness. Even then its applicability would seem limited to normative theory.

If there were no exogenous influences, the endowment would move in the "right" direction, that is, the direction in which utility increases fastest, constraint permitting. Ordinarily, though, the driver will be nonnull. Ordinarily then, $\mathbf{x}$ will move in the "wrong" direction, knocked off course by the driver. And although the endowment immediately sets about to counter the driver's push and pull, it is always catching up, always slightly behind the times. You might say that the motion law, as it now stands, is a *Myopic Law.*

The Myopic Law has an obvious alternative, suggesting a shrewder consumer. This alternative, the *Rational Law,* is based on the idea that it is more efficient for the consumer to take the exogenous influences into account *ex ante* rather than *ex post.* By anticipating the exogenous influences, the consumer will always be able to send his endowment in the best direction that his constraint permits. Figure 5 illustrates this: given $\mathbf{b}$ and ∇u, the consumer makes $\mathbf{a}$ so long that $\mathbf{a} + \mathbf{b}$ points in the direction of ∇u.

Although the Rational Law sounds promising, the solution it proposes does not always exist and can lead to absurd behavior when it does exist. See Figure 6. Because ∇u is nearly parallel to the budget line, the consumer will have to make $\mathbf{a}$ very long—meaning that he has to act very fast—if $\mathbf{a} + \mathbf{b}$ is to point in the direction of ∇u. And if ∇u is exactly parallel to the budget line (a possibility that Model One permits), the Rational Law is impossible to obey.

Nor is this all. It is shown later, in Part III, that the Rational Law is based on faulty logic. The Myopic Law is thus the right one, notwithstanding its apparent inefficiency, and notwithstanding its connotations. Judging by

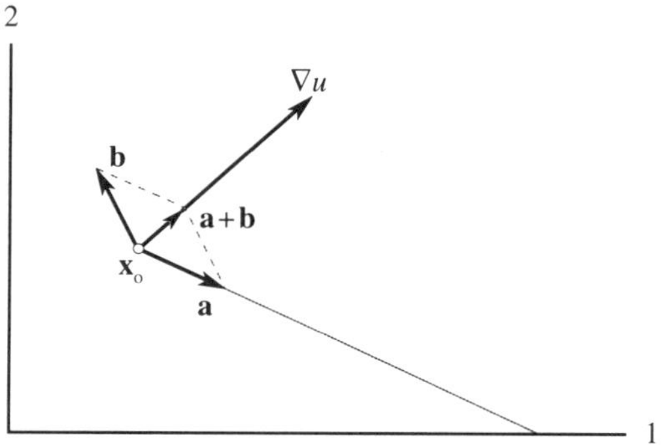

Figure 5. Illustrating the benefits of rationality.

connotations, the Myopic Law should be inferior to the Rational Law; actually, it is the other way around. Rational is bad, myopic is good.

From here on, "the motion law" means the Myopic Law.

The motion law implies that *the speed of* **x** *is always finite* (and typically positive rather than zero). It is a thoroughly untraditional feature, absent from neoclassical utility theory. In fact, it is absent from every period-analytical model that leaves the period length unspecified. The reason is that, when the period length is indeterminate, the only meaningful speeds are zero and infinity. "Six widgets per period" sounds admirably precise, but it means nothing if we do not know how long the period is. Not coincidentally, zero and infinity are the only speeds found in neoclassical utility theory: the Paretian endowment either does not move at all (zero speed) or adjusts instantaneously to a parametric change (infinite speed).

The biggest drawback of period-analytical models, at least of those that do not specify the period length, is that they need a *stationary equilibrium* to survive.

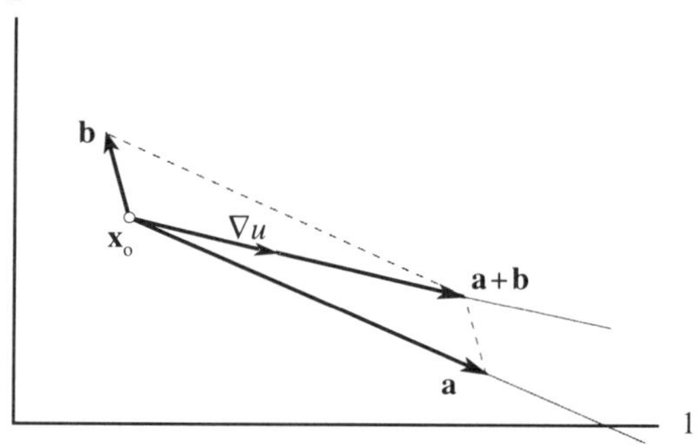

Figure 6. Illustrating why rationality does not work, after all.

For an illustration, consider Pareto's utility theory once more. Its protagonist, the endowment, moves with either zero speed or infinite speed. To preserve at least a semblance of realism, the model must rule out *explosive behavior*—must see to it that when the endowment moves with infinite speed, it covers no more than a finite distance. In other words, the model must guarantee the existence of a stationary equilibrium. In this undertaking, the model's main tool is the budget constraint. It is the budget constraint that keeps the consumer from attaining infinite wealth in finite time. Of course, the budget constraint also keeps the consumer from attaining even the slightest wealth increase (beyond what may fall into his lap through price changes and the like), but that cannot be helped. For if the consumer were allowed to gain from any particular trade, the postulate of utility maximization would compel him to carry out that trade infinitely often, on the instant, thus making him infinitely wealthy in the blink of a rapacious eye. Since such explosive behavior is unacceptable, the budget constraint must remain in place, unrealistic though it may be.

When the endowment moves with finite speed, as it does in Model One (and in the real world), explosive behavior is ruled out from the start. Model One can thus afford to relax or abolish some neoclassical constraints, gaining realism as it does so. Best of all, stationary equilibrium ceases to be a theoretical mainstay and a theoretical necessity. An endowment governed by Model One behaves plausibly even if there is no equilibrium. Depending on how the driver is specified, the endowment *may* approach a static or moving or stochastic equilibrium; but it does not have to.

QUESTION 4. *How is the consumer constrained between trips to the market?*

Between trips to the market, the budget constraint does not operate. What takes its place?

As noted in Chapter 4, a better, more general constraint is that of activity analysis. Of course, activity analysis concerns the doings of producers rather than consumers, but that is merely a matter of connotations. The important thing is that actions are mathematically indistinguishable from activities. Connotational differences are irrelevant.

Chapter 6 has the mathematical details. Meanwhile, if you have forgotten what the feasible set of activity analysis looks like, you may want to take another look at pp. 78–79. Three possible shapes are sketched there.

QUESTION 5. *Every producer becomes a consumer now and then, and goes back to being a producer a while later; when does he make these changes?*

The traditional answer is that the changes are probably made sometime between Mondays, when neoclassical theory is taking a break. Implied is that any search for a more precise answer is bound to fail.

But there is no period analysis in Model One, no break between Mondays, no gap in theoretical coverage. Model One puts the consumer under permanent surveillance. And that closes some easy but illegitimate exits. Many modeling questions that could earlier be swept under the neoclassical rug now refuse to go away. One of them is Question 5.

It may be useful to recall that the consumer of theory is a robot, who does only as he is told. When the consumer switches roles and becomes a producer, it is not because he wants a change of scenery. It is because theory says that this is what he should do. Or, more precisely, when the endowment stops obeying utility theory and starts obeying producer theory, it is because utility theory says so. Later, when the endowment goes back to behaving according to utility theory, it is because producer theory says so.

With all that established, we ask again, when does role switching happen? Intuition has no answer. But logic does.

The logical answer, due to Scitovsky, is that role switching never happens. It means that there is no room for two model-robots, the consumer and the producer. They cease to exist. All the things that the two of them used to do are now done by a single model-robot. This versatile newcomer is the neutrally named *agent.* Before, the consumer used to buy apples and sell oranges; now it is the agent who does that. Before, the producer used to build cars and repair shoes; now it is the agent who does that. And strong divisibility implies that the agent does all these things both simultaneously and continually. Every second of every day he is busy buying apples, selling oranges, building cars, repairing shoes.

If there is to be only one theory of individual economic behavior, there can be only one objective function and only one constraint. Except for a few small changes, the activity-analytical constraint is universal enough to fit all behavior. That leaves the objective function.

We take the objective function to be utility. Insofar as the agent acts as a consumer, this is an unremarkable choice. What if he acts as a producer?

As argued earlier, the neoclassical theory of the profit-maximizing producer is normative; it explains what producers should do if they want to maximize profit. Our interest, on the other hand, lies with positive theory. We want to know how producers behave, not how they ought to behave. It is in this light that the following arguments are meant to be seen.

Some writers have pointed out that the best of all monopoly profits is a quiet life. Others have said that what producers really want is to keep the stockholders happy. Still others hold that producers are mere satisficers, meaning that they aim for satisfactory results rather than optimum results. What these views amount to is that producers pursue happiness, like everybody else. But then it is reasonable to let the producer's objective function be the same as everybody else's. It is reasonable, in other words, to let the *agent's* objective function be utility.

If the idea that producers are driven by utility seems at first absurd, it is because the connotations of "utility" and "producer" clash. "Utility" suggests usefulness, markets, commodities. "Producer" conjures up images of industrial production, the boardroom, the factory floor. All these connotations might have some relevance if the producer of theory were a living being, a man in a three-piece suit and a hardhat. As it is, the producer of theory is a robot. He is, moreover, an unimportant robot. It is the endowment that runs the show. And the endowment is just a moving point, virtually connotation-free.

As for "utility," its associations do not matter either. Utility is merely a function guiding the endowment's behavior. It is not a reflection of preferences; endowments do not have preferences. Nor is utility another word for usefulness; endowments do not know what usefulness means. In fact, that the objective function carries the name "utility" is entirely unimportant. What matters is that there is only one objective function, not two.

As said, the irrelevance of the connotations of "utility" is demonstrated in the next chapter, where the nine testable results are derived. All nine would be unchanged if utility were redefined as a minimand.

If, after all this, it still seems that producers differ from consumers, consider the following.

The interpretation of neoclassical theory carries the suggestion that all individual economic behavior falls under either utility theory or producer theory. This is misleading. Some behavior falls under both, and some under neither. For example, a restaurant owner who dines in his own establishment while keeping an eye on the staff is acting as both a consumer and a producer. The same can be said for the house painter who, when ordering paint from a wholesaler, includes a gallon or two to spruce up his own kitchen. As for behavior not covered by either theory, an example is eating. It is not a trivial example—eating, it was pointed out, is important because it is the only action to produce energy.

That the two theories are neither mutually exclusive nor exhaustive in their coverage is unsurprising. After all, they evolved from entirely different eighteenth-century beginnings and remained apart as they matured. Given such uncoordinated development, an occasional imperfection is to be expected.

The purpose of these remarks is to underscore that *the producer/consumer dichotomy is a historical accident. It is not a carefully reasoned piece of model building. It is a product of chance, rather than logic*. Had logic taken a hand, two centuries ago, it could very well have produced the argument that, since all people are constructed according to the same physiological principles, there is neither need nor room for two theories of individual economic behavior, each with its own objective function and its own constraint. And that argument might then have led to a theory like Model

One—a single, unified theory, with a single objective function and a single constraint.

SUMMARY

The agent is a consumer and a producer and a little more. His role in Model One is minimal. What matters is his endowment.

The endowment travels along a smooth curve, its behavior dictated by a law of motion. This motion law involves (*i*) a unified objective function called utility, (*ii*) exogenous influences embodied in a vector called the driver, and (*iii*) a unified constraint that is very nearly the constraint of activity analysis.

Actions produce and consume; the agent does not.

According to the utility-maximization postulate, utility is *always* a maximum, and adjustment to changes in prices and other parameters is instantaneous. According to the motion law of Model One, the endowment can carry submaximum utility and may adjust to parametric changes at its leisure.

The motion law implies that the endowment always moves with finite speed. This makes it unnecessary to postulate the existence of any kind of equilibrium.

Questions

1. In connection with Figure 2 it was said that if the increase of the beer price p is not too large, the second element of $\mathbf{P}\nabla u$ becomes larger in absolute value. Demonstrate this graphically.
2. (Continuation) It was also said that, in the circumstances just described, the consumer's demand rate for beer is inelastic. Prove this algebraically.
3. (Continuation) "If the increase of the beer price is large enough, the second element of $\mathbf{P}\nabla u$ will become *smaller* in absolute value. In that case then, the consumer's demand rate for beer is elastic." Discuss.
4. For the function $g(p) = (2p^2 - 5p + 4)/(p^2 - 3p + 3)$, find the extrema and corresponding extremizers, if any. Find the horizontal asymptotes, if any. Find the zeros of the function, if any. (A zero of g is a value of p for which $g(p) = 0$.) Sketch the graph of $g(p)$.
5. Define $g(p) = (Ap^2 + Bp + C)/(Dp^2 + Ep + F)$, with $Dp^2 + Ep + F$ positive definite. Prove that g has at most two extrema. Prove also that if g does have two extrema, one is a maximum and one is a minimum.

6. The own-price demand function for beer is

$$f(p) = (Bp + C)/(Dp^2 + Ep + 1), p \geq 0.$$

Show that its graph bends backward if and only if all three of B, C, and $B - CE$ are positive.

7. (Continuation) As $p \to \infty$, what is the limit of the demand rate for beer, and what is the limit of the expenditure rate for beer?

8. (Continuation) As $p \to \infty$, what is the limit of the p-elasticity of the demand rate for beer, and what is the limit of the p-elasticity of the expenditure rate for beer?

9. (Continuation) Since supply and demand differ only in sign, the own-price supply function of money should have the same form as the own-price demand function for beer. That is to say, it should be the quotient of a linear numerator and a quadratic denominator. On the other hand, the rate at which the consumer pays for the beer he buys is p times the demand rate, meaning his money supply function is $pf(p)$, and $pf(p)$ is the quotient of a *quadratic* numerator and a quadratic denominator. How can this be?

10. (Continuation) Show that, if there are only two goods and marginal utilities are positive, the own-price demand function can bend backward only if measurement units are present.

11. The motion law says that, in the absence of exogenous influences, the endowment's velocity is $\gamma \mathbf{PH}^{-1}\nabla u$. Seeing that ∇u is unknown anyway, why can we not submerge γ in ∇u, thereby simplifying $\gamma \mathbf{PH}^{-1}\nabla u$ to $\mathbf{PH}^{-1}\nabla u$?

12. "It has long been known that there is a certain amount of overlap between the theory of the consumer and the theory of the producer; think of household production functions, for example. The area of overlap has been thoroughly analyzed. There is thus no reason to make a fuss over the unification of consumer theory and producer theory; it has been done." Discuss.

13. "So perhaps utility maximization has no place in positive theory. Normative theory is different, though. Suppose that people were to ask some academic for the best way to maximize utility. The answer would be a normative theory of utility maximization." Discuss.

6

Model One

This chapter translates into mathematics what Chapter 5 had to say about six model ingredients: endowment, action, driver, utility, feasible set, and motion law.

The *endowment,* also called the *current endowment* and the *endowment at time* t, is written $\mathbf{x}(t)$ or, sometimes, $\mathbf{x}$. It is, roughly, Model One's version of "initial endowment." Model One has no equivalent of "final endowment." Traditionally, the final endowment is what the agent has at the end of the period, but since there is no period analysis in this book, there is no such thing as "the end of the period," and therefore no final endowment in the traditional sense. Nor, it will be seen, does Model One assume or imply that the agent's endowment ever reaches a state of rest, and so there is no final endowment in that sense either.

The endowment's time path is continuous everywhere, and differentiable everywhere except perhaps at those instants at which (*a*) a parameter change occurs, or (*b*) the time path enters or leaves a coordinate (hyper)-plane. Case (*b*) means of course that a zero stock becomes positive or a positive stock becomes zero.

Wherever its time path is differentiable, the endowment moves with a well-defined velocity. That velocity, written $d\mathbf{x}(t)/dt$, $d\mathbf{x}/dt$, or $\dot{\mathbf{x}}$, is found as follows.

At time t the endowment's location is $\mathbf{x}(t)$. A little later, at $t + \Delta t$, the location is $\mathbf{x}(t + \Delta t)$. The endowment's displacement between t and $t + \Delta t$ is therefore $\mathbf{x}(t + \Delta t) - \mathbf{x}(t)$, commonly shortened to $\Delta\mathbf{x}(t)$ or $\Delta\mathbf{x}$. Division by Δt gives the average velocity of $\mathbf{x}$ during the interval from t to $t + \Delta t$. If we next let Δt go to zero, $\Delta\mathbf{x}(t)/\Delta t$ becomes $d\mathbf{x}(t)/dt$, the velocity of $\boldsymbol{x}$ at t.

Elements of $d\mathbf{x}$ are flows, measured in bottles (b), cans (c), dollars (d), and so on. The differential $d\mathbf{x}$ is thus a vector in the action space A. Elements of $\dot{\mathbf{x}}$ are flow rates. It means that $\dot{\mathbf{x}}$ belongs to the space of vectors whose elements are measured in b/h, c/h, d/h, and so on. That space—which is not A—plays so small a role that we will not bother giving it a name and a symbol of its own.

Because $\dot{\mathbf{x}}$ does not lie in A, vectors $\dot{\mathbf{x}}$ and $\mathbf{x}$ cannot appear in the same picture. Vectors $d\mathbf{x}$ and $\mathbf{x}$ can.

The motion of $\mathbf{x}$ is due in part to the agent's own actions and in part to the exogenous influences. The part of $\dot{\mathbf{x}}$ that is caused by what the agent does is the *action rate at time* t, written $d\mathbf{a}(t)/dt$ or $d\mathbf{a}/dt$ or $\dot{\mathbf{a}}$. The part of $\dot{\mathbf{x}}$ that is caused by exogenous influences is the *driver rate at time* t, written $d\mathbf{b}(t)/dt$ or $d\mathbf{b}/dt$ or $\dot{\mathbf{b}}$. In all then,

$$\dot{\mathbf{x}} = \dot{\mathbf{a}} + \dot{\mathbf{b}}.$$

Multiplying the action rate by dt gives $d\mathbf{a}(t)$ or $d\mathbf{a}$, the *action at time* t. Integrating the action rate from 0 to t gives the *action between times* 0 *and* t, written $\mathbf{a}(t) - \mathbf{a}(0)$. We define $\mathbf{a}(0) = \mathbf{0}$, as interpretation suggests. With that, the action between times 0 and t simplifies to $\mathbf{a}(t)$.

Multiplying the driver rate by dt gives $d\mathbf{b}(t)$ or $d\mathbf{b}$, the *driver at time* t. Integrating the driver rate from 0 to t gives the *driver between times* 0 *and* t, written $\mathbf{b}(t) - \mathbf{b}(0)$. We define $\mathbf{b}(0) = \mathbf{0}$, as interpretation suggests. With that, the driver between times 0 and t simplifies to $\mathbf{b}(t)$.

Vectors $d\mathbf{a}$ and $\mathbf{a}(t)$, whose elements are flows, belong to the action space A. Not in A is $\dot{\mathbf{a}}$: its elements are flow rates. A diagram with $\mathbf{x}(t)$ in it can thus depict $d\mathbf{a}$ and $\mathbf{a}(t)$, but not $\dot{\mathbf{a}}$.

Vectors $d\mathbf{b}$ and $\mathbf{b}(t)$, whose elements are flows, belong to the action space A. Not in A is $\dot{\mathbf{b}}$: its elements are flow rates. A diagram with $\mathbf{x}(t)$ in it can thus show $d\mathbf{b}$ and $\mathbf{b}(t)$, but not $\dot{\mathbf{b}}$.

(In last chapter's Figures 3 through 6, the vectors $\mathbf{a}$ and $\mathbf{b}$ should have been $d\mathbf{a}$ and $d\mathbf{b}$. But at the time, labeling them that way would have been mystifying.)

Equivalent to $\dot{\mathbf{x}} = \dot{\mathbf{a}} + \dot{\mathbf{b}}$ are $d\mathbf{x} = d\mathbf{a} + d\mathbf{b}$ and $\mathbf{x}(t) = \mathbf{x}(0) + \mathbf{a}(t) + \mathbf{b}(t)$.

The driver's elements are functions of time, specifiable in several ways. Simplest is to take $d\mathbf{b}(t)$ constant. Less simple, but more realistic, is to define the elements of $d\mathbf{b}(t)$ as periodic functions, or as sums of periodic functions, to reflect the rhythms of everyday life. Still another possibility is to make $d\mathbf{b}(t)$ a stochastic process, meaning that the elements of $d\mathbf{b}(t)$ are taken to be irregular ("random") functions of t. Choosing this last option will add some realistic caprice to the endowment's time path.

A useful interpretation of $\dot{\mathbf{x}} = \dot{\mathbf{a}} + \dot{\mathbf{b}}$ is that, given $\dot{\mathbf{b}}$, knowledge of $\dot{\mathbf{a}}$ implies knowledge of $\dot{\mathbf{x}}$, and vice versa. In fact, given $\dot{\mathbf{b}}$, knowledge of $\dot{\mathbf{a}}$ or $\mathbf{a}(t)$ or $\dot{\mathbf{x}}$ or $\mathbf{x}(t)$ implies knowledge of the other three.

So much for endowment, action, and driver. The fourth model ingredient is *utility*.

Utility is defined as a differentiable function $u{:}X \rightarrow E^1$, independent of time. Differentiability of u means that the first-order partial derivatives of u not only exist but are continuous. Those first-order partial derivatives do not have to be positive; second-order partial derivatives need not exist;

strict quasiconcavity is unnecessary. Even the derivation of the nine testable results, in the next chapter, asks no more than differentiability.

It is important to distinguish between the utility function and its value. Think of the utility surface as the curved roof of a cave, and of the endowment as a point moving about on the floor. As the endowment moves, the height of the roof above it—that is, $u(\mathbf{x}(t))$—changes. The value of u thus varies with time. But u itself does not: the roof stays where it is.

Two model ingredients remain to be discussed. One is the feasible set. The other is the motion law.

The constraint of Model One says that $d\mathbf{a}(t)$ must belong, for all t, to the *feasible set,* denoted F. Rather than simply defining F and moving on to the next topic, we start with the neoclassical constraint, $\mathbf{p}'\mathbf{x} = \mathbf{p}'\mathbf{x}_0$, and gradually transform it into F. Doing so helps to bring out that the gap between Model One and neoclassical utility theory is much smaller than it might otherwise seem.

As a first step, replace the initial endowment, $\mathbf{x}_0$, with the current endowment, $\mathbf{x}(t)$. This turns the Paretian constraint into

$$\mathbf{p}'\mathbf{x} = \mathbf{p}'\mathbf{x}(t). \tag{1}$$

Equivalent is $d^{-1}\mathbf{p}'(\mathbf{x} - \mathbf{x}(t)) = 0$, where d stands for dollar, as before. Being the difference of two endowments, $\mathbf{x} - \mathbf{x}(t)$ is an action. Call it $\mathbf{a}$. (By interpretation, $\mathbf{a}$ is of course a transaction.) Equation (1) now becomes $d^{-1}\mathbf{p}'\mathbf{a} = 0$. Economically interpreted, $d^{-1}\mathbf{p}'\mathbf{a} = 0$ means that undertaking $\mathbf{a}$ makes the agent neither richer nor poorer.

For further detail, suppose there are only two goods, tuna and money, in that order. The price of tuna is p_1. The price of money is $p_2 \equiv 1$. Of the two, only p_2 is a real number; p_1 is the product of a real number and a measurement unit, the unit being dollars per can.

From here on, and until further notice, measurement units are suppressed. It is easier on the eyes.

Define $\mathbf{a} = (1, -p_1)'$. By interpretation, $\mathbf{a}$ is "buying one can of tuna," and $c\mathbf{a} = (c, -cp_1)'$ is "buying c cans of tuna." Since $\mathbf{p}'\mathbf{a}$ is zero, $\mathbf{a}$ is feasible; since $\mathbf{p}'(c\mathbf{a}) = c\mathbf{p}'\mathbf{a}$ is zero, all scalar multiples of $\mathbf{a}$ are feasible too.

Figure 1 illustrates the argument. When there are only two goods, as here, (1) represents a line. The current endowment is depicted, rather arbitrarily, as a point on the vertical axis. At time t therefore, the agent has money but no tuna. Arrow $\mathbf{a}$ represents action $\mathbf{a}$. All scalar multiples of $\mathbf{a}$ lie on the budget line, at least when they are affixed at $\mathbf{x}(t)$.

Equivalent to (1) is

$$\mathbf{x} = \mathbf{x}(t) + c\mathbf{a}. \tag{2}$$

Note that $\mathbf{x}$ in (2) forms the entire left side, whereas $\mathbf{x}$ in (1) is part of the

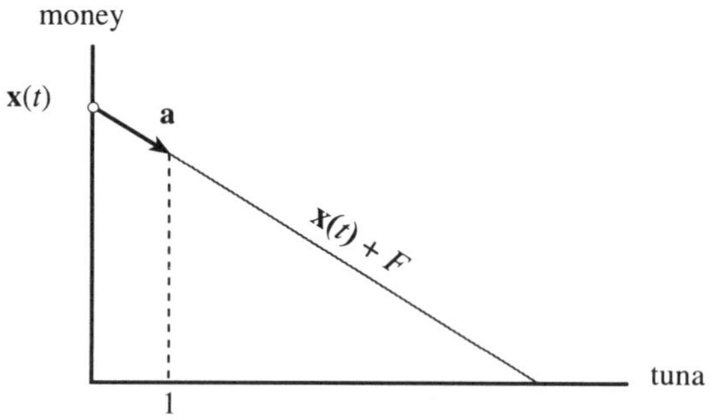

Figure 1. Transaction interpretation of the budget line.

left side. More formally, $\mathbf{x}$ is written implicitly in (1), explicitly in (2). Equation (2) can thus be seen as the general solution of (1).

Because of its dependence on prices, (1) fits market behavior only, and so is inapplicable to Model One. Equation (2) comes closer to the ideal, in that it avoids all reference to prices. Prices continue to exist, of course. They are merely no longer mentioned. Already they have begun their march to the periphery of the puzzle.

In the situation to which (2) refers, the feasible set is the set of $\mathbf{a}$'s scalar multiples. At this point then, F is not yet the pointed, convex, polyhedral cone it will eventually become.

The set of endowments defined by (2) can be written $\mathbf{x}(t) + F$. It is a useful (and standard) piece of notation, reflecting that every $\mathbf{x}$ in the set is the sum of $\mathbf{x}(t)$ and some action in F. The notation was used before, in Chapter 2, MT 18.

Arrow $\mathbf{a}$ in Figure 1 has both length and direction. Its direction is important but its length is not: the budget line would be unaffected if $\mathbf{a}$ were replaced with any nonzero scalar multiple $c\mathbf{a}$. Put differently, every nonzero scalar multiple of $\mathbf{a}$ can be a basis vector for F, can serve as the *basic action.* The most natural choice is $\mathbf{a}$, but it would be perfectly acceptable to let the basic action be $3\mathbf{a}$, say.

The next example is like the preceding one, except that it concerns three goods. Instead of a budget line we thus now have a budget plane. See Figure 2. The three goods are beer, tuna, and money, in that order. Let the prices be $p_1 = 3$, $p_2 = 2$, and $p_3 \equiv 1$. This time there are two basic actions. One, "buying a bottle of beer," is $\mathbf{a}_1 = (1,0,-p_1)' = (1,0,-3)'$. The other, "buying a can of tuna," is $\mathbf{a}_2 = (0,1,-p_2)' = (0,1,-2)'$. It is easy to verify that $\mathbf{p}'\mathbf{a}_1 = \mathbf{p}'\mathbf{a}_2 = 0$. Both $\mathbf{a}_1$ and $\mathbf{a}_2$ are thus feasible, are vectors in F. Also easy to see is that $\mathbf{a}_1$ and $\mathbf{a}_2$ are linearly independent. (If they were not, it would be misleading to call them "basic actions.") The current endowment is again put on the vertical axis, implying that at time t the agent has money but neither beer nor tuna.

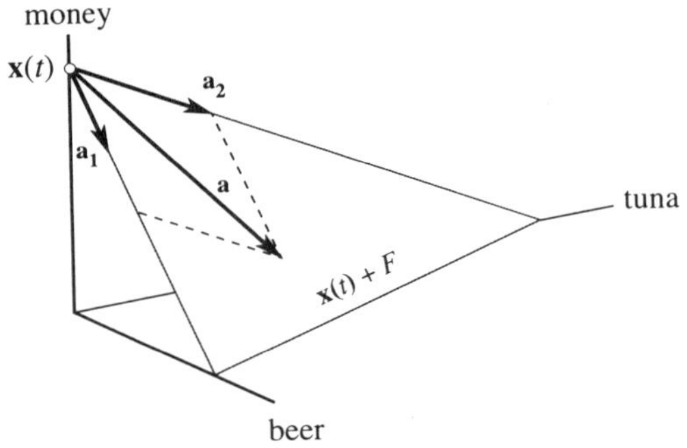

Figure 2. Transaction interpretation of the budget plane.

Suppose the agent buys c_1 bottles of beer and c_2 cans of tuna. It means that he undertakes the action $\mathbf{a} = c_1\mathbf{a}_1 + c_2\mathbf{a}_2$, a linear combination of the two basic actions. (In Figure 2, $c_1 = 2$ and $c_2 = 1$.) From $\mathbf{p}'\mathbf{a} = \mathbf{p}'(c_1\mathbf{a}_1 + c_2\mathbf{a}_2) = c_1(\mathbf{p}'\mathbf{a}_1) + c_2(\mathbf{p}'\mathbf{a}_2) = 0 + 0 = 0$ follows that $\mathbf{a}$ is a feasible action. Of course the proof holds in general: every linear combination of the basic actions is feasible. In the situation of Figure 2, therefore, the feasible set F is the set of all linear combinations of $\mathbf{a}_1$ and $\mathbf{a}_2$. Evidently, F is still not a pointed cone. It is a plane.

The budget plane in Figure 2 is given by both (1) and

$$\mathbf{x} = \mathbf{x}(t) + c_1\mathbf{a}_1 + c_2\mathbf{a}_2. \tag{3}$$

Every point $\mathbf{x}$ satisfying (3) for some c_1 and c_2 is an *attainable endowment,* a self-explanatory term.

Because the vectors $c_1\mathbf{a}_1 + c_2\mathbf{a}_2$ make up the feasible set F, the set of attainable endowments can also be written, again, as $\mathbf{x}(t) + F$.

The next step is a slight generalization. In Figure 2, each basic action has a zero element, is parallel to a coordinate plane. This condition is now dropped; from here on, the two basic actions may be *any* two vectors in the budget plane, so long as they are linearly independent. Equation (3) is unaffected. So is its interpretation: $\mathbf{x}$ still represents any attainable endowment.

For an example, suppose a store sells beer and tuna, but only in the form of Party Paks and Family Paks. A Party Pak consists of one bottle of beer and one can of tuna, and costs \$5. A Family Pak contains two bottles of beer and three cans of tuna, and costs \$12. "Buying a Party Pak" is $\mathbf{a}_1 = (1,1,-5)'$. "Buying a Family Pak" is $\mathbf{a}_2 = (2,3,-12)'$. Vectors $\mathbf{a}_1$ and $\mathbf{a}_2$ are easily seen to be linearly independent (and *not* parallel to any coordinate plane). Further, solving $\mathbf{p}'\mathbf{a}_1 = \mathbf{p}'\mathbf{a}_2 = 0$ gives $p_1 = 3$ and $p_2 = 2$. The price of beer is thus \$3 per bottle, and the price of tuna is \$2 per can. Those are also the prices of beer and tuna in the preceding example, the one that

Figure 2 illustrates. Apparently then, the budget plane is unchanged: if $\mathbf{a}_1 = (1,1,-5)'$ and $\mathbf{a}_2 = (2,3,-12)'$ were depicted in Figure 2, as arrows affixed at $\mathbf{x}(t)$, both would lie in the budget plane shown there.

In the just-completed example, beer and tuna cannot be bought separately. Neither therefore has a market price. Only Party Paks and Family Paks have market prices. Prices found by solving $\mathbf{p}'\mathbf{a}_1 = \mathbf{p}'\mathbf{a}_2 = 0$ are *imputed prices.* The imputed price of beer is $p_1 = 3$, and the imputed price of tuna is $p_2 = 2$.

Suppose the agent wishes to undertake some feasible action $\mathbf{a}$. Because the basic actions—$\mathbf{a}_1$ and $\mathbf{a}_2$—are linearly independent, there is only one way to write $\mathbf{a}$ as a linear combination of the $\mathbf{a}_i$. Or: the equation $\mathbf{a} = \mathbf{a}_1c_1 + \mathbf{a}_2c_2$ has only one solution c_1, c_2. This uniqueness is essential. For suppose the $\mathbf{a}_i$ were linearly dependent. Then $\mathbf{a} = \mathbf{a}_1c_1 + \mathbf{a}_2c_2$ would have infinitely many solutions c_1, c_2. Since Model One has no mechanism to decide which of those solutions the agent should actually select, the theory would be so ambiguous as to be useless. Linear independence of the $\mathbf{a}_i$ is thus necessary.

Necessary, but not sufficient. Suppose John buys a toaster, reconsiders, and takes back his purchase for a refund. Meanwhile, Joan neither buys nor sells a toaster but otherwise behaves exactly like John. Since Joan and John act differently, theory should describe them as acting differently. But it does not. If "buying a toaster" is $\mathbf{a}$, theory depicts both John and Joan as having undertaken $0\mathbf{a}$. In John's case, that $0\mathbf{a}$ is the sum of $\mathbf{a}$ and $-\mathbf{a}$.

The root of the problem is that John is being allowed to reverse his purchase. If the theory is to produce unique behavior, it must take away the agent's ability to undo his actions—it must make all feasible actions irreversible. You remember what that means: $c\mathbf{a}$ is feasible for every $c \geq 0$ and infeasible for every $c < 0$.

Is it realistic to declare feasible actions irreversible? Strictly, the question is academic. After all, even if irreversibility were utterly unrealistic, it still would have to be imposed, to guarantee uniqueness of behavior. It is therefore more to the point to ask whether irreversibility can be made to *look* realistic. Here the answer is yes. Every feasible action requires some effort, uses up some energy; and that energy is permanently lost. It is the reason, or one of the reasons, that feasible actions are irreversible. John can take the toaster back to the store and have his money cheerfully refunded, but he will not regain the energy he spent in making his original purchase. (Quite the contrary. Returning the toaster consumes still more energy.) Thus, if "buying a toaster" is $\mathbf{a}$, "returning the toaster" is *not* $-\mathbf{a}$.

Figure 3 illustrates the effect of irreversibility. The feasible set F, formerly a plane, is now a pointed cone. Figure 3 shows $\mathbf{x}(t) + F$. Vectors $\mathbf{a}_1$ and $\mathbf{a}_2$, the basic actions, span the *edges* of F. Every feasible action can be written as $c_1\mathbf{a}_1 + c_2\mathbf{a}_2$ for some $c_1 \geq 0$ and $c_2 \geq 0$. Conversely, every action that can be so written is feasible.

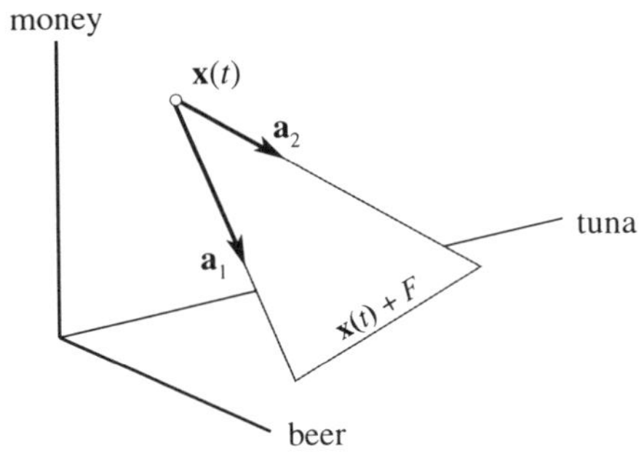

Figure 3. What is left of the budget plane when transactions are irreversible.

An important difference between Figures 2 and 3 is this. Suppose, for the duration of this paragraph, that the driver is null. The budget plane of Figure 2 then remains motionless throughout, and the current endowment moves within it. Also, all endowments in the plane are attainable. In Figure 3, on the other hand, the entire set $\mathbf{x}(t) + F$ moves whenever $\mathbf{x}(t)$ moves. This is because F is attached to $\mathbf{x}(t)$, like a beam to a flashlight. A parenthetical note: if the beam-and-flashlight simile is to be accurate, the flashlight must always point in the same direction, even when moving, for the edges of F always shift parallel to themselves.

We stay with Figure 3 a little longer. Since the entire set $\mathbf{x}(t) + F$ moves, an endowment that is attainable one moment (illuminated by the beam, so to speak) may well be unattainable (in the dark) the next. Attainability thus ceases to be a useful notion. This is particularly true if the driver is not parallel to the plane containing $\mathbf{x}(t) + F$; for then that plane will shift, over time, parallel to itself. No endowment is then attainable for more than the merest fraction of a second—no endowment spends more than a single instant in the glare.

Now that attainability has become irrelevant, the $\mathbf{x}$ on the left in (3) has no longer an economic interpretation. Its role is purely mathematical.

The following piece of notation will smooth the rest of the road to the definition of F. Figure 3 serves as an illustration.

Let $\mathbf{A}$ be the *action matrix,* that is, the 3×2 matrix whose columns are the basic actions. Further, let $\mathbf{c} = (c_1, c_2)'$. Then $c_1\mathbf{a}_1 + c_2\mathbf{a}_2 = \mathbf{Ac}$. The set F thus consists of all vectors of the form $\mathbf{Ac}$ with $\mathbf{c} \geq \mathbf{0}$. Equation (3), which is $\mathbf{x} = \mathbf{x}(t) + c_1\mathbf{a}_1 + c_2\mathbf{a}_2$, can also be written as

$$\mathbf{x} = \mathbf{x}(t) + \mathbf{Ac}, \quad \text{with } \mathbf{Ac} \geq \mathbf{0}.$$

As in (3), $\mathbf{x}$ is without economic interpretation.

The final definition of F is now only three quick generalizations away.

First, moving from the three-goods case to the n-goods case, we take $\mathbf{A}$ to be $n \times (n-1)$, rather than just 3×2. The action space A now has dimension n, and the pointed cone F is a subset of a hyperplane in A. Every feasible action can be written as $c_1\mathbf{a}_1 + c_2\mathbf{a}_2 + \cdots + c_{n-1}\mathbf{a}_{n-1}$ for certain scalars $c_1, c_2, \ldots, c_{n-1}$, all nonnegative. Equivalently, every feasible action can be written as $\mathbf{Ac}$ for some $\mathbf{c} \geq \mathbf{0}$.

As a moment's reflection will show, the requirement that the number of basic actions be $n - 1$ is merely a neoclassical legacy, a relic left by the $(n-1)$-dimensional budget hyperplane. Neither economic interpretation nor methodological rectitude asks that $\mathbf{A}$ have exactly $n - 1$ columns. So long as the columns of $\mathbf{A}$ are linearly independent, we have all we need.

This then is the second generalization: $\mathbf{A}$ is $n \times k$ and has rank k. A familiar implication is $k \leq n$. We also take $k > 0$, rather than $k \geq 0$. Taking $k > 0$ is an insignificant restriction, whose sole purpose is to shorten and simplify the exposition.

Formally the same as before is that every feasible action can be written as $\mathbf{Ac}$ with $\mathbf{c} \geq \mathbf{0}$. This time, of course, $\mathbf{Ac}$ means $c_1\mathbf{a}_1 + c_2\mathbf{a}_2 + \cdots + c_k\mathbf{a}_k$. Figure 4 sketches the case $n = k = 3$. The case $n = 3$ and $k = 2$ was already illustrated in Figure 3. If $n = 3$ and $k = 1$, F is a ray. In fact, F is a ray whenever $k = 1$, regardless of n.

Before turning to the third generalization, we need a few remarks about the just-redefined action matrix $\mathbf{A}$. That $\mathbf{A}$ may have fewer than $n - 1$ columns has a consequence of considerable interest and scope. To illustrate, let $n = 3$ and $k = 1$. The action space A is thus three-dimensional (since $n = 3$), and the feasible set F is a ray in A (since $k = 1$). Let the three goods be beer, tuna, and money, in that order. A Family Pak consists of two bottles of beer and three cans of tuna, and costs \$12. "Buying a Family Pak" is thus the action $\mathbf{a} = (2,3,-12)'$. Suppose $\mathbf{a}$ spans F. What are the prices of beer and tuna?

For an answer we solve $\mathbf{a}'\mathbf{p} = 0$ for $\mathbf{p}$. Because $\mathbf{a}'\mathbf{p} = 0$ is only one equation and $\mathbf{p}$ has three unknowns, there are infinitely many solutions. It

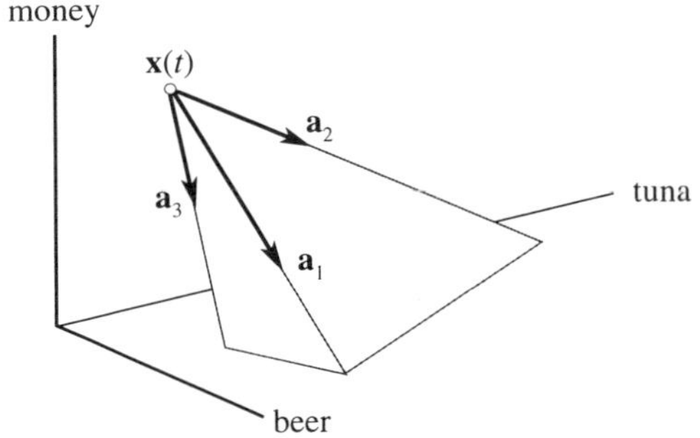

Figure 4. A three-dimensional feasible set when actions are irreversible.

is easy to verify that those solutions are the vectors **p** that can be written as $\lambda(-3,2,0)' + \mu(6,0,1)'$. To normalize, let $p_3 \equiv 1$. Since $p_3 = \lambda(0) + \mu(1) = \mu$, setting $p_3 \equiv 1$ is the same as setting $\mu = 1$. With that, **p** simplifies to $\lambda(-3,2,0)' + (6,0,1)'$; but this *still* describes infinitely many vectors. Setting $\lambda = 1$, for example, gives $p_1 = 3$ and $p_2 = 2$; setting $\lambda = 1/2$ gives $p_1 = 9/2$ and $p_2 = 1$; setting $\lambda = 1/3$ gives $p_1 = 5$ and $p_2 = 2/3$; and so on.

Finding an infinity of prices is disconcerting only if you believe that every good must have one and only one price. It is not disconcerting at all if you accept the earlier assertion that, from a theoretical point of view, prices are insignificant, are Bright Pieces that belong near the edge of the puzzle.

Finally, the third generalization. It is one of interpretation: from now on, the $\mathbf{a}_i$ need no longer represent transactions only. Some basic actions may represent production processes, for example.

A difficulty arises here. Suppose that tuna, energy, and money are the only goods, so that $n = 3$. There are then at most $k = 3$ basic actions. Consider an agent who is able to buy tuna ($\mathbf{a}_1$), to turn tuna into energy by eating ($\mathbf{a}_2$), and to sell his energy for money ($\mathbf{a}_3$). That exhausts his basic-action allotment. Should he develop a desire to expend energy in fishing for tuna ($\mathbf{a}_4$), or to buy energy (that is, pay someone to help him, $\mathbf{a}_5$), or to sell tuna ($\mathbf{a}_6$), theory would have to disappoint him: the six vectors $\mathbf{a}_i$ cannot possibly be linearly independent. It is an unsatisfactory state of affairs, to remain without remedy until Part III.

While we are highlighting flaws in Model One, here is another. Nothing said so far prevents the driver from being, at times or always, a nonnegative linear combination of the basic actions. It is thus possible for the driver to be a feasible action. This spells grief, for it means that some actions can be both exogenous and endogenous. Evidently, what is needed is a mathematical distinction between the driver and a feasible action, between exogeneity and endogeneity. Model One is too primitive to permit such a distinction. Model Two does better, however. Part III has details.

The feasible set, whose discussion is now completed, is formally described in Definition 1. Measurement units are reinstated.

DEFINITION 1. Given are k linearly independent vectors, the *basic actions,* all belonging to the action space A. The basic actions are the columns of the $n \times k$ matrix $\mathbf{A}$, the *action matrix.* A *feasible action* is a nonnegative linear combination of the basic actions. The *feasible set* is the set of feasible actions, $F = \{\mathbf{a}\colon \mathbf{a} = \mathbf{A}\mathbf{c} \text{ for some } \mathbf{c} \geq \mathbf{0}\}$.

The basic actions are constant over time, except perhaps for occasional parametric changes.

As already hinted in Chapter 4, the here defined F differs in two ways from the feasible set of activity analysis. First, our $\mathbf{A}$ has full column rank; activity analysis allows the columns of its $\mathbf{A}$ to be linearly dependent.

Second, Definition 1 permits free access, meaning that F may contain nonnegative vectors other than $\mathbf{0}$; activity analysis prohibits free access.

Both activity analysis and Model One keep the agent from becoming infinitely rich in an instant. Activity analysis does so by ruling out free access. Model One does it by ensuring, through its motion law, that the endowment always moves with finite speed.

The activity-analytical term for free access is "production *ex nihilo.*" Now that producers no longer form a separate category, the term sounds inappositely narrow. It is the reason that Model One uses "free access" instead.

Figures 1 through 4 could suggest that the feasible set F ends where it meets a coordinate plane of X. This is not so. In fact, the set depicted is not even F. It is $\mathbf{x}(t) + F$, in all four diagrams. The main difference between F and $\mathbf{x}(t) + F$ is that F is a subset of A whereas $\mathbf{x}(t) + F$ is a subset of X (since endowment + action = endowment). And F is always unbounded, for if $\mathbf{a}$ is feasible, all nonnegative multiples of $\mathbf{a}$ are feasible too.

Figures 1 through 4 could suggest that the set $\mathbf{x}(t) + F$ is always bounded. Even that is not true. Free access is possible, after all, and where free access exists, $\mathbf{x}(t) + F$ is unbounded.

It should be added that whenever $\mathbf{x}(t) + F$ happens to be bounded, its boundedness is virtually irrelevant. The reason is that only a small part of F has theoretical significance, namely, the part in the immediate vicinity of F's vertex, $\mathbf{0}$. As some reflection will show, this is just another way of saying that the important thing about a feasible action is its direction, not its length.

The last paragraph drives home that the right way to look at Model One is to look at $\mathbf{x}(t)$ in extreme close-up. After all, the essence of Model One is concentrated in and near $\mathbf{x}(t)$. There is not even a utility-maximizing location, nearby or far away, to distract your eye, for utility maximization is no longer relevant. At every instant, the endowment is made to move by the action at that instant and the driver at that instant, and nothing else; consequently, what you want to observe is the push and pull of those two forces, and nothing else.

That the essence of Model One is concentrated in and near $\mathbf{x}(t)$ can also be expressed this way: If you knew the endowment's location and velocity at time t_o, if you also knew the driver's time path for all $t \geq t_o$, and if no parametric changes of any kind were to occur after t_o, you would be able to compute the entire time path of the endowment from t_o until doomsday.

Finally, the *motion law.*

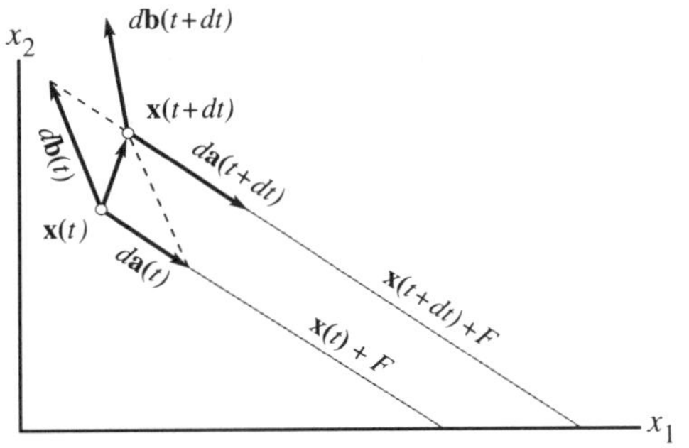

Figure 5. The motion law at work: comparing $\mathbf{x}(t)$ with $\mathbf{x}(t + dt)$.

Definition 2 (motion law for Model One).

(*i*) $d\mathbf{x}(t) = d\mathbf{a}(t) + d\mathbf{b}(t)$.

(*ii*) The direction of $d\mathbf{a}(t)$ is that in which u increases fastest, constraint permitting. The length of $d\mathbf{a}(t)$ is proportional to the slope of u in that direction. Vector $d\mathbf{b}(t)$ is exogenously given.

The proportionality factor will be written γdt.

Figure 5 illustrates the two-goods case. The cone F is a ray. Adding $d\mathbf{x}(t) = d\mathbf{a}(t) + d\mathbf{b}(t)$ to $\mathbf{x}(t)$ gives $\mathbf{x}(t + dt)$. As the diagram reflects, the direction of $d\mathbf{a}$ at $t + dt$ is the same as the direction of $d\mathbf{a}$ at t. Not so the length: the length of $d\mathbf{a}(t + dt)$ may differ from the length of $d\mathbf{a}(t)$. Vector $d\mathbf{b}(t + dt)$ can differ from $d\mathbf{b}(t)$ in direction, length, both, or neither.

Figure 6, too, illustrates the two-goods case. To keep the picture simple, the driver is assumed permanently null: $d\mathbf{b}(t) \equiv \mathbf{0}$. Also for simplicity, the situation depicted is that at time t only, not at time $t + dt$. The novelty

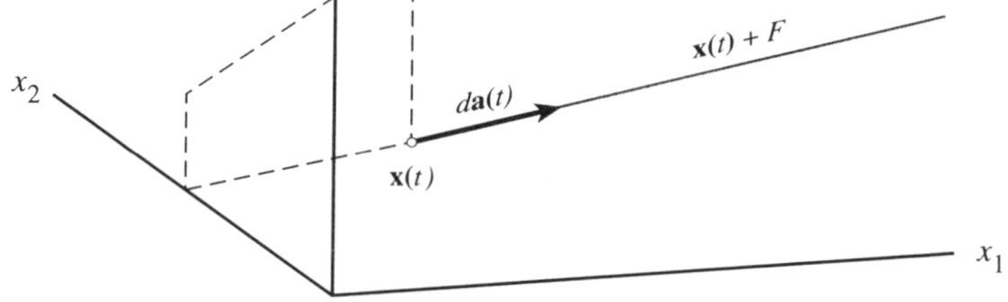

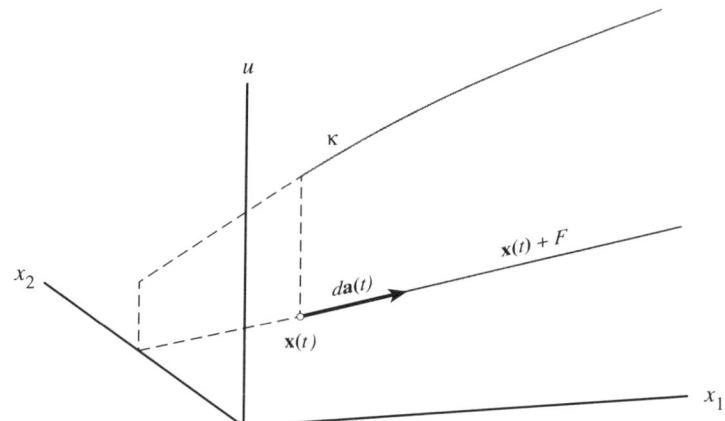

Figure 6. Existence of a constrained utility maximum is no longer necessary.

here is that $\mathbf{x}(t) + F$ is unbounded. Figure 6 makes the point that a utility maximum, even a constrained one, need not exist. The endowment set X is the floor of the diagram. Utility is measured along the vertical axis. Since the driver is for all t null, $\mathbf{x}(t) + F$ lies for all t on the same line. Suppose, additionally, that all marginal utilities are positive. Utility then reaches no maximum on that line. Yet this poses no problem. The endowment's location is at all times determinate, and the endowment's speed is at all times finite.

By the motion law, and since the driver is by assumption identically null, the endowment in Figure 6 moves at forever declining speed as time goes on. This is because the curve κ climbs at a forever decreasing rate. But κ does not have to have this form. Both neoclassical utility theory and Model One allow κ to climb at an increasing rate, for instance. If κ does so, the endowment will travel at forever increasing (but always finite) speed. Although such behavior seems implausible, nothing is gained by ruling it out.

Figure 7 depicts the three-goods case, again with $d\mathbf{b}(t) = \mathbf{0}$. Each good has its own coordinate axis, leaving no room for a utility axis. There are three basic actions. In the diagram, $d\mathbf{a}(t)$ is a linear combination of $\mathbf{a}_1$ and $\mathbf{a}_2$ alone, implying that $\mathbf{a}_3$ is unhelpful. Apparently, if the agent were to undertake all three basic actions, instead of just the first two, his endowment would not move in the direction in which utility increases fastest, feasible set permitting.

We continue with Figure 7. The triangular facet containing $d\mathbf{a}(t)$ is part

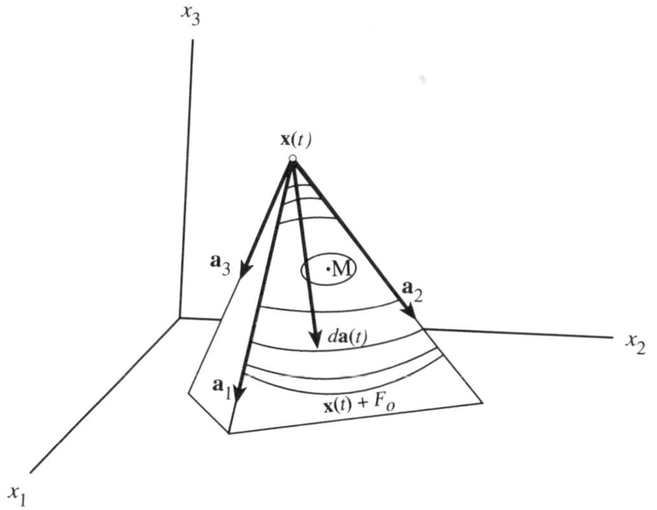

Figure 7. At $\mathbf{x}(t)$, the action is perpendicular to the constrained indifference curve through $\mathbf{x}(t)$.

of a plane. That plane intersects some indifference surfaces along closed curves. A few of these constrained indifference curves are shown.

Vector $d\mathbf{a}(t)$ is orthogonal, at $\mathbf{x}(t)$, to the constrained indifference curve through $\mathbf{x}(t)$. (See Chapter 2, Question 34.) More generally, if the driver were null, the endowment's path would cross the constrained indifference curves—those that it does cross—at right angles.

Near $\mathbf{x}(t)$, the constrained indifference curves are relatively dense, in Figure 7. It signifies that utility increases quickly there (in the direction of $d\mathbf{a}(t)$, of course). Arrow $d\mathbf{a}(t)$ is thus relatively long. If the driver were null, the endowment would move roughly in the direction of M, where the constrained indifference curves are shown as less dense. Near M, therefore, $d\mathbf{a}(t)$ is shorter.

In the n-goods case, the mechanism is the same as in the three-goods case.

Two more comments.

First, traditional utility theory, too, has a motion law, which is a special case of ours. To see this, consider that traditional theory has no driver and declares the endowment to be the utility-maximizing one, at all times. That there is no driver means $\dot{\mathbf{b}} = \mathbf{0}$. That the endowment always maximizes utility means two things. First, it means that the endowment does not move: $\dot{\mathbf{x}} = \mathbf{0}$. Second, it means that the steepest constrained ascent is always perpendicular to the budget (hyper)plane: $\mathbf{PH}^{-1}\nabla u = \mathbf{0}$, therefore $\dot{\mathbf{a}} = \mathbf{0}$. Thus, since $\dot{\mathbf{a}} = \dot{\mathbf{b}} = \dot{\mathbf{x}} = \mathbf{0}$, it is indeed true that $\dot{\mathbf{x}} = \dot{\mathbf{a}} + \dot{\mathbf{b}}$.

Second, it is tempting to regard $d\mathbf{a}(t)$ as the utility-maximizing action, and crucial to see that there is no such thing. For, since utility is a function of endowments, it can be maximized only by an endowment. It is thus mathematically impossible for $d\mathbf{a}(t)$, or any other action, to maximize utility, regardless of what intuition says. Besides, utility maximization has stopped playing a role. In fact, we saw that even a constrained utility maximum need no longer exist.

The next order of business is to express $d\mathbf{a}(t)$, the action at time t, in terms of the $\mathbf{a}_i$, the basic actions.

In the preceding chapter, the action rate at t was $\dot{\mathbf{a}} = \gamma\mathbf{PH}^{-1}\nabla u$. The action at t was therefore $d\mathbf{a}(t) = \gamma\mathbf{PH}^{-1}\nabla u dt$. In these formulas, $\mathbf{P}$ represented projection onto the budget (hyper)plane, $\mathbf{p}'\mathbf{x} = \mathbf{p}'\mathbf{x}_0$. Vector $\mathbf{PH}^{-1}\nabla u$ is of course the steepest constrained ascent (Chapter 2, MT 24).

Under Definition 2 (the motion law), the action rate at t is still $\dot{\mathbf{a}} = \gamma\mathbf{PH}^{-1}\nabla u$, and the action at t is still $d\mathbf{a}(t) = \gamma\mathbf{PH}^{-1}\nabla u dt$. But $\mathbf{P}$ now has a different interpretation. This time, $\mathbf{P}$ represents projection onto the feasible set F. Vector $\mathbf{PH}^{-1}\nabla u$ is thus, of all vectors in F, the one closest to $\mathbf{H}^{-1}\nabla u$. If $\mathbf{H}^{-1}\nabla u$ lies *in* the set F, this is obvious, for $\mathbf{PH}^{-1}\nabla u$ and $\mathbf{H}^{-1}\nabla u$ are then the same vector. If $\mathbf{H}^{-1}\nabla u$ does not lie in F, your intuition probably tells you that, indeed, F contains a vector closest to $\mathbf{H}^{-1}\nabla u$. Your intuition probably also tells you that this vector is unique. If you want proof rather than intuition, note that F is closed, and use Chapter 2, MT 27, Theorem 1, to prove existence; next, note that F is convex, and use Chapter 2, MT 27, Theorem 2, to prove uniqueness.

To find out how $\mathbf{P}$ depends on the basic actions, we need some notation. Because the action at t must be feasible, $d\mathbf{a}(t)$ is a nonnegative linear combination of the basic actions. The scalar weights in this linear combination will be written $dc_i(t)$, elements of $d\mathbf{c}(t)$:

$$d\mathbf{a}(t) = \mathbf{a}_1 dc_1(t) + \mathbf{a}_2 dc_2(t) + \cdots + \mathbf{a}_k dc_k(t) \quad \text{for certain } dc_i(t) \geq 0.$$

Equivalently, $d\mathbf{a}(t) = \mathbf{A}d\mathbf{c}(t)$ for some $d\mathbf{c}(t) \geq \mathbf{0}$. When there is no risk of misunderstanding, we leave off the argument t and write $d\mathbf{a} = \mathbf{A}d\mathbf{c}$ for some $d\mathbf{c} \geq \mathbf{0}$.

The action rate at t is $d\mathbf{a}(t)/dt = \mathbf{A}d\mathbf{c}(t)/dt$, or $d\mathbf{a}/dt = \mathbf{A}d\mathbf{c}/dt$, or $\dot{\mathbf{a}} = \mathbf{A}\dot{\mathbf{c}}$. The action between 0 and t is $\mathbf{a}(t) = \mathbf{A}\mathbf{c}(t)$ or $\mathbf{a} = \mathbf{A}\mathbf{c}$, with $\mathbf{c}(0) = \mathbf{0}$.

Each dc_i may vary over time. If, for instance, the driver varies from one moment to the next, the agent's response does so too. It is thus possible for the direction of $d\mathbf{a}$ to vary, not only now and then, but continually.

Basic action $\mathbf{a}_i$ will be called *attractive* (at time t) if its coefficient dc_i is positive, and *unattractive* if its coefficient is zero. Attractive basic actions are thus actually undertaken, and unattractive basic actions are not. In Figure 7, $d\mathbf{a}$ lies in the side of F that is spanned by $\mathbf{a}_1$ and $\mathbf{a}_2$; apparently, $\mathbf{a}_1$ and $\mathbf{a}_2$ are attractive and $\mathbf{a}_3$ is unattractive. (It gives you some idea of the whereabouts of ∇u.) The side of F containing $d\mathbf{a}$ is the *attractive facet* of F. More generally, the attractive facet of F is the set of nonnegative linear combinations of the attractive basic actions.

In practice, ∇u is unknown. In practice, therefore, it is impossible to determine which basic actions are attractive and which are unattractive. This is not the drawback that it appears to be. For suppose we specified u. In theory we could then compute ∇u and, next, find out which of the basic actions are attractive. Actually carrying out this program is another matter. Merely specifying someone's action matrix $\mathbf{A}$ in complete, numerical detail can be expected to require a prodigious effort, with the payoff unlikely to be worth the cost. And that would be only half the job. What all this adds up to is that even if ∇u were known we would not be able to use the information.

Let the number of attractive basic actions be k_o. To avoid trivialities we assume $k_o \geq 1$. The attractive $\mathbf{a}_i$ are the columns of $\mathbf{A}_o$, an $n \times k_o$ submatrix of $\mathbf{A}$. The corresponding dc_i, all positive, form $d\mathbf{c}_o$. Clearly, $\mathbf{A}d\mathbf{c} = \mathbf{A}_o d\mathbf{c}_o$, from which, in obvious notation, $\mathbf{A}\dot{\mathbf{c}} = \mathbf{A}_o\dot{\mathbf{c}}_o$. The attractive facet is F_o. If $k_o = k$, all basic actions are attractive. In that case, $d\mathbf{a}$ lies in the interior of the cone F, and $\mathbf{A}_o = \mathbf{A}$, and $d\mathbf{c}_o = d\mathbf{c}$, and F_o is the entire cone F. In Figure 7, the triangular facet closest to you is $\mathbf{x}(t) + F_o$.

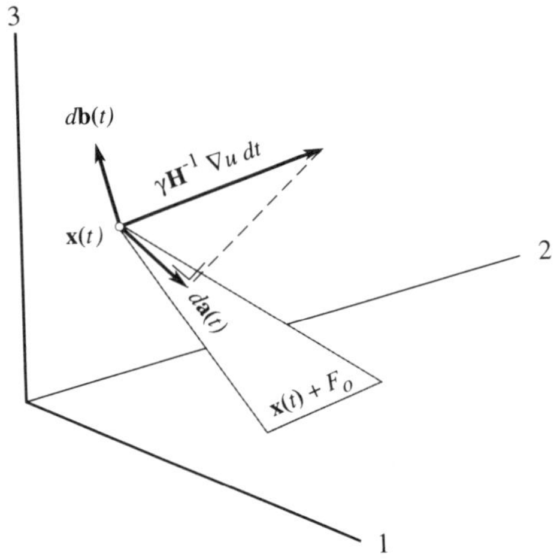

Figure 8. Illustrating the motion law.

Define **P** through

$$\mathbf{P} = \mathbf{A}_o(\mathbf{A}_o'\mathbf{H}\mathbf{A}_o)^{-1}\mathbf{A}_o'\mathbf{H}.$$

Matrix **P** thus represents projection onto the attractive facet (Chapter 2, MT 19). The original definitions, $\mathbf{P} = \mathbf{A}(\mathbf{A}'\mathbf{H}\mathbf{A})^{-1}\mathbf{A}\mathbf{H}$ and $\mathbf{P} = \mathbf{A}(\mathbf{A}'\mathbf{A})^{-1}\mathbf{A}$, are discarded.

Definition 2 can now be reformulated, more specifically, as

DEFINITION 2′ (MOTION LAW FOR MODEL ONE).

$$d\mathbf{x}(t) = d\mathbf{a}(t) + d\mathbf{b}(t),$$
$$\text{with } d\mathbf{a}(t) = \mathbf{A}_o d\mathbf{c}_o = \gamma\mathbf{P}\mathbf{H}^{-1}\nabla u dt \text{ and } d\mathbf{b}(t) \text{ exogenously given.} \quad (4)$$

Figure 8 summarizes the motion law graphically.

Definition 2′ is the core of Model One. In fact, it is only a slight exaggeration to say that Definition 2′ *is* Model One.

SUMMARY

Endowments are points **x** in a point set X. Actions are vectors **a** in a vector space A. The connection between the two is that the difference of two endowments is an action. Utility is a real-valued, differentiable function, defined over X.

The endowment owes its velocity in part to what the agent does and in part to exogenous influences: $\dot{\mathbf{x}} = \dot{\mathbf{a}} + \dot{\mathbf{b}}$, or $d\mathbf{x} = d\mathbf{a} + d\mathbf{b}$. Vector $d\mathbf{a}$, the action at time t, belongs to the feasible set $F = \{\mathbf{a}: \mathbf{a} = \mathbf{Ac} \text{ for } \mathbf{c} \geq \mathbf{0}\}$. More precisely, $d\mathbf{a}$ is a constant multiple (γdt) of the vector in F that is closest to $\mathbf{H}^{-1}\nabla u$. You can also say that $d\mathbf{a}$ is the vector in F that is closest to $\gamma\mathbf{H}^{-1}\nabla u dt$. See Figure 8.

Questions

1. Seeing that the driver is determined by reality, do we have the freedom to specify the functional form of its elements? Or does Nature take care of that?
2. Suppose all quantities are real. Show that if

$$\mathbf{A} = \begin{pmatrix} 1 & 3 \\ -1 & 1 \\ 2 & -1 \end{pmatrix},$$

   then at least one (imputed) price is negative.
3. (Continuation) It follows that $\mathbf{A}$ cannot be an action matrix. True or false?
4. (Continuation) Find at least one feasible action with all elements positive.
5. Suppose all quantities are real. It was said that "buying a Party Pak," $(1, -1, 5)'$, and "buying a Family Pak," $(2, 3, -12)'$, are linearly independent. Prove this algebraically.
6. Describe the attractive facet of F if $\nabla u = (2/b, 2/f, 7/k)'$ and $k_o = 0$.
7. Use Eq. (4) to express $\dot{\mathbf{c}}_o$ in terms of $\mathbf{A}_o$, $\mathbf{H}$, ∇u, and γ. (Do not assume that $\mathbf{A}_o$ is square.)
8. Suppose all quantities are real. Let the action matrix be

$$\mathbf{A} = \begin{pmatrix} 1 & -1 & 2 \\ 2 & 0 & 1 \\ 3 & 1 & -1 \end{pmatrix}.$$

   Is $\mathbf{v}_1 = (1, 2, 2)$ feasible? Is $\mathbf{v}_2 = (2, 4, 1)'$ feasible? Is $\mathbf{v}_3 = (1, 2, 1)'$ feasible?
9. (Continuation) Replace $\mathbf{a}_1$, the first column of $\mathbf{A}$, with $-\mathbf{a}_1$. Now which of the three $\mathbf{v}_i$ is or are feasible?
10. Figure 5 appears to imply that $\mathbf{x}(t) + d\mathbf{a}(t) + d\mathbf{b}(t) = \mathbf{x}(t + dt)$. Does this equation indeed hold?
11. If the cone F has three edges, how many feasible actions are there?

7

The Short-Response Function

The purpose of this chapter is to find out how certain dependent variables respond to parametric changes of some basic-action element.

Recall that the action at time t is $d\mathbf{a} = \mathbf{A}d\mathbf{c} = \Sigma \mathbf{a}_i dc_i$.

Every dependent variable to be considered is either a flow or a flow rate. If a flow, it is either an element of an $\mathbf{a}_i dc_i$ or the sum of several such elements. If a flow rate, it is either an element of an $\mathbf{a}_i dc_i/dt$ or the sum of several such elements. Since flows and flow rates differ only by a factor dt, there is no need to examine both. We concentrate on flow rates. Effectively then, all dependent variables in this chapter are flow rates.

The function describing how any flow rate reacts to a parametric change of a basic-action element will be called the *short-response function.* Among its special cases are the nine testable results promised earlier: all four demand functions (consumer/own-price, consumer/cross-price, producer/own-price, producer/cross-price), all four supply functions (consumer/own-price, consumer/cross-price, producer/own-price, producer/cross-price), and the quasi-Engel function, which describes how the demand rate for a good depends on the wage.

If some basic-action element changes at time t_o, the short-response function describes how the dependent variable is affected at t_o, and only at t_o. Part III introduces the *long-response function,* which describes how the dependent variable reacts not only at t_o but also afterward.

The short-response function is given by the equation $\dot{q} = f(p)$. We interpret first p and then $\dot{q}$. After that, the form of $f(p)$ is derived.

All but one of the basic actions are assumed constant. To streamline the exposition, suppose the basic actions have been ordered so that the variable one is $\mathbf{a}_1$.

All but one of the elements of $\mathbf{a}_1$ are assumed constant. To streamline the exposition, suppose the commodities have been ordered so that the variable element of $\mathbf{a}_1$ is the first, a_{11}.

For notational simplicity, a_{11} is written p. This p, which may be negative, is the independent variable in the short-response function. There is no need for p to be a price; p can be any basic-action element—any input in a production process, for instance.

Strictly, p *cannot* be a price. A price is a quotient of two action elements, with sign suppressed, whereas p is a single action element. To illustrate, let $\mathbf{a}_1$ be "buying a gallon of milk," with a milk element of $1g$ and a money element of $-2d$. The price of milk is thus $(2d)/(1g)$. When $-2d$ is abbreviated to p, and $2d$ to $-p$, the price of milk becomes $-p/(1g)$; which is still a far cry from p. But it is accurate to say that *changes* of the milk price are represented by *changes* of p. From here on, references to "the price p" are meant to be interpreted in that sense.

With one exception, the diagrams of economics follow mathematical practice by measuring independent variables along the horizontal axis. The exception is when the independent variable is a price; economics then follows Marshallian practice by putting price on the vertical axis. All this works very well so long as it is clear whether one's independent variable is a price or not. But that has ceased to be clear: p may or may not be a price. It is thus no longer possible to obey both mathematical custom and Marshallian custom. Forced to choose, we go with the mathematicians. In this book then, the p-axis is always horizontal.

So much for the interpretation of the independent variable, p. The interpretation of the dependent variable, $\dot{q}$, is next.

The action rate at time t is $\dot{\mathbf{a}} = \mathbf{A}\dot{\mathbf{c}} = \dot{c}_1\mathbf{a}_1 + \dot{c}_2\mathbf{a}_2 + \cdots + \dot{c}_k\mathbf{a}_k$. Its elements are

$$
\begin{aligned}
\dot{a}_1 &= \dot{c}_1 a_{11} + \dot{c}_2 a_{21} + \cdots + \dot{c}_k a_{k1} \\
\dot{a}_2 &= \dot{c}_1 a_{12} + \dot{c}_2 a_{22} + \cdots + \dot{c}_k a_{k2} \\
&\ \ \vdots \\
\dot{a}_n &= \dot{c}_1 a_{1n} + \dot{c}_2 a_{2n} + \cdots + \dot{c}_k a_{kn}.
\end{aligned}
$$

Each of the n right-hand sides consist of k flow rates, all of the form $\dot{c}_i a_{ij}$ for some i and j. The general flow rate $\dot{c}_i a_{ij}$, with i and j unspecified, is the $\dot{q}$ in $\dot{q} = f(p)$.

In the field of economics, $\dot{q}$ is the dandelion. As the following examples illustrate, almost every rate of economic significance is either a flow rate of the form $\dot{c}_i a_{ij}$ or the sum of several such flow rates.

Demand and *supply,* perhaps more accurately called *demand rate* and *supply rate,* are either flow rates or sums of flow rates. If apples are good 3, if you get all your apples by buying them at FoodPlace, and if "buying an apple at FoodPlace" is $\mathbf{a}_i$, your demand rate for apples is $\dot{c}_i a_{i3}$. If you buy apples not only at FoodPlace ($\mathbf{a}_i$) but also at FoodCorner ($\mathbf{a}_j$), and if in addition you borrow apples from one neighbor ($\mathbf{a}_k$) and steal apples from another ($\mathbf{a}_l$), your demand rate for apples is $\dot{c}_i a_{i3} + \dot{c}_j a_{j3} + \dot{c}_k a_{k3} + \dot{c}_l a_{l3}$. If money is good 1, your *expenditure rate* for apples is $\dot{c}_i a_{i1} + \dot{c}_j a_{j1}$. This rate is negative; you may prefer to follow custom and define the expenditure rate for apples as $|\dot{c}_i a_{i1} + \dot{c}_j a_{j1}|$.

More examples: If you have both a day job ($\mathbf{a}_f$) and a night job ($\mathbf{a}_g$), and if energy is good 7, your *supply rate* of energy is $\dot{c}_f a_{f7} + \dot{c}_g a_{g7}$, or its absolute value if you prefer. Being paid wages in both jobs, you have an *income rate* of $\dot{c}_f a_{f1} + \dot{c}_g a_{g1}$, assuming that money is still good 1. If you pay taxes ($\mathbf{a}_h$) on your earned income, the rate at which you do so—your *tax payment rate*—is $\dot{c}_h a_{h1}$, or its absolute value if you prefer. Your *disposable-income rate* is then $\dot{c}_f a_{f1} + \dot{c}_g a_{g1} + \dot{c}_h a_{h1}$.

Still more examples: If chairs are good 4, and "making a chair" is $\mathbf{a}_p$, and you make chairs, your *output rate* is $\dot{c}_p a_{p4}$. The corresponding *revenue rate* is $\dot{c}_p a_{p1}$, assuming that you sell the chairs you make, and assuming that money is still good 1. If cars are good 8, and "selling a car" is $\mathbf{a}_q$, and you sell cars, your *sales rate* is $\dot{c}_q a_{q8}$, or its absolute value if you prefer.

And so on.

Every own-price demand function is of the form $\dot{q} = f(p)$, with p representing a price and $\dot{q}$ being both a demand rate and an element of $\mathbf{a}_1\dot{c}_1$. Every cross-price demand function is of the form $\dot{q} = f(p)$, with p representing a price and $\dot{q}$ being both a demand rate and *not* an element of $\mathbf{a}_1\dot{c}_1$.

Every own-price supply function is of the form $\dot{q} = f(p)$, with p representing a price and $\dot{q}$ being both a supply rate and an element of $\mathbf{a}_1\dot{c}_1$. Every cross-price supply function is of the form $\dot{q} = f(p)$, with p representing a price and $\dot{q}$ being both a supply rate and *not* an element of $\mathbf{a}_1\dot{c}_1$.

It should be amply clear by now that $f(p)$ is a good deal more than a demand or supply function in the traditional sense, whether own-price or cross-price. The short-response function also describes how the income rate depends on the wage p, or on the price p of tea. And it describes how the output rate of cars varies with the labor input (that is, the quantity p of energy needed to make one car). And it describes how the agent's consumption rate of peanut butter sandwiches varies with the quantity p of peanut butter on each sandwich. In brief, $f(p)$ describes how *any* flow rate responds to changes in *any* basic-action element.

The derivation of $f(p)$ is next. A numerical example serves as introduction. For simplicity, all quantities are temporarily assumed dimensionless. Both A and A^0 are thus R^3, for the time being.

The numerical example involves $k = 2$ basic actions and $n = 3$ goods. The basic actions are $\mathbf{a}_1 = (2, -1, 3)'$ and $\mathbf{a}_2 = (-1, 1, 2)'$, columns of

$$\mathbf{A} = \begin{pmatrix} 2 & -1 \\ -1 & 1 \\ 3 & 2 \end{pmatrix}.$$

Also given is $\gamma\nabla u = (6, 7, 4)'$. In real life, of course, you never have this kind of information.

For a picture, see Figure 8 in Chapter 6 (with $\mathbf{H} = \mathbf{I}$).

Projecting $\gamma\nabla u$ onto the plane spanned by $\mathbf{a}_1$ and $\mathbf{a}_2$ gives $\mathbf{P}(\gamma\nabla u) = \mathbf{A}(\mathbf{A}'\mathbf{A})^{-1}\mathbf{A}'(\gamma\nabla u)$. Gambling that both basic actions are attractive (and prepared to start over if it turns out otherwise), we set this equal to $\mathbf{A}\dot{\mathbf{c}}$, to get $\mathbf{A}\dot{\mathbf{c}} = \mathbf{A}(\mathbf{A}'\mathbf{A})^{-1}\mathbf{A}'(\gamma\nabla u)$. To simplify, premultiply both sides by $\mathbf{A}'$. This gives $\mathbf{A}'\mathbf{A}\dot{\mathbf{c}} = \mathbf{A}'(\gamma\nabla u)$, which is a linear system in the unknowns $\dot{c}_1$, $\dot{c}_2$. Using the givens turns the system into

$$14\dot{c}_1 + 3\dot{c}_2 = 17$$

$$3\dot{c}_1 + 6\dot{c}_2 = 9.$$

Its solution is $\dot{c}_1 = \dot{c}_2 = 1$. As hoped, both $\dot{c}_i$ are positive. Both basic actions are thus attractive. Equivalently, $\dot{\mathbf{c}} = \dot{\mathbf{c}}_0$.

For the next step toward the short-response function, we change $\mathbf{a}_1$ from $(2, -1, 3)'$ to $(p, -1, 3)'$. The system $\mathbf{A}'\mathbf{A}\dot{\mathbf{c}} = \mathbf{A}'(\gamma\nabla u)$ thereby becomes

$$\begin{aligned}(p^2 + 10)\dot{c}_1 + (5 - p)\dot{c}_2 &= 5 + 6p\\ (5 - p)\dot{c}_1 + \qquad 6\dot{c}_2 &= 9.\end{aligned}$$

Solving by Cramer's Rule gives

$$\dot{c}_1 = \begin{vmatrix} 5 + 6p & 5 - p \\ 9 & 6 \end{vmatrix} \div \begin{vmatrix} p^2 + 10 & 5 - p \\ 5 - p & 6 \end{vmatrix}$$

$$\dot{c}_2 = \begin{vmatrix} p^2 + 10 & 5 + 6p \\ 5 - p & 9 \end{vmatrix} \div \begin{vmatrix} p^2 + 10 & 5 - p \\ 5 - p & 6 \end{vmatrix},$$

from which

$$\dot{c}_1 = \dot{c}_1(p) = \frac{9p - 3}{p^2 + 2p + 7}$$

$$\dot{c}_2 = \dot{c}_2(p) = \frac{3p^2 - 5p + 13}{p^2 + 2p + 7}.$$

For a quick description, let Q, L, and K stand for "a quadratic form in p," "a linear form in p," and "a constant." Also, let Q_o represent the quadratic form that is the common denominator of the $\dot{c}_i$. Then $\dot{c}_1 = L/Q_o$ and $\dot{c}_2 = Q/Q_o$.

The results just found are typical, in the following sense. Suppose the variable basic action (in the example, $\mathbf{a}_1$) is attractive. As will be shown in a moment, the element of $\dot{\mathbf{c}}_o$ that is associated with the variable basic action (in the example, $\dot{c}_1$) is a quotient of a linear form and a quadratic form, not just here but in general. All other elements of $\dot{\mathbf{c}}_o$ are quotients of two quadratic forms. Further, all elements of $\dot{\mathbf{c}}_o$ have the same denominator, Q_o. Elements of $\dot{\mathbf{c}}$ not in $\dot{\mathbf{c}}_o$ are, as you know, zero.

Now that we know how the $\dot{c}_i$ depend on p, it is easy to find out how the various flow rates $\dot{c}_i a_{ij}$ depend on p. First, $i = 1$: since the three elements of $\mathbf{a}_1$ are p, -1, and 3, the three flow rates in $\dot{c}_1\mathbf{a}_1$ have the form pL/Q_o, L/Q_o, and L/Q_o. Next, $i = 2$: since the three elements of $\mathbf{a}_2$ are constants, all three flow rates in $\dot{c}_2\mathbf{a}_2$ have the form Q/Q_o.

Note that pL is a Q with its constant term lopped off. You might say that all flow rates have the form Q/Q_o, except that the flow rates in $\dot{c}_1\mathbf{a}_1$ have "deficient numerators": the numerator of $\dot{c}_1 a_{11}$ is a Q without a constant term, and the numerators of the other $\dot{c}_1 a_{1i}$ are Q's without a quadratic term.

This completes the example. Generalization follows, in the form of Theorem 1. Measurement units are reinstated.

THEOREM 1. *Let* $\dot{\mathrm{q}} = \dot{\mathrm{c}}_\mathrm{i}\mathrm{a}_\mathrm{ij}$. *The short-response function is*

$$\dot{q} = f(p) = Q/Q_o = \frac{Ap^2 + Bp + C}{Dp^2 + Ep + 1}, \tag{1}$$

where A, B, C, D, *and* E *are parameters. For flow rates that are elements of* $\dot{\mathrm{c}}_1\mathbf{a}_1$, *the function simplifies: if* $\dot{\mathrm{q}} = \mathrm{c}_1\mathrm{a}_{11}$ $(= \dot{\mathrm{c}}_1\mathrm{p})$, *the numerator lacks a constant term* (C = 0), *and if* $\dot{\mathrm{q}}$ *is any other element of* $\dot{\mathrm{c}}_1\mathbf{a}_1$, *the numerator lacks a quadratic term* (A = 0).

Parameters A, B, *and* C *vary with* i *and* j. *Parameters* D *and* E *are the same for all* i *and* j.

Proof. First, a refresher. Recall that basic action $\mathbf{a}_j$ is attractive (at t) if it appears with positive weight dc_j in $d\mathbf{a} = \mathbf{a}_1 dc_1 + \mathbf{a}_2 dc_2 + \cdots + \mathbf{a}_k dc_k = \mathbf{A}d\mathbf{c}$. The attractive basic actions form $\mathbf{A}_o$. The positive dc_i form $d\mathbf{c}_o$. The action at t, which is $d\mathbf{a}$, thus equals not only $\mathbf{A}d\mathbf{c}$ but also $\mathbf{A}_o d\mathbf{c}_o$. Division by dt gives the action rate at t: $\dot{\mathbf{a}} = \mathbf{A}_o\dot{\mathbf{c}}_o$.

By the motion law for Model One—see Chapter 6, Definition 2′—we have $\dot{\mathbf{a}} = \mathbf{A}_o\dot{\mathbf{c}}_o = \gamma\mathbf{P}\mathbf{H}^{-1}\boldsymbol{\nabla}u = \gamma\mathbf{A}_o(\mathbf{A}_o'\mathbf{H}\mathbf{A}_o)^{-1}\mathbf{A}_o'\boldsymbol{\nabla}u$. Premultiplying by $\mathbf{A}_o'\mathbf{H}$ gives

$$\mathbf{A}_o'\mathbf{H}\mathbf{A}_o\dot{\mathbf{c}}_o = \gamma\mathbf{A}_o'\boldsymbol{\nabla}u. \tag{2}$$

Equation (2) is a linear system of k_o equations in the k_o unknown elements $\dot{c}_i$ of $\dot{\mathbf{c}}_o$. (Elements of $\dot{\mathbf{c}}$ not in $\dot{\mathbf{c}}_o$ are known: they are all zero.) To make the argument easier to follow, we take $k_o = 3$ and let the three attractive basic actions be $\mathbf{a}_1$, $\mathbf{a}_2$, and $\mathbf{a}_3$. Nothing essential is lost by these assumptions: as the story unfolds, it will become clear that the reasoning is quite general and applies equally well to all other possible values of k_o and to all other possible collections of attractive basic actions.

The coefficient matrix in (2), which is $\mathbf{A}_o'\mathbf{H}\mathbf{A}_o$, has general element $\mathbf{a}_i'\mathbf{H}\mathbf{a}_j$. This is quadratic in p if $i = j = 1$, linear in p if either $i = 1$ or $j = 1$, and constant otherwise. On the right, the ith term is $\gamma\mathbf{a}_i'\boldsymbol{\nabla}u$. This is linear in p if $i = 1$ and constant otherwise. System (2) can thus be written, symbolically, as

$$\begin{pmatrix} Q & L & L \\ L & K & K \\ L & K & K \end{pmatrix} \begin{pmatrix} \dot{c}_1 \\ \dot{c}_2 \\ \dot{c}_3 \end{pmatrix} = \begin{pmatrix} L \\ K \\ K \end{pmatrix}. \tag{3}$$

When (3) is solved by Cramer's Rule, each $\dot{c}_i$ emerges as a quotient of determinants. The three *denominators* are the same; each is the determinant of the coefficient matrix. To see how this determinant depends on p, expand with respect to the first row. You find that

$$\begin{aligned} \det(\mathbf{A}_o'\mathbf{H}\mathbf{A}_o) &= Q \begin{vmatrix} K & K \\ K & K \end{vmatrix} + L \begin{vmatrix} L & K \\ L & K \end{vmatrix} + L \begin{vmatrix} L & K \\ L & K \end{vmatrix} \\ &= Q + L(L) + L(L) = Q_o. \end{aligned}$$

The three *numerators* are handled the same way. They are

$$\begin{vmatrix} L & L & L \\ K & K & K \\ K & K & K \end{vmatrix} = L, \quad \begin{vmatrix} Q & L & L \\ L & K & K \\ L & K & K \end{vmatrix} = Q, \text{ and } \begin{vmatrix} Q & L & L \\ L & K & K \\ L & K & K \end{vmatrix} = Q.$$

In all then,

$$\dot{c}_1 = L/Q_o, \text{ and } \dot{c}_2 = Q/Q_o, \text{ and } \dot{c}_3 = Q/Q_o.$$

The first element of $\mathbf{a}_1$ is p, and the other elements are constant. The flow rate $\dot{c}_1 a_{11}$ thus has the form pL/Q_o, and all other flow rates $\dot{c}_1 a_{1i}$ have the form L/Q_o.

The elements of $\mathbf{a}_2$ and $\mathbf{a}_3$ are constant. All flow rates $\dot{c}_2 a_{2i}$ and $\dot{c}_3 a_{3i}$ thus have the form Q/Q_o.

Let $Q_o = Dp^2 + Ep + F$. Since $Q_o = \det(\mathbf{A}_o'\mathbf{H}\mathbf{A}_o)$ is positive, F cannot be zero. (Nor, for that matter, can D.) It is thus permissible to divide all numerators (L or Q) and all denominators (Q_o) by F. Equivalently, we may set $F = 1$, as is done in (1). P.O.C.

Discussion. (*i*) Figure 1 shows a sample graph of (1). Figure 2 shows a sample graph of (1) with $A = 0$. Figures 3 and 4 show sample graphs of (1) with $A = 0$ and $p \geqq 0$. Note that Q/Q_o can be written as $L/Q_0 + K$, so that every graph of (1) is a vertical translate of the graph of some L/Q_o. It means that you can get a good idea of the possible graphs of Q/Q_o by inspecting graphs of L/Q_o, like Figures 2, 3, and 4.

(*ii*) For an illustration of Theorem 1, let $\mathbf{a}_1$ be "buying a gallon of milk." Let its milk element be $+1g$ and its money element p. Milk is good 5, say. Since $p = a_{11}$, by convention, money is good 1. Suppose that "buying a

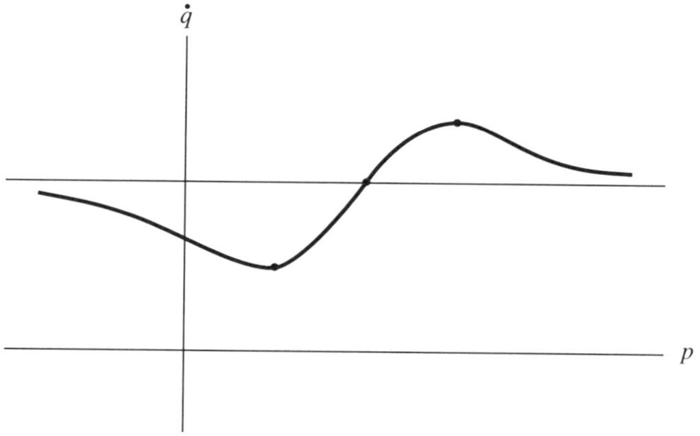

Figure 1. A short-response function.

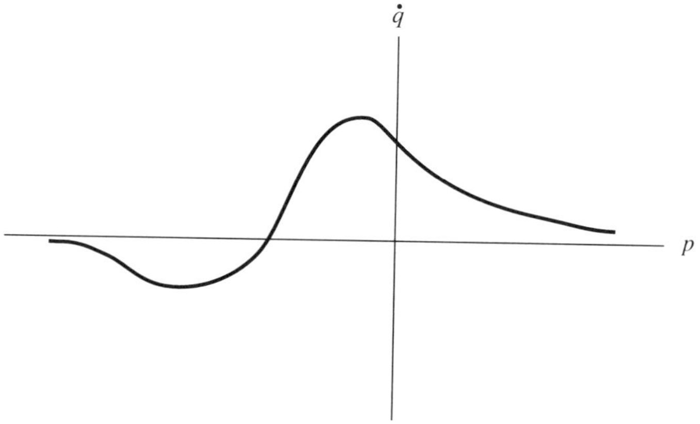

Figure 2. A short-response function with $A = 0$.

loaf of bread" is one of the basic actions. The rate $\dot{q}$ at which the agent buys bread depends on the price of milk according to (1). In fact, every cross-price demand function has the form Q/Q_o.

The flow rate $\dot{c}_1 a_{15}$ is the rate at which the agent buys milk, at time t. Since $\dot{c}_1 a_{15}$ is an element of $\dot{c}_1 \mathbf{a}_1$ other than $\dot{c}_1 a_{11}$, its dependence on p is given by L/Q_o. The own-price demand function for milk is thus of the form (1) with $A = 0$. Obviously, every own-price demand function will be of that form.

The flow rate $\dot{c}_1 a_{11} = \dot{c}_1 p$, or its absolute value, is the rate at which the agent pays for the milk he buys. By Theorem 1, this expenditure rate obeys (1) with $C = 0$.

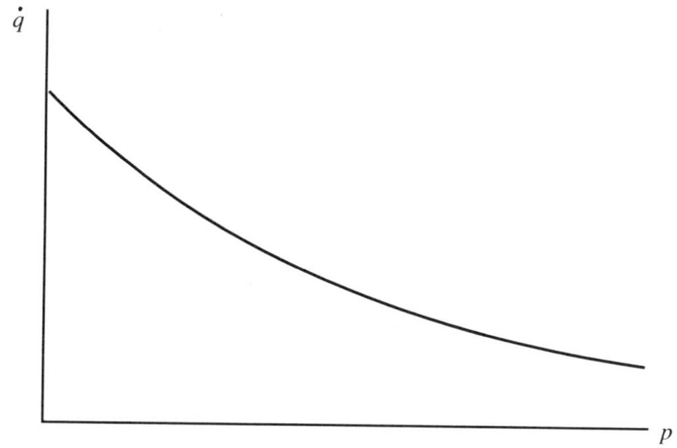

Figure 3. A short-response function interpretable as a demand function.

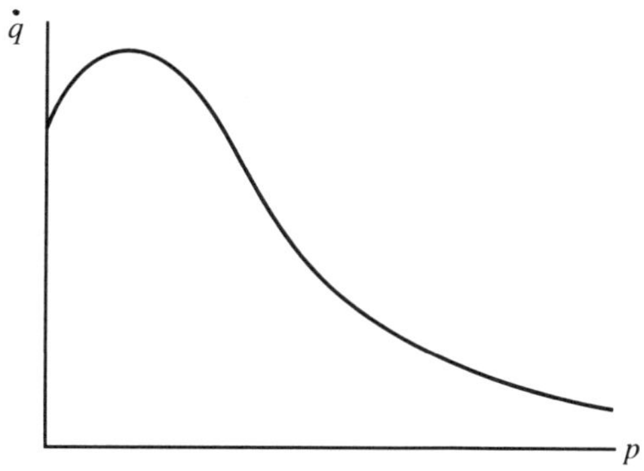

Figure 4. A short-response function interpretable as a Giffenesque demand function.

(*iii*) For another illustration, let $\mathbf{a}_1$ be "working for a wage." Let its energy element be $-1e$ (= 1 erg) and its money element p. A change of p thus represents a wage change. Energy is good 6, say. Money is good 1, as before. Noted again is that this book interprets supplying as selling, rather than as merely offering for sale.

The flow rate $\dot{c}_1 a_{16}$, or its absolute value, is the rate at which the agent supplies energy, at time t. Since $\dot{c}_1 a_{16}$ is an element of $\dot{c}_1 \mathbf{a}_1$ other than $\dot{c}_1 a_{11}$, its dependence on p is given by L/Q_o. The own-price supply function of energy, more commonly called the labor-supply function, is thus of the form (1) with $A = 0$. The labor-supply curve can bend backward, or downward rather (now that p is on the horizontal axis). As you saw in

Question 6 at the end of Chapter 5, the labor-supply curve bends downward if and only if all three of B, C, and $B - CE$ are positive.

The flow rate $\dot{c}_1 a_{11} = \dot{c}_1 p$ is the rate at which the agent receives money for the energy he sells—his income rate, in other words. By Theorem 1, this income rate depends on the wage according to (1) with $C = 0$.

(*iv*) For yet another illustration, let $\mathbf{a}_1$ again be "working for a wage," and let $\mathbf{a}_2$ be "buying a loaf of bread." Bread is good 8. Money is again good 1. As before, a change of p represents a wage change.

The *quasi-Engel function* for bread describes how the demand rate for bread, $\dot{c}_2 a_{28}$, varies with the wage—varies with p, that is. The quasi-Engel

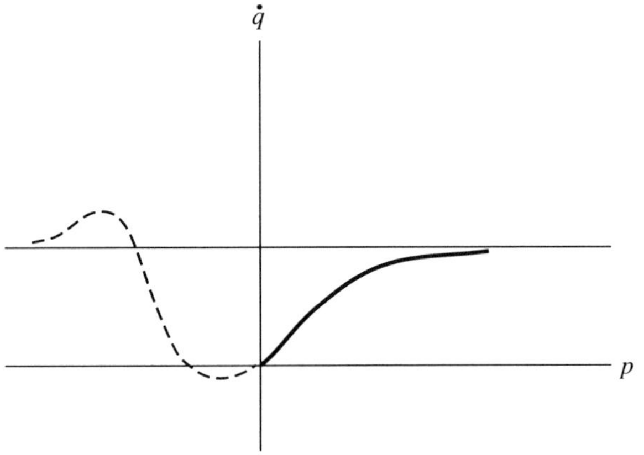

Figure 5. A quasi-Engel curve through the origin; p is the wage.

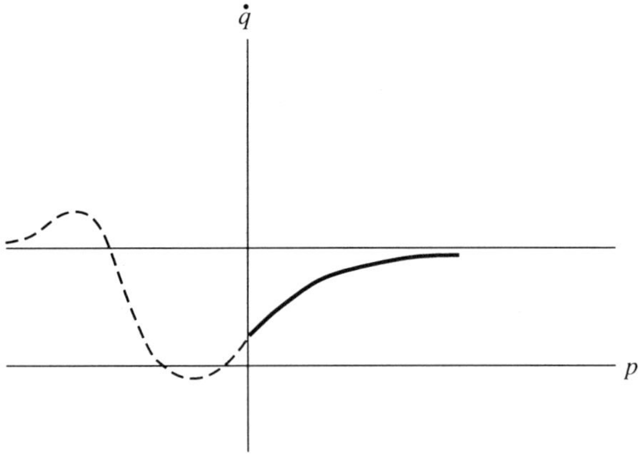

Figure 6. Quasi-Engel curve for a good bought even if the wage p is zero.

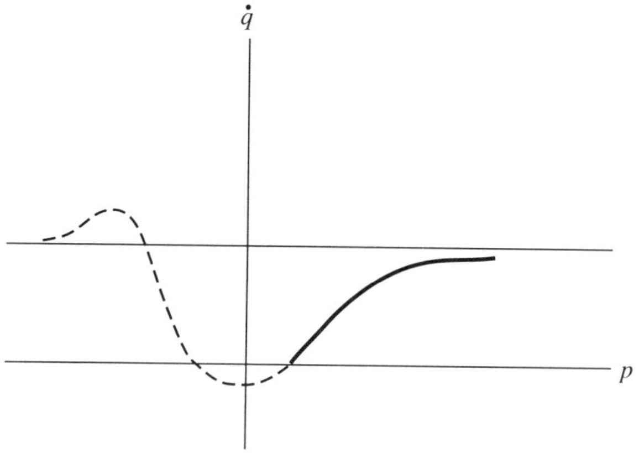

Figure 7. Quasi-Engel curve for a good bought only when the wage p exceeds a certain level.

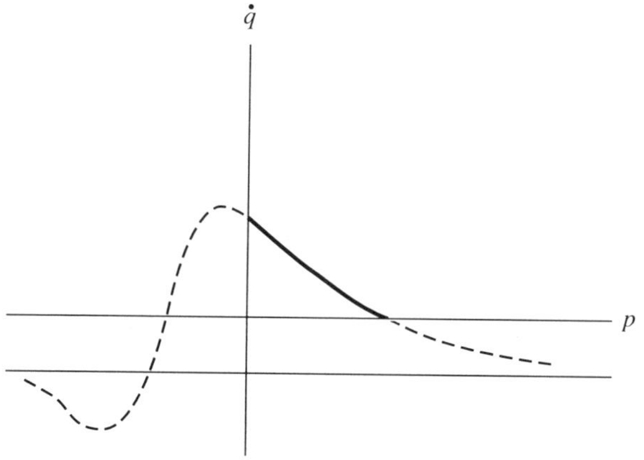

Figure 8. Quasi-Engel curve for a wage-inferior good, like cheap wine.

function is thus nothing but a cross-price demand function, of the form Q/Q_o. Figures 5–7 show three possible graphs.

Define a good as *wage-normal* or *wage-inferior* depending on whether the demand rate for it increases or decreases when the wage goes up. For contrast, normal and inferior goods will be called *income-normal* and *income-inferior.* Figures 5–7 concern wage-normal commodities, like expensive wine. Figure 8 shows a quasi-Engel function for a wage-inferior good, like cheap wine. Figure 9 shows a quasi-Engel function for a good that is initially wage-normal but eventually wage-inferior, like mid-priced wine.

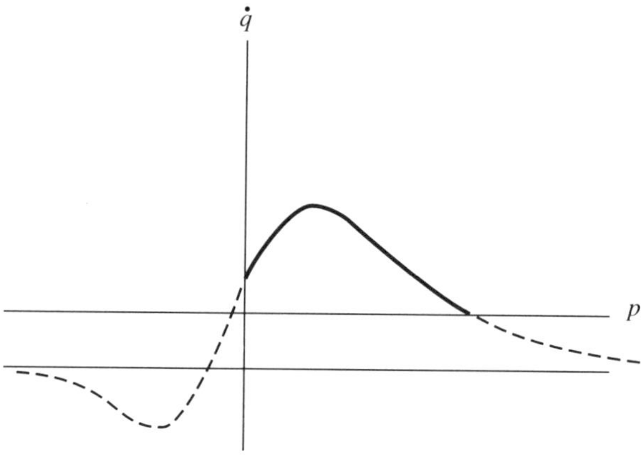

Figure 9. Quasi-Engel curve for midpriced wine.

(v) Introduction of the quasi-Engel function raises the question of where the ordinary Engel function fits in. The answer is that it does not. In Model One, the income rate is a flow rate of the form $\dot{c}_i a_{ij}$, or a sum of several such flow rates—in short, a *dependent* variable. But the definition of the Engel function treats the income rate as an *independent* variable. By the standards of Model One, therefore, the Engel function is an illegitimate construction. And not just according to Model One, either. It is well known that the Engel function is not single-valued, meaning it is not a function.

Still, for many workers, the income rate is nearly proportional to the wage. Thus, if one of those workers' income rate were plotted against that worker's demand rate for some commodity, the resulting graph would closely resemble that of the quasi-Engel function. In particular, graphs concerning income-normal goods would likely have the sigmoid shape you see in Figures 5–7. This is of more than passing interest: many empirical studies have found Engel curves for income-normal goods to be sigmoidal.

(vi) A parenthetical note: Because this book views income as a dependent variable, it has no way of dealing with any notion that treats income as an independent variable. The Engel function is of course one of these. The income elasticity of demand is another. The income effect is a third.

(vii) Parameters A through E in (1) are dimensioned. To see how, we note first that since the inner product on A is real-valued, all elements of $\mathbf{A}_o'\mathbf{H}\mathbf{A}_o$ are real. Det($\mathbf{A}_o'\mathbf{H}\mathbf{A}_o$) $= Q_o$ is thus real too. It follows that if p is measured in bottles (b), parameters D and E are measured in $1/b^2$ and $1/b$. As for the numerator, $Ap^2 + Bp + C$, suppose that $\dot{q}$ is measured in cans per hour, c/h. Then all three of Ap^2, Bp, and C must be so measured. In consequence, the unit of A is c/b^2h, and that of B is c/bh.

(*viii*) Because the five parameters in (1) depend on unknown quantities, like the marginal utilities and the elements of **H**, their values should be considered obtainable solely by estimation, rather than by computation or direct observation. To see how such estimation might be performed, suppose, for concreteness, that $\dot{q} = f(p)$ is an own-price demand function. In neoclassical utility theory, observations on p and $\dot{q}$ would be made on Mondays only, and the agent would have to have the same initial endowment each time. But for two slight differences, it is the same here. First, there is no need to limit the observing of p and $\dot{q}$ to Mondays, or even to regularly spaced instants. Second, at all observations the endowment $\mathbf{x}$ must be the same (or else ∇u will differ at different observations, affecting the parameter values to be estimated). Incidentally, the $\mathbf{x}$ here referred to can be any endowment. It does not have to be the initial endowment. In fact, there is no such thing as an initial endowment in Model One.

The requirement that $\mathbf{x}$ be the same at all observations needs a small modification. Flow rates, like $\dot{q} = dq/dt$, cannot actually be observed. But you can observe $\Delta q/\Delta t$. Doing so requires that the commodity stock of interest be measured *twice*, once at some instant t and once a little later, at $t + \Delta t$. Barring exceptional circumstances, $\mathbf{x}(t + \Delta t)$ will differ from $\mathbf{x}(t)$, and $\nabla u(t + \Delta t)$ will differ from $\nabla u(t)$. Since the endowment's time path is continuous, the difference between $\mathbf{x}(t + \Delta t)$ and $\mathbf{x}(t)$ is small if Δt is. Further, u is differentiable, meaning that all marginal utilities not only exist but are continuous; this implies that the difference between $\nabla u(t + \Delta t)$ and $\nabla u(t)$ is small if Δt is. In all then, $\Delta q/\Delta t$ will be a reasonable approximation of dq/dt so long as Δt is small.

Continuity of the marginal utilities plays no role in Model One itself. It is only when Model One is put to the test, and actual observations are needed for parameter estimation, that continuity becomes important. Existence of the marginal utilities is essential, however. Without it, there would be no ∇u.

More on estimation in Part III.

(*ix*) If two flow rates, $\dot{q}_1$ and $\dot{q}_2$, are measured in the same units, they can be added. Suppose that both are written as functions of p, and $\dot{q}_1 + \dot{q}_2$ is too. Since $\dot{q}_1$ and $\dot{q}_2$ have the same denominator Q_o, the denominator of $\dot{q}_1 + \dot{q}_2$ will be that same Q_o. Further, since the numerators of $\dot{q}_1$ and $\dot{q}_2$ are polynomials of degree 2 or less, the numerator of $\dot{q}_1 + \dot{q}_2$ is too. It follows that $\dot{q}_1 + \dot{q}_2$ is a flow rate in its own right, its dependence on p given by (1). For example, if wine and milk are both measured in gallons, and if p is the price of milk (or rather, the number of dollars you need to buy a gallon of milk), the demand rate for wine plus the demand rate for milk depends on p according to $Q/Q_o + L/Q_o = Q/Q_o$. For another example, let $\mathbf{a}_1$ be a production process producing two goods, both measured in tons. If the goods are 2 and 3—more to the point, if neither is good 1—the sum of the output rates, $\dot{c}_1 a_{12} + \dot{c}_1 a_{13}$, will depend on $a_{11} = p$ according to $L/Q_o + L/Q_o = L/Q_o$.

(*x*) A few comments about the domain of $f(p)$. The domain is not necessarily the entire p-axis. There are two reasons.

First, it is possible—rather easy, in fact—to construct an example in which the basic actions lose their linear independence once the change of p is big enough. When that happens, Q_o vanishes, and $f(p)$ ceases to be defined.

Second, as p varies, an attractive basic action may become unattractive, and vice versa. At isolated moments then, $\mathbf{A}_o$ may gain or lose a column, changing the value of k_o. The model continues to apply, and $f(p)$ retains its analytical form; but some postchange parameter values will differ from the prechange ones. Interpretation suggests that, in the real world, changes of k_o are infrequent.

Since the basic actions are observable, it is possible, in principle, to find the p-values (if any) at which the $\mathbf{a}_i$ become linearly dependent. But it is unlikely that this can be done in practice. There exist hundreds of thousands of goods, making it next to impossible to specify someone's action matrix $\mathbf{A}$, let alone manipulate it in computations.

It is even more difficult to find the p-values at which k_o changes. In fact, it is impossible, for ∇u determines which basic actions are attractive, and ∇u is unknown.

What all this adds up to is that both the domain of $f(p)$ and the specification of $\mathbf{A}_o$ should be considered unknowable.

(*xi*) Supppose $\mathbf{a}_1$ is unattractive, and p varies so little that $\mathbf{a}_1$ remains unattractive. Changes in p then have no effect. For instance, an agent who dislikes broccoli is unlikely to respond if the broccoli price p drops a bit. The demand rate for broccoli still follows (1), but with $A = B = C = 0$. Of course, if p goes down a lot the agent might reconsider and start buying broccoli. In that case he adjusts all other flow rates too.

(*xii*) Suppose that two or more elements of $\mathbf{a}_1$ are variable—say, $a_{11} = p_1$ and $a_{15} = p_2$. Tracing the proof of Theorem 1, you find that, with one proviso, $\dot{c}_1$ still has the form L/Q_o, and all other $\dot{c}_i$ still have the form Q/Q_o. The proviso is that L and Q must be reinterpreted as linear and quadratic forms in *two* variables, p_1 and p_2. It follows immediately that $\dot{q} = \dot{c}_1 a_{11}$ has the form $p_1 L/Q_o$, that $\dot{q} = \dot{c}_1 a_{15}$ has the form $p_2 L/Q_o$, that all other elements of $\dot{c}_1 \mathbf{a}_1$ have the form L/Q_o, and that all elements of all other $\dot{c}_i \mathbf{a}_i$ have the form Q/Q_o.

(*xiii*) Now that the individual own-price demand function is known in explicit analytical detail, the Slutsky equation has lost its relevance. Still, it is only natural to be curious about what the Slutsky equation would look like when recast in the terminology of Model One.

Because income is not in Model One's vocabulary, a precise parallel does not exist. There are, however, several formulations that more or less resemble the Slutsky equation. Probably the simplest of these is: If a basic-action element changes, and if at the same time one or more other basic-action elements are made to change so that $d\mathbf{a}$ is again possible (compensation), then the postchange $\| d\mathbf{a} \|$ exceeds the original $\| d\mathbf{a} \|$. A proof follows. Since the result is of less than vital importance, the proof considers only the case of three goods and two basic actions. To simplify further, both basic actions are assumed attractive. The feasible set's attractive facet is thus the feasible set itself: $F_o = F$.

See Figure 10. The action at time t *is* $d\mathbf{a}$ = XB, found by projecting $\gamma\nabla u dt$ = XA onto F. Suppose that a basic-action element changes, at time t, and that as a result $d\mathbf{a}$ is no longer feasible. The set F thus changes its tilt. The new F—call it F_1—is not shown in Figure 10.

Also at time t, one or more basic-action elements are made to change so that $d\mathbf{a}$ is again feasible. The feasible set thus changes once more, from F_1 to F_2. Figure 10 does show F_2.

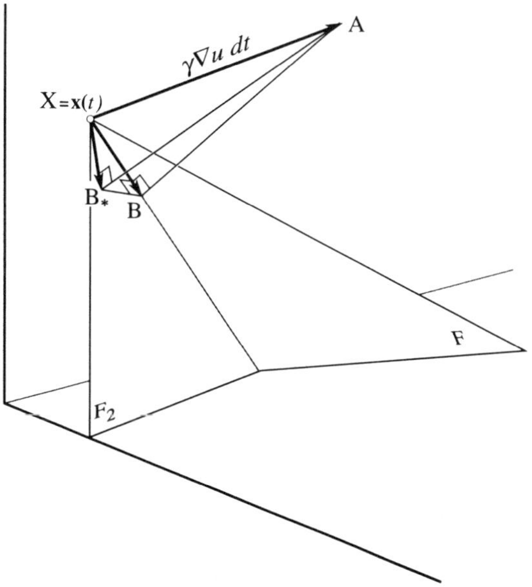

Figure 10. Illustrating a Model One version of the Slutsky equation.

Figure 10 also shows $d\mathbf{a}^* = \text{XB}^*$, which is the projection of $\gamma\nabla u dt$ onto F_2. Since XB lies not only in F but also in F_2, vectors AB* and XB are perpendicular. Since vectors AB and XB are also perpendicular, XB is perpendicular to the plane through AB and AB*. It follows that XB is perpendicular to BB*. Triangle XBB* thus has a right angle at B. This implies that $\| \text{XB}^* \| > \| \text{XB} \|$, or $\| d\mathbf{a}^* \| > \| d\mathbf{a} \|$. P.O.C.

SUMMARY

Almost all rates of economic interest are flow rates, of the form $\dot{q} = \dot{c}_i a_{ij}$.

By the law of motion, the action rate at time t satisfies $\dot{\mathbf{a}} = \mathbf{A}_o\dot{\mathbf{c}}_o = \gamma\mathbf{PH}^{-1}\nabla u$. From this can be inferred how the elements $\dot{\mathbf{c}}_i$ of $\dot{\mathbf{c}}_o$, and therefore all flow rates, depend on the basic-action element p.

Theorem 1 says that flow rates depend on p according to the short-response function, $f(p) = (Ap^2 + Bp + C)/(Dp^2 + Ep + 1)$. Among the interpretations of $f(p)$ are all demand and supply functions, both own-price and cross-price, as well as the quasi-Engel function. In fact, the quasi-Engel function is a cross-price demand function.

In certain special cases, $f(p)$ simplifies. All own-price demand functions, for example, obey $f(p)$ with $A = 0$. So do all own-price supply functions, if supplying is interpreted as selling.

Questions

1. Are preferences transitive, in Model One?
2. You just found out that there is a new theory of behavior claiming that consumers never destroy money. To falsify the theory, you burn a dollar bill, something you would not have done if you had not heard about the new theory. Compare this with the law of gravity, which you obey regardless of whether you know it or not. Now for the question: give an example of behavior that will falsify (*a*) Pareto's utility theory, (*b*) Model One. More on this subject in Chapter 8, when the falsifiability of Model Two is examined.
3. Suppose John's $\mathbf{A}_o$ never gains or loses a column. Roughly how many actions does John carry out during his lifetime?
4. A *permutation matrix* is what you get when you permute the columns of an identity matrix. For example, if $\mathbf{I} = (\mathbf{e}_1, \mathbf{e}_2, \mathbf{e}_3)$, then $\mathbf{M} = (\mathbf{e}_2, \mathbf{e}_3, \mathbf{e}_1)$ is a permutation matrix. Prove that if $\mathbf{M}$ is a permutation matrix, $\mathbf{M}'\mathbf{M} = \mathbf{M}\mathbf{M}' = \mathbf{I}$.
5. If you postmultiply $\mathbf{A}_o$ by a permutation matrix $\mathbf{M}$, what is the effect on $\mathbf{A}_o$, and what is the size of $\mathbf{M}$?

6. (Continuation) What, if anything, must you do to $\mathbf{H}$, $\mathbf{H}^{-1}$, $\dot{\mathbf{c}}_o$, $\mathbf{P}$, ∇u, the system $\mathbf{A}_o'\mathbf{H}\mathbf{A}_o\dot{\mathbf{c}}_o = \gamma\mathbf{A}_o'\nabla u$—which is Eq. (2)—and Theorem 1 if all results derived so far are to retain their economic interpretation?
7. If you premultiply $\mathbf{A}_o$ by a permutation matrix $\mathbf{M}$, what is the effect on $\mathbf{A}_o$, and what is the size of $\mathbf{M}$?
8. (Continuation) What, if anything, must you do to $\mathbf{H}$, $\mathbf{H}^{-1}$, $\dot{\mathbf{c}}_o$, $\mathbf{P}$, ∇u, the system $\mathbf{A}_o'\mathbf{H}\mathbf{A}_o\dot{\mathbf{c}}_o = \gamma\mathbf{A}_o'\nabla u$—which is Eq. (2)—and Theorem 1 if all results derived so far are to retain their economic interpretation?
9. Show that Theorem 1 would be unchanged if the utility function were a minimand rather than a maximand.

Part III

MODEL TWO

8

Model Two

After a sketchy and nonmathematical outline, this chapter formulates Model Two. Chapter 9 derives the long-response function. Chapter 10 tests it.

In the course of the argument, it will become clear that Model Two outperforms Model One in every way. For one thing, Model Two concerns all individual behavior, not just economic behavior. For another, Model Two has ten testable results, against Model One's nine. What is more, the testable results of Model Two are more detailed than those of Model One, in that they describe the effects of parameter changes not only at the time of their occurrence but also afterward (the "long response").

Individual behavior is governed by the mind. Neoclassical utility theory and Model One reflect it, if skimpily: both theories condense the mind's influence into a single number, $u(\mathbf{x})$.

Starting from the belief that the mind is too complex to be captured by just one number, Model Two uses m numbers, with m possibly very large. The m numbers are the coordinates of a point, called the *state of mind* (at time t). It is the state of mind, not the endowment, that acts as the model's protagonist. Model Two does have a place for the endowment (or rather, something like it), but it is a much smaller place than before. In Model One, the endowment came first, the mind second; in Model Two it is the other way around.

Whatever goes on inside the agent's mind (or brain—the terms are used interchangeably here) is assumed unobservable. This is a little stronger than necessary—it would be enough not to assume observability, rather than to assume unobservability—but it simplifies the language.

The mind constantly receives and processes information. Everything the agent perceives, through any of his senses, serves as input. The mind transforms the input into output, by ordering the mouth to eat, the feet to walk, the hands to move. Taking a guess at how the transforming mechanism works, Model Two postulates a motion law for the state of mind. Mathematically, the chosen motion law closely resembles that of Model One: input from the outside serves as the driver, pulling or pushing the state of mind this way and that; the state of mind counters by giving orders meant to make it—the state of mind—move in the direction of quickest improvement, constraint permitting, and with a speed proportional to the objective function's slope in that direction.

Much of what goes on inside the mind is linked to the outside world, in that it has concrete, observable consequences. One of the things Model Two must do is guess how the link works—how the visible tail is affixed to the unobservable dog. A sample question: If, as a result of a sudden parameter change, the state of mind were to start moving twice as fast, would the endowment also start to move twice as fast?

The connection between the mind and the outside world is actually two connections, an input link and an output link.

When the agent observes some exogenous event, his observation is transformed into stimuli affecting the state of mind. The transformation is the input link.

Right after the mind orders the mouth to eat, the mouth goes to work. We cannot witness the giving of the order, but we can see the soup disappear, and we know that the agent's hunger abates. The output link describes how the dwindling of the hunger is tied to the dwindling of the soup.

A picture is beginning to emerge. See Figure 1. In the center is a Black Box—the mind. Events occurring in the outside world are observed at the entrance of the Box, marked "input link," and translated into stimuli the mind can understand. The mind then processes the stimuli (which it does according to the motion law), turning them into instructions to various parts of the body. When those instructions are carried out, some of the consequences emerge on the right, where it says "output link," in the form of observable events. In all then, there is observable input at the beginning, observable output at the end, and, in between, the unobservable mechanism that turns input into output. The mechanism has three parts—input link, motion law, and output link—whose workings we must guess. Given the input and the three guesses, we can predict the output. If the guesses are

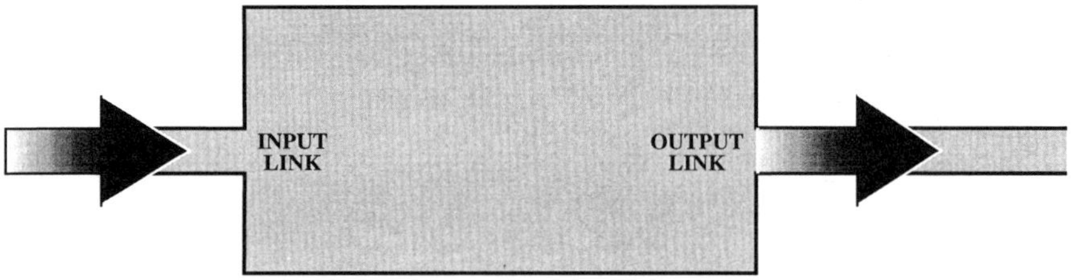

Figure 1. The Black Box for Model Two.

good, the prediction will be borne out by the facts. If the prediction is not borne out by the facts, at least one of the guesses must be bad.

The outline is not yet complete. Consider again the changes in the outside world that act as input to the agent's mind. So far, the discussion has implicitly taken for granted that those changes are wholly exogenous, forming what Model One called the driver. But there are other, not quite so exogenous changes, which the agent also perceives. They are the changes brought about by what he himself does.

For an example, suppose the agent is, once again, eating soup. As he does so, the stock of soup diminishes. The disappearing of the soup constitutes a change of the real world. The change is visible not only to you and me but also to the agent. Now when the agent observes *any* change in the real world, his state of mind is affected. In particular then, his state of mind is affected when he perceives the vanishing of the soup.

The soup example illustrates that output emerging from the Black Box—that is, observable consequences of the agent's own actions—acts as input. This phenomenon is known as *feedback,* and the information being fed back is *the feedback.*

Is the feedback endogenous or exogenous? You could argue either way. On the one hand, the news that the soup is disappearing enters the brain from the outside, through the eyes, suggesting that the change is exogenous. Then again, since the soup vanishes as a consequence of the agent's own actions, the change is plausibly considered endogenous.

Some reflection will show that the feedback is best regarded as endogenous. The argument is this. Suppose that for some reason the mind goes into higher gear, handing out orders for faster actions. The production of visible consequences—via the output link—then speeds up as well. In its turn, this increases the feedback volume. Information being fed back thus moves more or less in lockstep with the agent's own actions, and this makes the feedback endogenous. A useful implication is that when actions are (re)defined, as they shortly are, they can be made to include the feedback as a constituent part.

The following account of how the mind operates is fictional. It is not meant to be subjected to expert scrutiny, and would not survive if it were.

Sensations, like hunger and thirst, reach the brain in the form of electrochemical signals. Each signal puts one or more neurons into a stimulated state. Every neuron has its own wavelength, so to speak: some neurons react to hunger signals only, others react to thirst signals only, and so on. Thus, if there are m distinguishable sensations, there are, correspondingly, m distinct groups of neurons. These groups will be called *registers.* At every instant t, every register contains a possibly very large number of activated neurons. It is not assumed that m is observable, that the m register values are observable, or that the m sensations are identifiable by name.

Suppose that, if there are *more* than 50,000 activated neurons in the hunger register, the agent is hungry—a little bit hungry if the number of activated cells is barely above 50,000, very hungry if it is much greater than 50,000. (The number 50,000 is chosen for the sake of illustration only; no factual accuracy is implied.) Suppose further that, if there are *fewer* than 50,000 activated neurons in the hunger register, the agent feels the unpleasant sensation resulting from overeating—a little bit if the number is barely less than 50,000, a lot if the number is much less than 50,000. We now subtract 50,000 from the actual number, thereby replacing the old hunger quantity with a new measure. The old quantity was a nonnegative integer; the new one, still an integer, is positive, negative, or zero.

Let the new hunger measure be divided by 10,000 (also chosen arbitrarily). The result is a rational number. This number changes every time the agent's hunger varies, and each of those changes is a multiple of 1/10,000. Increments of that size are small enough to take the daring out of the next step: in what follows, the value of the hunger register is assumed to be a real number.

Applying the same procedure to the other registers (possibly with key numbers other than 50,000 and 10,000) yields, in the end, a collection of m real numbers, one for each register.

Simplifying further, we ignore from here on that the value of a register has a maximum and minimum. The value of any register is thus now a real number between $-\infty$ and $+\infty$. For the ith register, that number is written $\xi_i(t)$ or ξ_i.

The state of mind at time t is $(\xi_1(t),\xi_2(t), \ldots ,\xi_m(t))'$, also written $\boldsymbol{\xi}(t)$ or $\boldsymbol{\xi}$. Although a column, $\boldsymbol{\xi}$ is a point, in E^m. (Chapter 2, MT 5 and MT 7.)

The time path of $\boldsymbol{\xi}$ is taken to be continuous everywhere and, except perhaps at a few isolated points, differentiable as well. Each of the m functions $\xi_i(t)$ is thus almost everywhere differentiable with respect to t, for all t.

Of all possible states of mind, $\boldsymbol{\xi} = \mathbf{0}$ is the most attractive. When $\boldsymbol{\xi}$ is null, no desire is overfilled, none underfulfilled. The point $\boldsymbol{\xi} = \mathbf{0}$ is a cousin of what utility theory calls the bliss point. It is a distant cousin: whereas the coordinates of the bliss point represent commodity stocks and are thus dimensioned quantities, the coordinates of $\boldsymbol{\xi}$ are real numbers. More briefly put, the bliss point belongs to X, and the state of mind belongs to E^m.

We assume that the key numbers—like the 50,000 and 10,000 in the example above—can be and have been chosen so that a thirst of 3 is as (un)pleasant as a hunger of 3. More generally, we assume that the key numbers can be and have been chosen so that two states of mind, $\boldsymbol{\xi}_1$ and $\boldsymbol{\xi}_2$, are equally (un)pleasant if and only if they are equally far removed from the origin—if and only if $\| \boldsymbol{\xi}_1 \| = \| \boldsymbol{\xi}_2 \|$.

Strictly speaking, $\| \boldsymbol{\xi} \|$ is undefined, for $\boldsymbol{\xi}$ is a point, not a vector. On the other hand, the difference between the point $\boldsymbol{\xi}$ and the point $\mathbf{0}$ is a vector, in R^m, so that $\| \boldsymbol{\xi} - \mathbf{0} \|$ does exist. We shorten $\boldsymbol{\xi} - \mathbf{0}$ to $\boldsymbol{\xi}$. From here on then, $\boldsymbol{\xi}$ is either a point in E^m or a vector in R^m, context deciding which is which.

The inner product on R^m is taken to be standard. By $\| \boldsymbol{\xi} \|$ is thus meant $\sqrt{\boldsymbol{\xi}'\boldsymbol{\xi}}$. Taking the inner product to be standard simplifies the formulas but is otherwise inessential. More to the point, if we were to define $\| \boldsymbol{\xi} \|$ not as $\sqrt{\boldsymbol{\xi}'\boldsymbol{\xi}}$ but as $\sqrt{\boldsymbol{\xi}'\mathbf{H}\boldsymbol{\xi}}$, with $\mathbf{H}$ an unspecified inner-product matrix of constants, all results derived below would remain the same. We therefore might as well keep things simple and choose $\mathbf{H} = \mathbf{I}$.

The objective function, to be called the *stress,* is

$$s(\boldsymbol{\xi}) = \| \boldsymbol{\xi} \|^2 = \boldsymbol{\xi}'\boldsymbol{\xi}.$$

The stress is a decrescend: its slope, rather than s itself, is to be minimized. Loosely speaking, the state of mind seeks to reduce stress, in the same sense that the endowment in Model One tried to increase utility. Details come later, when the motion law is introduced.

The contour surfaces of $s(\boldsymbol{\xi})$ are given by $s(\boldsymbol{\xi})$ = constant. They are circles if $m = 2$, spheres if $m = 3$, and hyperspheres if $m > 3$. They are to $s(\boldsymbol{\xi})$ what indifference curves or (hyper)surfaces are to $u(\mathbf{x})$. Of course, the equal-stress contours are collections of points in E^m, whereas indifference surfaces are collections of endowments, points in X.

Figure 2 illustrates the case $m = 2$. For concreteness, the two registers are called hunger and thirst. At every point of the circle, the stress is the same. At $\boldsymbol{\xi}_{(1)}$, hunger has the value 4, thirst has the value 3, and the stress is $3^2 + 4^2 = 25$. At $\boldsymbol{\xi}_{(2)}$, hunger is -5, thirst is 0, and the stress is 25. At $\boldsymbol{\xi}_{(3)}$, hunger is 3, thirst is -4, and the stress is again 25.

Specifying the objective function brings a vital benefit, in that it enables us to derive the analytical form of the long-response function. Details are given in the next chapter.

Why is it so easy to devise a justifiable specification of $s(\boldsymbol{\xi})$ when it is so hard to do the same for $u(\mathbf{x})$? The answer does not lie in the difference between stress and utility. It lies, rather, in the difference between a minimand and a maximand. As scientists have demonstrated time and again, minimands tend to be easily specifiable. The reason is that they can often be given an elementary, physical interpretation, namely, that of a distance, or maybe a simple function of a distance. Maximands lack an attractive feature of this sort. Nature abhors a maximand.

A misunderstanding could arise here. Since the slope of $s(\boldsymbol{\xi})$ is a minimand, the slope of $-s(\boldsymbol{\xi})$ is a maximand. This might suggest that the stress is an unnecessary addition to the list of concepts. More to the point, it might suggest that the need for an analytically specified objective function

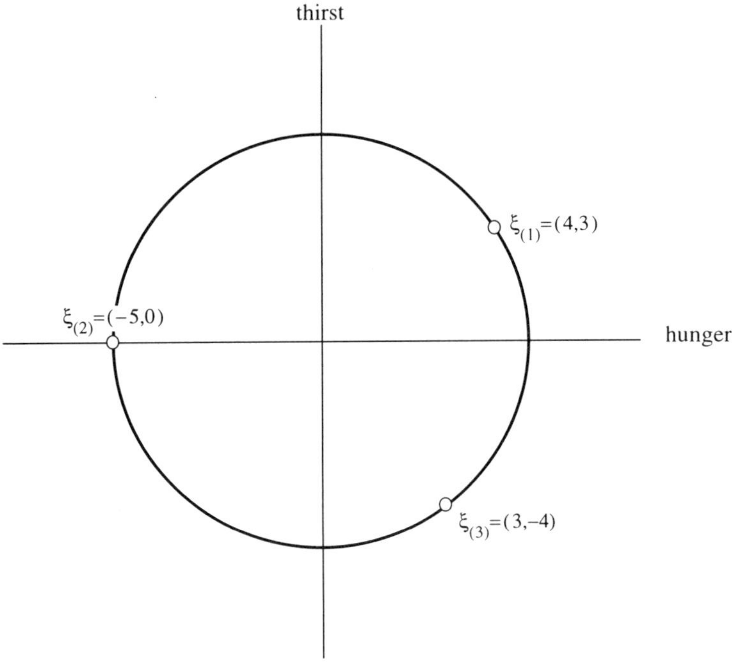

Figure 2. A stress contour.

can be met without introducing the stress: all we have to do is, first, redefine utility as a function of states of mind rather than endowments, and, second, choose $u = -\boldsymbol{\xi}'\boldsymbol{\xi}$. But it is not that simple. As said earlier, specifying the objective function is only half the job. Justifying the specification is the other half. And how the choice $u = -\boldsymbol{\xi}'\boldsymbol{\xi}$ might be justified is a question for which this book has no answer.

To define the output and input links, the feedback, and the motion law, we need some terminology and notation.

When the agent has a cup of soup, the value of his hunger register declines. His state of mind, $\boldsymbol{\xi}$, is thus affected. His endowment, $\mathbf{x}$, is affected too, because the soup stock shrinks. Having a cup of soup is thus plausibly represented by *two* vectors, one to be added to $\boldsymbol{\xi}$ and the other to be added to $\mathbf{x}$. If we write the former as $\boldsymbol{\alpha}$ and the latter as $\mathbf{a}$, having a cup of soup can be said to turn $\boldsymbol{\xi}$ into $\boldsymbol{\xi} + \boldsymbol{\alpha}$ and $\mathbf{x}$ into $\mathbf{x} + \mathbf{a}$. Equivalently, $(\boldsymbol{\xi}, \mathbf{x})$ is turned into $(\boldsymbol{\xi} + \boldsymbol{\alpha}, \mathbf{x} + \mathbf{a}) = (\boldsymbol{\xi}, \mathbf{x}) + (\boldsymbol{\alpha}, \mathbf{a})$.

The pair $(\boldsymbol{\xi}, \mathbf{x})$ or, more fully, $(\boldsymbol{\xi}(t), \mathbf{x}(t))$, is the *state* at time t. The state is a point, in the point set $E^m \times X$.

Actions, which so far have been vectors in A, now become pairs of vectors, $(\boldsymbol{\alpha}, \mathbf{a})$, with $\boldsymbol{\alpha}$ in R^m and $\mathbf{a}$ in A. If $(\boldsymbol{\alpha}, \mathbf{a})$ is any action, its *unobservable part* is $\boldsymbol{\alpha}$, and its *observable part* is $\mathbf{a}$. The shortly defined output link describes the connection between $\boldsymbol{\alpha}$ and $\mathbf{a}$.

The set of actions, $R^m \times A$, is the *action space.*

The *driver,* formerly $d\mathbf{b}(t)$ or $d\mathbf{b}$, becomes the pair $(d\boldsymbol{\beta}, d\mathbf{b})$. Its *unobservable part* is $d\boldsymbol{\beta}$. Its *observable part* is $d\mathbf{b}$. Connotations notwithstanding, the driver is an action, an element of the action space. The shortly defined input link describes the connection between $d\boldsymbol{\beta}$ and $d\mathbf{b}$.

First, the output link. There is no need, at this stage, to worry about the feedback.

DEFINITION 1 (OUTPUT LINK). Let $(\boldsymbol{\alpha}, \mathbf{a})$ and $(\boldsymbol{\alpha}_o, \mathbf{a}_o)$ be any actions, and let c be any scalar. Then $(\boldsymbol{\alpha}, \mathbf{a}) + (\boldsymbol{\alpha}_o, \mathbf{a}_o) = (\boldsymbol{\alpha} + \boldsymbol{\alpha}_o, \mathbf{a} + \mathbf{a}_o)$, and $c(\boldsymbol{\alpha}, \mathbf{a}) = (c\boldsymbol{\alpha}, c\mathbf{a})$.

The set of actions, $R^m \times A$, is thus closed under addition and scalar multiplication. It makes $R^m \times A$ a vector space, and $\{E^m \times X, R^m \times A\}$ a point space.

Because the set of actions is a vector space, an action is not just a pair of vectors but also a vector in its own right. (Recall that a vector need not be a column.)

To illustrate the output link, let $(\boldsymbol{\alpha}, \mathbf{a})$ and $(\boldsymbol{\alpha}_o, \mathbf{a}_o)$ be "having a cup of soup" and "eating a sandwich." Suppose that having a cup of soup reduces hunger by 7 and eating a sandwich reduces hunger by 10. Undertaking both actions then reduces hunger by $7 + 10 = 17$, and consuming two cups of soup reduces hunger by $2 \times 7 = 14$.

A word of caution may be in order. Because the two cups of soup contain the same number of calories, they are equal in their ability to lessen hunger. It should not be concluded that they are equal in their ability to give pleasure. Near the end of the chapter it is shown that the first cup of soup—indeed, the first sip—will ordinarily cause a bigger reduction of the stress than does the second. The first cup, or sip, is thus more enjoyable. It is the Model Two version of the Law of Diminishing Marginal Utility.

More terminology and notation:

The *basic actions,* formerly the given vectors $\mathbf{a}_1, \mathbf{a}_2, \ldots, \mathbf{a}_k$ in A, are now the given vectors $(\boldsymbol{\alpha}_1, \mathbf{a}_1), (\boldsymbol{\alpha}_2, \mathbf{a}_2), \ldots, (\boldsymbol{\alpha}_k, \mathbf{a}_k)$ in $R^m \times A$. For reasons to become clear later, the $\boldsymbol{\alpha}_i$ must be linearly independent, but the $\mathbf{a}_i$ need not be. In particular, one or more $\mathbf{a}_i$ may be null, reflecting that some actions have no visible consequences, have no effect on the endowment. "Thinking" and "planning" can serve as examples, if you are willing to ignore the small amounts of energy that these actions consume.

The unobservable parts of the basic actions are the columns of the $m \times k$ matrix $\underline{\mathbf{A}}$ ("alpha"). The observable parts are the columns of the $n \times k$ matrix $\mathbf{A}$. Thus, $\underline{\mathbf{A}} = (\boldsymbol{\alpha}_1, \ldots, \boldsymbol{\alpha}_k)$ and $\mathbf{A} = (\mathbf{a}_1, \ldots, \mathbf{a}_k)$. Linear combinations like $\Sigma\alpha_i c_i$ and $\Sigma a_i c_i$ can be written $\underline{\mathbf{A}}\mathbf{c}$ and $\mathbf{A}\mathbf{c}$. The definition of the output link implies that if an action's observable part is $\mathbf{A}\mathbf{c}$, its unobservable part must be $\underline{\mathbf{A}}\mathbf{c}$—the same $\mathbf{c}$—and vice versa.

The *feasible actions,* formerly the actions $\mathbf{Ac}$ with $\mathbf{c} \geq \mathbf{0}$, are now the actions $(\underline{\mathbf{A}}\mathbf{c}, \mathbf{Ac})$ with $\mathbf{c} \geq \mathbf{0}$.

The *action at time* t, formerly $d\mathbf{a}(t)$ or $d\mathbf{a}$, is now $(d\boldsymbol{\alpha}(t), d\mathbf{a}(t))$ or $(d\boldsymbol{\alpha}, d\mathbf{a})$. The constraint of Model Two is the same as that of Model One: the action at time t must be feasible. It means that $(d\boldsymbol{\alpha}, d\mathbf{a}) = (\underline{\mathbf{A}}d\mathbf{c}, \mathbf{A}d\mathbf{c})$ for some $d\mathbf{c} \geq \mathbf{0}$.

The *action rate at time* t, formerly $d\mathbf{a}/dt$ or $\dot{\mathbf{a}}$, is now $(d\boldsymbol{\alpha}/dt, d\mathbf{a}/dt)$ or $(\dot{\boldsymbol{\alpha}}, \dot{\mathbf{a}})$.

The *action between times* 0 *and* t, formerly $\mathbf{a}(t)$ with $\mathbf{a}(0) = \mathbf{0}$, is now $(\boldsymbol{\alpha}(t), \mathbf{a}(t))$ with $(\boldsymbol{\alpha}(0), \mathbf{a}(0)) = (\mathbf{0}, \mathbf{0})$. (The second $\mathbf{0}$ consists of dimensioned zeros.) Equivalent is $(\underline{\mathbf{A}}\mathbf{c}(t), \mathbf{Ac}(t))$ with $\mathbf{c}(0) = \mathbf{0}$.

The *driver rate at time* t, formerly $d\mathbf{b}/dt$ or $\dot{\mathbf{b}}$, is now $(d\boldsymbol{\beta}/dt, d\mathbf{b}/dt)$ or $(\dot{\boldsymbol{\beta}}, \dot{\mathbf{b}})$.

The *driver between times* 0 *and* t, formerly $\mathbf{b}(t)$ with $\mathbf{b}(0) = \mathbf{0}$, is now $(\boldsymbol{\beta}(t), \mathbf{b}(t))$ with $(\boldsymbol{\beta}(0), \mathbf{b}(0)) = (\mathbf{0}, \mathbf{0})$. The second $\mathbf{0}$ consists of dimensioned zeros.

The *feasible set,* formerly a convex cone in A, denoted F, is now a convex cone in R^m, denoted Φ. This Φ consists of all $\underline{\mathbf{A}}\mathbf{c}$ with $\mathbf{c} \geq \mathbf{0}$.

This brings us to the input link. Recall that the driver is $(d\boldsymbol{\beta}, d\mathbf{b})$.

The agent observes all changes of his endowment. He observes, in particular, the exogenous changes that make up $d\mathbf{b}$. Formally, "observing" is a transformation, one that turns vectors in A—in particular, $d\mathbf{b}$—into vectors in R^m. The transformed $d\mathbf{b}$ is $d\boldsymbol{\beta}$. The transformation itself is denoted by ω, for "observation." (Using o would be more accurate but also more likely to confuse.) Thus, $d\boldsymbol{\beta} = \omega(d\mathbf{b})$.

We take ω to be a linear function; see Chapter 2, MT20. Should the "real" ω—if there is such a thing—be nonlinear, our ω can always be viewed as a linear approximation.

Because ω is linear, $\omega(\mathbf{a})$ can be written as $\boldsymbol{\Omega}\mathbf{a}$ for some matrix $\boldsymbol{\Omega}$ of constants. Matrix $\boldsymbol{\Omega}$, left unspecified except for its fixity and its size, is the *observation matrix.*

DEFINITION 2 (INPUT LINK). The input link is defined through $d\boldsymbol{\beta} = \omega(d\mathbf{b}) = \boldsymbol{\Omega}d\mathbf{b}$:

$$d\boldsymbol{\beta} = \boldsymbol{\Omega}d\mathbf{b}. \tag{1}$$

We temporarily step out of the argument, for a brief sketch of how this apparatus can be used to model social or interactive behavior. When Smith takes the action $(d\boldsymbol{\alpha}, d\mathbf{a})$, the observable part, $d\mathbf{a}$, becomes part of Jones's $d\mathbf{b}$. Jones observes his $d\mathbf{b}$, meaning that his $d\mathbf{b}$ is transformed into $d\boldsymbol{\beta}$. Jones responds to his observation by taking an action—call it $(d\boldsymbol{\alpha}, d\mathbf{a})_J$. Smith observes Jones's $d\mathbf{a}$, meaning that Jones's $d\mathbf{a}$ becomes part of Smith's $d\mathbf{b}$; and so on. The story generalizes easily to any number of agents: everyone observes the doings of all agents around him and responds by taking an action; everyone observes all those actions and responds; and so on. Since all velocities are finite throughout, there is once again no need to postulate, through the imposition of special assumptions, the (unrealistic) existence of equilibrium.

Detour completed, we return to the main road. The feedback is next.

If the agent observes exogenous movements of $\mathbf{x}$, he surely also observes endogenous movements of $\mathbf{x}$. In particular, if he undertakes basic action $(\boldsymbol{\alpha}_i, \mathbf{a}_i)$, he is bound to observe $\mathbf{a}_i$, assuming that $\mathbf{a}_i$ is nonnull. His observing transforms $\mathbf{a}_i$ into $\omega(\mathbf{a}_i) = \boldsymbol{\Omega}\mathbf{a}_i$, a vector in R^m. This vector is the feedback. It is convenient to define $\boldsymbol{\Omega}\mathbf{a}_i$ as the feedback even if $\mathbf{a}_i$ is null—even if there is nothing to observe. In that case, the feedback is also null.

As noted earlier, $\boldsymbol{\alpha}_i$ and $\boldsymbol{\Omega}\mathbf{a}_i$ move in tandem, because $\boldsymbol{\alpha}_i$ and $\mathbf{a}_i$ do: multiplying $\boldsymbol{\alpha}_i$ by any scalar will also multiply $\mathbf{a}_i$, and therefore $\boldsymbol{\Omega}\mathbf{a}_i$, by that scalar. We can thus take the feedback to be an integral component of $\boldsymbol{\alpha}_i$, and will do so from now on. Concretely, this means that $\boldsymbol{\alpha}_i$ now consists of the feedback and a remainder. That remainder will be called the *core* of $\boldsymbol{\alpha}_i$, denoted $\boldsymbol{\alpha}_i^{\mathrm{c}}$. In all,

$$\boldsymbol{\alpha}_i = \boldsymbol{\alpha}_i^{\mathrm{c}} + \boldsymbol{\Omega}\mathbf{a}_i.$$

The $\boldsymbol{\alpha}_i^{\mathrm{c}}$, $i = 1, \ldots, k$, are taken to be linearly independent, like the $\boldsymbol{\alpha}_i$.

Not just $\boldsymbol{\alpha}_i$ but every feasible action's unobservable part consists of core and feedback. Definition 3 summarizes.

Definition 3 (feedback and core). Let $(\underline{\mathbf{A}}\mathbf{c}, \mathbf{A}\mathbf{c})$ be any feasible action, and define $\underline{\mathbf{A}}^{\mathrm{c}} = (\boldsymbol{\alpha}_1^{\mathrm{c}}, \boldsymbol{\alpha}_2^{\mathrm{c}}, \ldots, \boldsymbol{\alpha}_n^{\mathrm{c}})$, an $m \times k$ matrix. Vector $\underline{\mathbf{A}}\mathbf{c}$ is the sum of its core, $\underline{\mathbf{A}}^{\mathrm{c}}\mathbf{c}$, and the feedback, $\boldsymbol{\Omega}\mathbf{A}\mathbf{c}$. Thus,

$$\underline{\mathbf{A}}\mathbf{c} = \underline{\mathbf{A}}^{\mathrm{c}}\mathbf{c} + \boldsymbol{\Omega}\mathbf{A}\mathbf{c}. \tag{2}$$

The $\boldsymbol{\alpha}_i^{\mathrm{c}}$ are linearly independent, and constant under all parameter changes.

A feasible action of particular interest is $(d\boldsymbol{\alpha}, d\mathbf{a})$, the action at time t. Since $d\boldsymbol{\alpha} = \underline{\mathbf{A}}d\mathbf{c}$ and $d\mathbf{a} = \mathbf{A}d\mathbf{c}$, we have, by (2), that $\underline{\mathbf{A}}d\mathbf{c} = \underline{\mathbf{A}}^{\mathrm{c}}d\mathbf{c} + \boldsymbol{\Omega}\mathbf{A}d\mathbf{c}$. Writing $\underline{\mathbf{A}}^{\mathrm{c}}d\mathbf{c}$ as $d\boldsymbol{\alpha}^{\mathrm{c}}$ gives, equivalently,

$$d\boldsymbol{\alpha} = d\boldsymbol{\alpha}^{\mathrm{c}} + \boldsymbol{\Omega}d\mathbf{a}, \tag{3}$$

with core $d\boldsymbol{\alpha}^{\mathrm{c}}$ and feedback $\boldsymbol{\Omega}d\mathbf{a}$.

Breaking up a feasible action's unobservable part into core and feedback has operational consequences only when there is some parametric change in some basic action. For $\boldsymbol{\Omega}\mathbf{A}$ then may change (since $\mathbf{A}$ changes), whereas $\underline{\mathbf{A}}^{\mathrm{c}}$ stays the same. At all other times—that is, when all basic actions are constant—the analysis of $\underline{\mathbf{A}}\mathbf{c}$ into its constituent parts serves no practical purpose.

The motion law is next. We begin with a memory freshener, in the form of a brief trip back to Model One.

The motion law of Model One consisted of two equations. One was $d\mathbf{x} = d\mathbf{a} + d\mathbf{b}$, the other, $d\mathbf{a} = \gamma\mathbf{P}\mathbf{H}^{-1}\boldsymbol{\nabla}u dt$. In the last equation, γ, $\mathbf{P}$, and

$\mathbf{H}^{-1}\nabla u$ had these meanings: γ is a proportionality constant, $\mathbf{P}$ is a projection matrix, and $\mathbf{H}^{-1}\nabla u$ is the steepest ascent. The role of dt is merely to make the units come out right.

You remember that the steepest ascent is the vector whose direction is that in which utility increases fastest and whose length is the slope of the utility function in that direction. Interpretation suggests that the direction of the steepest ascent is, as a rule, not feasible. If indeed it is not, the best direction is that of the steepest *constrained* ascent, which is the projection of the steepest ascent onto the feasible set. That projection is $\mathbf{P}(\mathbf{H}^{-1}\nabla u)$. The direction of $\mathbf{PH}^{-1}\nabla u$ is that in which utility increases fastest, constraint permitting, and its length equals the slope of the utility function in that direction.

The motion law for Model Two is based on the same ideas. It too consists of two equations. The first one is $d\boldsymbol{\xi} = d\boldsymbol{\alpha} + d\boldsymbol{\beta}$. The second one says that the direction of $d\boldsymbol{\alpha}$ is that in which the stress s decreases fastest, constraint permitting, and the length of $d\boldsymbol{\alpha}$ is, but for sign, proportional to the slope of s in that direction. Letting the proportionality constant be $\frac{1}{2}\gamma dt$ (the reason for the factor $\frac{1}{2}$, which is purely cosmetic, will become clear in a moment), we have

$$d\boldsymbol{\alpha} = -\tfrac{1}{2}\gamma\boldsymbol{\Pi}\nabla s dt. \tag{4}$$

Here, dt has its usual meaning, ∇s is the gradient of the stress, and $\boldsymbol{\Pi}$ is the matrix of projection onto the feasible set Φ. (Matrix $\boldsymbol{\Pi}$ is thus to Φ what, back in Model One, $\mathbf{P}$ was to F.) To explain the minus sign in (4), consider that ∇s points in the direction in which the stress *increases* fastest. The direction in which the stress *decreases* fastest is thus that of $-\nabla s$. And this is precisely the direction that the state of mind would like to take.

We have reached the point at which Model Two begins to pull ahead of Model One. The reason is that, unlike the utility function, the stress is specified, as $s(\boldsymbol{\xi}) = \|\boldsymbol{\xi}\|^2 = \boldsymbol{\xi}'\boldsymbol{\xi}$. The gradient of s is thus also specified, where that of u was not; in fact, $\nabla s = 2\boldsymbol{\xi}$, as is easy to see. It means we can take (4) one step further:

$$d\boldsymbol{\alpha} = -\tfrac{1}{2}\gamma\boldsymbol{\Pi}(2\boldsymbol{\xi})dt = -\gamma\boldsymbol{\Pi}\boldsymbol{\xi}dt. \tag{5}$$

Note how the inelegant factor $\frac{1}{2}$ makes itself useful here. Had it not been present in (4), there would now be an inelegant factor 2 in (5).

Definition 4 summarizes, and Figure 3 illustrates.

Definition 4 (motion law for model two).

$$d\boldsymbol{\xi}(t) = d\boldsymbol{\alpha}(t) + d\boldsymbol{\beta}(t),$$

with $d\boldsymbol{\alpha}(t) = -\gamma\boldsymbol{\Pi}\boldsymbol{\xi}dt$ and $d\boldsymbol{\beta}(t)$ exogenously given.

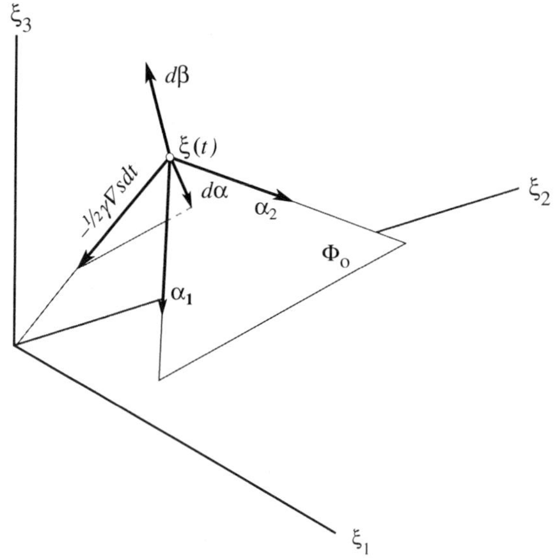

Figure 3. Illustrating the motion law for Model Two.

Vectors $d\boldsymbol{\xi}(t)$, $d\boldsymbol{\alpha}(t)$, and $d\boldsymbol{\beta}(t)$ belong to R^m. Definition 4 can also be expressed in terms of velocities $\dot{\boldsymbol{\xi}}$, $\dot{\boldsymbol{\alpha}}$, $\dot{\boldsymbol{\beta}}$—all it takes is to divide through by dt. Of course the setting is then no longer R^m.

Recall that $\mathbf{\Pi}$ represents projection onto Φ. It should thus be possible to express $\mathbf{\Pi}$ in terms of the basic actions. More precisely, it should be possible to express $\mathbf{\Pi}$ in terms of the $\boldsymbol{\alpha}_i$. Indeed it is. Details follow.

The action at time t, $(d\boldsymbol{\alpha}, d\mathbf{a})$ or $(\underline{\mathbf{A}}d\mathbf{c}, \mathbf{A}d\mathbf{c})$, must be feasible. It means that $d\mathbf{c}$ must be nonnegative. Let k_o be the number of elements of $d\mathbf{c}$ that are actually positive. To rule out trivialities, we take $k_o \geq 1$.

As in Part II, $d\mathbf{c}_o$ is defined as the k_o-vector that remains after the zero elements of $d\mathbf{c}$ have been cast out. Casting out the corresponding columns of $\underline{\mathbf{A}}$ and $\mathbf{A}$ leaves $\underline{\mathbf{A}}_o$ and $\mathbf{A}_o$, each with k_o columns. Those columns are the *attractive* $\boldsymbol{\alpha}_i$ and the *attractive* $\mathbf{a}_i$. Pairing them gives the *attractive basic actions.* Matrix $\mathbf{\Pi}$ can now be described in greater detail: $\mathbf{\Pi} = \underline{\mathbf{A}}_o(\underline{\mathbf{A}}_o'\underline{\mathbf{A}}_o)^{-1}\underline{\mathbf{A}}_o'$. All elements of $\mathbf{\Pi}$ are real, as is easy to see. Existence of $(\underline{\mathbf{A}}_o'\,\underline{\mathbf{A}}_o)^{-1}$ is guaranteed by the linear independence of the $\boldsymbol{\alpha}_i$.

It will be clear that $(\underline{\mathbf{A}}d\mathbf{c}, \mathbf{A}d\mathbf{c}) = (\underline{\mathbf{A}}_o d\mathbf{c}_o, \mathbf{A}_o d\mathbf{c}_o)$. Division by dt gives $(\underline{\mathbf{A}}\dot{\mathbf{c}}, \mathbf{A}\dot{\mathbf{c}}) = (\underline{\mathbf{A}}_o\dot{\mathbf{c}}_o, \mathbf{A}_o\dot{\mathbf{c}}_o)$.

The *attractive facet* of Φ, written Φ_o, is the set of nonnegative linear combinations of the attractive $\boldsymbol{\alpha}_i$.

If $k_o = k$, all basic actions are attractive. In that case then, $(\underline{\mathbf{A}}_o, \mathbf{A}_o) = (\underline{\mathbf{A}}, \mathbf{A})$, and $d\mathbf{c}_o = d\mathbf{c}$, and Φ_o is all of Φ.

As a mathematical construction—the kind of thing the Scientist wants—Model Two is now finished. But the interpretation of Model Two—the kind of thing the Visitor cares about—still needs some comment.

Each model term comes out of the dictionary. Inevitably then, each carries some connotations. In some cases those connotations are harmful, in that they suggest something far more specific than what the term's mathematical definition allows. Probably the worst offender is *endowment.* By connotation, an endowment is a collection of commodity quantities in the agent's possession. This is an unnecessarily narrow interpretation of what an endowment really is: a point.

From here on, **x** will be called the *surround.* Its coordinates are *aspects.* Connotationally speaking, "surround" and "aspect" are nearly empty vessels, which is of course the reason for their introduction. How the vessels are filled is up to the Visitor; anything that fits the definition of a point can serve as the surround, or as part of the surround. More generally, Model Two is a purely mathematical construction, and the Visitor is free to interpret all of its mathematical notions in any way he likes.

Here are some examples of things that until now did not seem to fit Model Two, but which do fit now that "endowment" has been changed to "surround."

(*i*) A man used to running an hour every day wakes up one morning to find that his leg hurts. He therefore decides to run only half an hour that day. Model Two applies, assuming that there is some way to quantify "hurt."

This example is a special case of a much more general phenomenon: when some action becomes less pleasant, you reduce the rate at which you undertake that action. An equally special case of that same phenomenon is the Law of Demand: when the price of widgets goes up and you regard that as unpleasant, you reduce the rate at which you buy widgets.

(*ii*) A child likes to play outside for long hours on balmy days, but not quite so long when it is cold, and also not quite so long when it is hot. If this were described graphically, with the temperature as p, the result would be what psychologists call a preference–aversion curve, and what economists call a Giffen curve. As this example illustrates, Giffen behavior is not rare at all. Admittedly it is rare in the marketplace (at least on the demand side). But not all behavior is economic behavior, p is not always a price, and an increase of p is not always unpleasant.

(*iii*) A worker is most productive when his workplace is lit just right and less productive when the place is either too dim or too bright. If p is the amount of light, this example has the same structure as the preceding one.

(*iv*) A baby drinks only a little bit when its formula is cold, more when it is the right temperature, and less again when it is too warm. This too is like (*ii*), if p is the temperature of the formula.

(*v*) Thanks to the new interpretation of $\mathbf{x}$, Model Two can now deal with issues involving (changes of) *location.* Traveling, for example, is naturally and plausibly described as an action affecting most or all coordinates of the surround. Earlier, when $\mathbf{x}$ was the endowment, such a description would not have been plausible at all.

In the travel example, and indeed in all instances of locational change, it is probably easiest on your intuition if you treat the location of the agent's mind as fixed and the world as moving.

(*vi*) Now that the endowment—in the sense of a collection of assets—no longer plays a role, Model Two fits animal behavior as well. This is important for testing. See Chapter 10 for details.

Three pieces of unfinished business are left. First, Part II pointed out some weaknesses of Model One and said that Model Two would do better. Details remain to be supplied. Second, Part II showed that the alternative motion law, called the Rational Law, is untenable and said that Part III would present another argument leading to the same conclusion. That argument is still to come. Third, earlier in this chapter it was claimed that the first soup sip will as a rule be more enjoyable than the second, the second more than the third, and so on—the Model Two version of the Law of Diminishing Marginal Utility. A proof was promised, but has not yet been delivered.

The first weakness of Model One is this. Model One demanded that the k basic actions (which back then were $\mathbf{a}_1, \mathbf{a}_2, \ldots, \mathbf{a}_k$) be linearly independent. The requirement implied $k \leq n$, meaning that there cannot be more basic actions than there are goods. As was shown in Chapter 6, just before Definition 1, this is unacceptably limiting.

Model Two takes the $\boldsymbol{\alpha}_i$ to be linearly independent and allows the $\mathbf{a}_i$ to be linearly dependent. It follows that k cannot exceed m, but may exceed n. Or: there cannot be more basic actions than there are registers, but it is possible to have more basic actions than goods. The earlier problem is thus resolved.

The second weakness of Model One is that its definition of the driver, as $d\mathbf{b}$, partially overlapped the definition of a feasible action. Model One thus left open the possibility for an action to be, unacceptably, both exogenous and endogenous.

To see whether Model Two does better, we assume that the driver is a feasible action and see whether a contradiction will emerge. Our starting point is thus $(d\boldsymbol{\beta}, d\mathbf{b}) = (\underline{\mathbf{A}}\mathbf{c}, \mathbf{A}\mathbf{c})$ for some $\mathbf{c} \geq \mathbf{0}$.

Since $d\boldsymbol{\beta} = \boldsymbol{\Omega} d\mathbf{b}$, by (1), we must have $\underline{\mathbf{A}}\mathbf{c} = \boldsymbol{\Omega}\mathbf{A}\mathbf{c}$. Now by (2), the difference between $\underline{\mathbf{A}}\mathbf{c}$ and $\boldsymbol{\Omega}\mathbf{A}\mathbf{c}$ is the core $\underline{\mathbf{A}}^c\mathbf{c}$, and so the core is null in this case. By assumption, $\underline{\mathbf{A}}^c$ has full column rank, implying that the core is null if and only if $\mathbf{c}$ is null. It is thus still possible for the driver to be a feasible action, but only if it is $(\mathbf{0}, \mathbf{0})$. Even that small ambiguity could be removed, by defining the driver as nonnull. But it does not seem worth the trouble: a driver that is a feasible action only when it is null is not going to cause methodological difficulties.

Another weakness of Model One, not mentioned before, is that it—Model One—is at times forced to represent two or more quite different actions by one and the same **a**. For example, although "losing a dollar" is different from "giving a dollar to a beggar," which in turn is different from "paying a child its $1 allowance," Model One represents each of these three actions by the vector **a** whose money element is $-1d$ and whose other elements are all zero. Model Two does better. In Model Two, actions that are different in interpretation are also different in representation. The reason for the increased flexibility is of course that actions now have an unobservable part.

Next, the Myopic Law/Rational Law controversy.

Models One and Two are both governed by the Myopic Law, which portrays the agent as short-sighted, always forgetting to take the effects of the driver into account, never learning from the experience, forever scrambling *ex post* to adjust and correct. The alternative is the Rational Law, which depicts a wilier agent, capable of anticipating the effects of the driver and adjusting for them *ex ante.* As shown in Part II, however, the Rational Law does not always work—in certain circumstances, the recipe it prescribes is mathematically impossible.

The Rational Law has another, much more basic flaw: its very rationality. The law implicitly depicts the agent as examining the stimuli coming into his brain and making a quick calculation to see what is his best course of action, his best response. For the agent to do so, however, requires that he be able to step back, putting some distance between his observing self and the brain he wishes to observe. And stepping away from his brain is precisely what he cannot do. The agent *is* his brain.

To put it another way, the Rational Law depicts the agent as thinking before every action. This means, *since thinking is itself an action,* that the agent thinks before he thinks, and thinks before he thinks before he thinks, and so on. It is an impossible picture, similar to the one you get when you hold that everything we do is the outcome of a choice or decision. Since choosing and deciding are among the things we do, it follows that we choose to choose, decide to decide, choose to choose to choose, decide to decide to decide, and so on. Meanwhile, dinner is getting cold.

Just as rationality is the weakness of the Rational Law, so is *un*rationality the strength of the Myopic Law. According to the Myopic Law, there is no essential difference between the mind and a physical particle. The particle's motion is completely determined by natural laws, and so are the goings-on inside the brain. The particle does not choose or decide or think, and neither does the brain. Of course, we are used to *saying* that people can think, choose, and decide, just as we are used to saying that people have souls, egos, beliefs, ideas, abilities, and free will. But this does not mean that all these things are concrete enough to play a role in social science. Our forefathers were certain that light was carried by "the ether," that physiology was largely a matter of "humors," that unhappiness was caused by "the vapors." Ideas like these we now regard as archaic. But "soul," "free will," and the like are just as antiquated. If they have a place at all, it is in everyday conversation. They do not belong in any theoretical vocabulary.

Viewing people as automatons, wholly driven by electrochemical laws, does not come easy. If you wish to think some more about this issue—a contradiction in terms?—the first thing to keep in mind is that the agent and his brain (or you and your brain) are *not* separate entities. A corollary recommendation is therefore, Never use "I" and "my brain" in the same sentence. Except this one.

Finally, the Model Two version of the Law of Diminishing Marginal Utility.

Let "having a cup of soup" be $(\boldsymbol{\alpha}, \mathbf{a})$, and suppose, for simplicity, that the driver is null. When the agent undertakes $(\boldsymbol{\alpha}, \mathbf{a})$, the stress changes from $s(\boldsymbol{\xi}) = \boldsymbol{\xi}'\boldsymbol{\xi}$ to $s(\boldsymbol{\xi} + \boldsymbol{\alpha}) = (\boldsymbol{\xi} + \boldsymbol{\alpha})'(\boldsymbol{\xi} + \boldsymbol{\alpha})$. The very fact that the action was undertaken implies that the stress has declined. Thus, $s(\boldsymbol{\xi}) - s(\boldsymbol{\xi} + \boldsymbol{\alpha}) = \boldsymbol{\xi}'\boldsymbol{\xi} - (\boldsymbol{\xi} + \boldsymbol{\alpha})'(\boldsymbol{\xi} + \boldsymbol{\alpha}) = -2\boldsymbol{\alpha}'\boldsymbol{\xi} - \boldsymbol{\alpha}'\boldsymbol{\alpha}$ is positive. Now if $2\boldsymbol{\alpha}'\boldsymbol{\xi}$ were positive or zero, $-2\boldsymbol{\alpha}'\boldsymbol{\xi} - \boldsymbol{\alpha}'\boldsymbol{\alpha}$ would be negative (since $-\boldsymbol{\alpha}'\boldsymbol{\alpha}$ is negative). Evidently then, $2\boldsymbol{\alpha}'\boldsymbol{\xi}$ must be negative: $\boldsymbol{\xi}$ and $\boldsymbol{\alpha}$ must form an obtuse angle. Figure 4 shows that this is plausible. Note that, in Figure 4, eating soup not only reduces hunger but also increases thirst. Perhaps the soup is too salty.

Suppose the agent has a second cup of soup. The stress then changes again, this time from $s(\boldsymbol{\xi} + \boldsymbol{\alpha}) = (\boldsymbol{\xi} + \boldsymbol{\alpha})'(\boldsymbol{\xi} + \boldsymbol{\alpha})$ to $s(\boldsymbol{\xi} + 2\boldsymbol{\alpha}) = (\boldsymbol{\xi} + 2\boldsymbol{\alpha})'(\boldsymbol{\xi} + 2\boldsymbol{\alpha})$. The difference, $s(\boldsymbol{\xi} + \boldsymbol{\alpha}) - s(\boldsymbol{\xi} + 2\boldsymbol{\alpha}) = -2\boldsymbol{\alpha}'\boldsymbol{\xi} - 3\boldsymbol{\alpha}'\boldsymbol{\alpha}$, must be positive, for the same reason as before.

Eating the first sandwich has reduced the stress by $-2\boldsymbol{\alpha}'\boldsymbol{\xi} - \boldsymbol{\alpha}'\boldsymbol{\alpha}$; eating the second sandwich has reduced the stress by $-2\boldsymbol{\alpha}'\boldsymbol{\xi} - 3\boldsymbol{\alpha}'\boldsymbol{\alpha}$. The first reduction exceeds the second (by $2\boldsymbol{\alpha}'\boldsymbol{\alpha}$, in fact). Or as it was expressed earlier, the agent enjoyed the first cup of soup more than the second.

Reinterpreting $(\boldsymbol{\alpha}, \mathbf{a})$ as "having a spoonful of soup" shows that the agent enjoyed the first spoonful more than the second.

So far, the driver has been assumed null. If the driver is not null, the superiority of the first cup of soup (or spoonful) ceases to be a certainty. Indeed, if the driver is erratic enough, the second cup might become *more* enjoyable than the first, particularly if the agent takes a long break in between. An unambiguous conclusion is thus impossible in this case. Blame the passage of time.

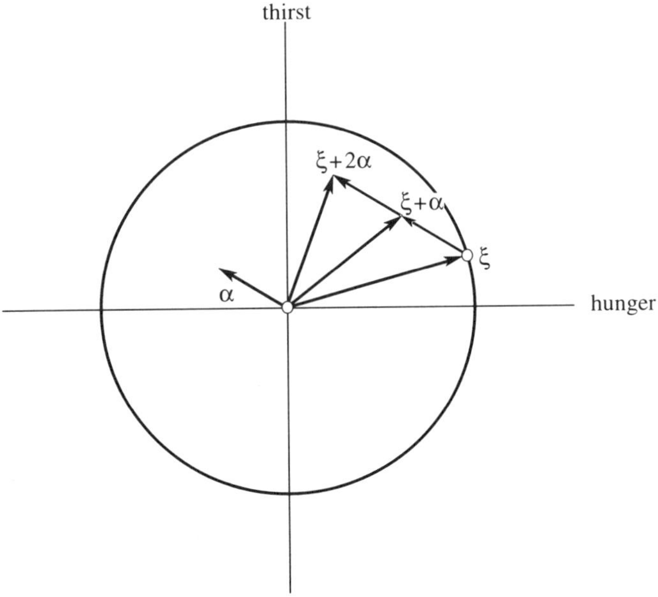

Figure 4. Illustrating the Model Two version of the Law of Diminishing Marginal Utility.

But there is a way to keep the passage of time from confusing the issue. All it takes is to recast the story in calculus terms. Details follow. For simplicity, and without loss of generality, we normalize $\boldsymbol{\alpha}$ by setting $\| \boldsymbol{\alpha} \| = 1$.

Undertaking $(\boldsymbol{\alpha}, \mathbf{a})$ decreases the stress. By Chapter 2, MT 22, the rate at which it does so is $D_{\alpha}s(\boldsymbol{\xi}) = \boldsymbol{\alpha}'\nabla s = 2\boldsymbol{\alpha}'\boldsymbol{\xi}$. This quantity is thus negative. See again Figure 4.

To be shown is that as the agent continues to undertake $(\boldsymbol{\alpha}, \mathbf{a})$, the stress decreases at a decreasing rate. Informally put, "the stress decreases at a decreasing rate" means that the negative quantity $D_{\alpha}s(\boldsymbol{\xi})$ becomes less negative. Formally put, it means that $D_{\alpha}D_{\alpha}s(\boldsymbol{\xi})$ is positive. It is not difficult to verify that $D_{\alpha}D_{\alpha}s(\boldsymbol{\xi}) = 2 > 0$. P.O.C.

SUMMARY

Model Two concerns all individual behavior, not just individual economic behavior. At its center is the state of mind, $\boldsymbol{\xi}(t)$. Much less important is the endowment, $\mathbf{x}(t)$; goods are no more than instruments allowing the agent to carry out his actions. Toward the end, goods lost even that small role, when "endowment" became "surround" and "commodity stock" became "aspect."

The state at time t is $(\boldsymbol{\xi}(t), \mathbf{x}(t))$, or $(\boldsymbol{\xi}, \mathbf{x})$ for short. Its change at time t, $(d\boldsymbol{\xi}, d\mathbf{x})$, is the sum of two components, the action $(d\boldsymbol{\alpha}, d\mathbf{a})$ and the driver $(d\boldsymbol{\beta}, d\mathbf{b})$. Action $(d\boldsymbol{\alpha}, d\mathbf{a})$ must be feasible, meaning that it must be a linear combination of the basic actions—the $(\boldsymbol{\alpha}_i, \mathbf{a}_i)$—with nonnegative weights.

The agent observes both $d\mathbf{a}$ and $d\mathbf{b}$. His observing is a transformation, changing $d\mathbf{a}$ and $d\mathbf{b}$ into $\boldsymbol{\Omega} d\mathbf{a}$ and $\boldsymbol{\Omega} d\mathbf{b}$, vectors that are unobservable to the outsider. Vector $\boldsymbol{\Omega} d\mathbf{b}$ equals $d\boldsymbol{\beta}$, but vector $\boldsymbol{\Omega} d\mathbf{a}$ (the feedback) does not equal $d\boldsymbol{\alpha}$. Rather, $\boldsymbol{\Omega} d\mathbf{a}$ is only part of $d\boldsymbol{\alpha}$, the remainder being the invariant core, $d\boldsymbol{\alpha}^c$.

The objective function is the stress, $s(\boldsymbol{\xi})$, specified as $\boldsymbol{\xi}'\boldsymbol{\xi}$. Since s is a minimand—strictly, a decrescend—the state of mind's preferred (but generally infeasible) direction is that of $-\boldsymbol{\nabla} s = -2\boldsymbol{\xi}$. The motion law says that $d\boldsymbol{\alpha}$ is a constant multiple of $\boldsymbol{\Pi}(-2\boldsymbol{\xi})$, the feasible action closest to $-2\boldsymbol{\xi}$. More precisely, $d\boldsymbol{\alpha} = -\gamma \boldsymbol{\Pi} \boldsymbol{\xi} dt$.

Questions

1. Prove that $d\boldsymbol{\xi} = d\boldsymbol{\alpha}^c + \boldsymbol{\Omega} d\mathbf{x}$.
2. Let $(\boldsymbol{\alpha}, \boldsymbol{\alpha})$ and $(\boldsymbol{\alpha}_o, \mathbf{a}_o)$ be feasible actions, and let c be any scalar. Show that $(\boldsymbol{\alpha} + \boldsymbol{\alpha}_o)^c = \boldsymbol{\alpha}^c + \boldsymbol{\alpha}_o{}^c$ and that $(c\boldsymbol{\alpha})^c = c(\boldsymbol{\alpha}^c)$.
3. Suppose that, instead of postulating that ω is a linear function, we were to stipulate that $(\boldsymbol{\alpha} + \boldsymbol{\alpha}_o)^c = \boldsymbol{\alpha}^c + \boldsymbol{\alpha}_o{}^c$ and $(c\boldsymbol{\alpha})^c = c(\boldsymbol{\alpha}^c)$ for any feasible actions $(\boldsymbol{\alpha}, \mathbf{a})$ and $(\boldsymbol{\alpha}_o, \mathbf{a}_o)$ and any scalar c. Would it follow that ω is linear?
4. Is Model Two falsifiable? That is, now that you know what the theory says, could you change your behavior so as to contradict Model Two?
5. The specification of the stress as $\| \boldsymbol{\xi} \|^2$ is to some extent arbitrary; other specifications could conceivably perform as well. One of these is $\| \boldsymbol{\xi} \|$. Analyze.
6. Prove that $d\mathbf{a}$ and $d\boldsymbol{\alpha}^c$ are linear functions of $d\boldsymbol{\alpha}$.

9

The Long-Response Function

Let basic action ($\boldsymbol{\alpha}_1$, $\mathbf{a}_1$) be attractive. As before, a_{11} is abbreviated to p. Suppose that p changes, parametrically, at some instant. It is convenient to let that instant be the origin of the time axis, $t = 0$. The *long-response function,* $\dot{q} = f(p,t)$, describes how the change affects any flow rate $\dot{q}$, not only at $t = 0$ but also afterward.

Figure 1 offers an illustration. The surface shown is the graph of the long-response function. Curve AB, which depicts $\dot{q} = f(p,0)$, is the graph of the short-response function. (With hindsight, Model One's short-response function should have been written $f(p,0)$, or perhaps $f(p,t_o)$, rather than $f(p)$. But confusion seems unlikely at this stage, particularly because Model One has been discarded.) Suppose that $p = p_o$ during the entire interval from $t = 0$ to $t = \tau > 0$. Curve CD depicts $\dot{q} = f(p_o,t)$ for all t in that interval. The time coordinate of point D is τ.

This chapter derives $f(p,t)$. Part II could not do so because deriving $f(p,t)$ requires an analytically specified objective function, which Part II lacked.

Integrating $\dot{q} = f(p,t)$ from 0 to t gives $q = F(p,t) - F(p,0)$, the *cumulative-response function.* Define $F(p,0) = 0$, as interpretation suggests. The cumulative-response function thereby simplifies to $q = F(p,t)$. Whereas $\dot{q}$ is a flow rate, q is a flow. All information contained in f is of course also contained in F, and vice versa. For an illustration of $q = F(p,t)$, see Chapter 10, Figure 1. (In that diagram, the t-axis is hidden behind the surface, and the q-axis has been omitted, to minimize clutter.)

Remember that the action at t is $(d\boldsymbol{\alpha}, d\mathbf{a}) = (\underline{\mathbf{A}}d\mathbf{c}, \mathbf{A}d\mathbf{c})$, a linear combination of the basic actions ($\boldsymbol{\alpha}_i$, $\mathbf{a}_i$), with nonnegative weights dc_i. Differentiation gives $(\dot{\boldsymbol{\alpha}}, \dot{\mathbf{a}}) = (\underline{\mathbf{A}}\dot{\mathbf{c}}, \mathbf{A}\dot{\mathbf{c}})$, the action rate at t.

As before, the general flow rate is $\dot{q} = \dot{c}_i a_{ij}$, where $\dot{c}_i$ is an element of $\dot{\mathbf{c}}$ and a_{ij} is an element of $\mathbf{a}_i$. Except for $a_{11} = p$, all a_{ij} are constant. The hard part of deriving $f(p,t)$—that is, finding out how $\dot{c}_i a_{ij}$ depends on p and t—is thus to find out how $\dot{c}_i$ depends on p and t. Which is why most of the proof of Theorem 1, below, concerns just that question.

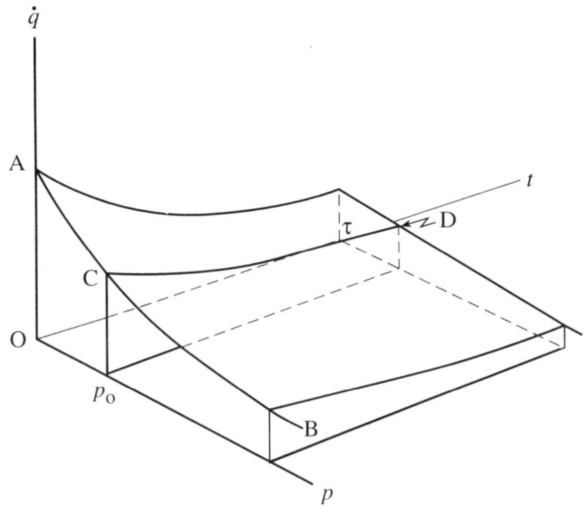

Figure 1. A long-response surface.

The starting point for the proof of Theorem 1 is the motion law for Model Two,

$$\dot{\boldsymbol{\alpha}}(t) = -\gamma \boldsymbol{\Pi} \boldsymbol{\xi}(t). \tag{1}$$

Recall that $\boldsymbol{\Pi} = \underline{\mathbf{A}}_o(\underline{\mathbf{A}}_o'\underline{\mathbf{A}}_o)^{-1}\underline{\mathbf{A}}_o'$ represents projection onto Φ_o, the attractive facet of the cone Φ.

Matrix $\boldsymbol{\Pi}$ can vary in several ways. First, $\boldsymbol{\Pi}$ varies (continuously) with p. To see this, consider that $\boldsymbol{\Pi}$ depends on $\underline{\mathbf{A}}_o$; which depends on its own first column, $\boldsymbol{\alpha}_1$; which equals $\boldsymbol{\alpha}_1^c + \boldsymbol{\Omega}\mathbf{a}_1$ and so depends on $\mathbf{a}_1$; whose first element is $\mathbf{a}_{11} = p$. Second, $\boldsymbol{\Pi}$ varies (abruptly) when the collection of attractive basic actions gains or loses a member. Such an event, if it occurs at all, is caused by the wanderings of the driver. Third, $\boldsymbol{\Pi}$ varies (abruptly) if the changes in p are so large as to make the $\boldsymbol{\alpha}_i$ lose their linear independence. When this happens, $\boldsymbol{\Pi}$ ceases to be defined—a rather extreme form of abrupt variation.

Every time $\boldsymbol{\Pi}$ changes abruptly, the values of some parameters of $f(p,t)$ vary too. Which parameters vary, and when, is most plausibly regarded as unknowable.

Throughout this chapter, it is assumed that $\boldsymbol{\Pi}$ undergoes continuous changes only, through variations in p. Abrupt changes are thus ruled out: the collection of basic actions stays the same, and changes of p are modest enough for the $\boldsymbol{\alpha}_i$ to remain linearly independent.

Certain functions of t play an important role. They will be called t-functions.

DEFINITION. Let $K_0, K_1, \ldots, K_m$ be any constants. A *t-function* is a function of the form

$$e^{-\gamma t}[K_0 + \int_0^t e^{\gamma\tau}\sum_i K_i \dot{b}_i(\tau)d\tau]. \tag{2}$$

As before, Q, L, and K mean "a quadratic form in p," "a linear form in p," and "a constant" (or, more fully, "a constant function of p"). By $Q(t)$ is meant a quadratic form in p whose coefficients are t-functions. Analogously defined are $L(t)$ and $K(t)$. The typical $Q(t)$ thus has the form $A(t)p^2 + B(t)p + C(t)$, the typical $L(t)$ is $B(t)p + C(t)$, and $K(t)$ is itself a t-function.

THEOREM 1. *Let* $\dot{\text{q}} = \dot{\text{c}}_\text{i}\text{a}_\text{ij}$. *The long-response function is*

$$\dot{q} = f(p,t) = Q(t)/Q_o = \frac{A(t)p^2 + B(t)p + C(t)}{Dp^2 + Ep + 1}, \tag{3}$$

where A(t), B(t), *and* C(t) *are* t*-functions. All three of* A(t), B(t), *and* C(t) *vary with* i *and* j. *(In fact, all constants* $\text{K}_0, \text{K}_1, \text{K}_2, \ldots$ *in* A(t), B(t), *and* C(t)*—see (2)—vary with* i *and* j.*) Parameters* D *and* E, *which are independent of time, are the same for all* i *and* j.

For flow rates that are elements of $\dot{\text{c}}_1\mathbf{a}_1$, *the long-response function simplifies: if* $\dot{\text{q}} = \dot{\text{c}}_1\text{a}_{11}$ $(= \dot{\text{c}}_1\text{p})$ *then* $\text{C(t)} \equiv 0$, *and if* $\dot{\text{q}}$ *is any other element of* $\dot{\text{c}}_1\mathbf{a}_1$ *then* $\text{A(t)} \equiv 0$.

The cumulative-response function, F(p,t), *is found from* f(p,t) *by replacing the* t*-functions* A(t), B(t), *and* C(t) *with their integrals* $\int_0^t \text{A}(\tau)\text{d}\tau$, $\int_0^t \text{B}(\tau)\text{d}\tau$, *and* $\int_0^t \text{C}(\tau)\text{d}\tau$.

Proof. Using $\boldsymbol{\xi}(t) = \boldsymbol{\xi}(0) + \boldsymbol{\alpha}(t) + \boldsymbol{\beta}(t)$ in (1) gives $\dot{\boldsymbol{\alpha}}(t) = -\gamma\mathbf{\Pi}[\boldsymbol{\xi}(0) + \boldsymbol{\alpha}(t) + \boldsymbol{\beta}(t)]$ or

$$\dot{\boldsymbol{\alpha}}(t) = -\gamma\mathbf{\Pi}\boldsymbol{\alpha}(t) - \gamma\mathbf{\Pi}[\boldsymbol{\xi}(0) + \boldsymbol{\beta}(t)]. \tag{4}$$

This is a differential equation—or a system of differential equations, if you prefer—in $\boldsymbol{\alpha}(t)$.

You can see where the argument is going. First, (4) is solved for $\boldsymbol{\alpha}(t)$. Differentiation then gives $\dot{\boldsymbol{\alpha}}$. Better still, it gives $\dot{\mathbf{c}}_o$, for $\dot{\boldsymbol{\alpha}} = \underline{\mathbf{A}}_o\dot{\mathbf{c}}_o$. (Elements of $\dot{\mathbf{c}}$ not in $\dot{\mathbf{c}}_o$ are zero.) After that, all we have to do is figure out how those elements of $\dot{\mathbf{c}}_o$ depend on p.

There is a small shortcut. Premultiplying (4) by $\underline{\mathbf{A}}_o'$ and using $\underline{\mathbf{A}}_o'\mathbf{\Pi} = \underline{\mathbf{A}}_o'\underline{\mathbf{A}}_o(\underline{\mathbf{A}}_o'\underline{\mathbf{A}}_o)^{-1}\underline{\mathbf{A}}_o' = \underline{\mathbf{A}}_o'$ gives

$$\underline{\mathbf{A}}_o'\dot{\boldsymbol{\alpha}}(t) = -\gamma\underline{\mathbf{A}}_o'\boldsymbol{\alpha}(t) - \gamma\underline{\mathbf{A}}_o'[\boldsymbol{\xi}(0) + \boldsymbol{\beta}(t)],$$

which is a differential equation in $\underline{\mathbf{A}}_o'\boldsymbol{\alpha}(t)$. By Chapter 2, MT 25, its solution is

$$\underline{\mathbf{A}}_o'\boldsymbol{\alpha}(t) = e^{-\gamma t}\underline{\mathbf{A}}_o'\boldsymbol{\alpha}(0) - (1 - e^{-\gamma t})\underline{\mathbf{A}}_o'\boldsymbol{\xi}(0) - \underline{\mathbf{A}}_o'\boldsymbol{\beta}(t) + e^{-\gamma t}\int_0^t e^{\gamma\tau}\underline{\mathbf{A}}_o'\dot{\boldsymbol{\beta}}(\tau)d\tau.$$

Since $\boldsymbol{\alpha}(0) = \mathbf{0}$, the first term on the right drops out. Differentiation gives next

$$\underline{\mathbf{A}}_o'\dot{\boldsymbol{\alpha}} = -\gamma e^{-\gamma t}[\underline{\mathbf{A}}_o'\boldsymbol{\xi}(0) + \int_0^t e^{\gamma\tau}\underline{\mathbf{A}}_o'\dot{\boldsymbol{\beta}}(\tau)d\tau].$$

Equivalently,

$$\underline{\mathbf{A}}_o'\underline{\mathbf{A}}_o\dot{\mathbf{c}}_o = \underline{\mathbf{A}}_o'\boldsymbol{\sigma}, \quad \text{with } \boldsymbol{\sigma} = -\gamma e^{-\gamma t}[\boldsymbol{\xi}(0) + \int_0^t e^{\gamma\tau}\dot{\boldsymbol{\beta}}(\tau)d\tau]. \tag{5}$$

Neither $\mathbf{A}$ nor $\underline{\mathbf{A}}$ appears in $\boldsymbol{\sigma}$. Vector $\boldsymbol{\sigma}$ is thus independent of $\mathbf{a}_1$, and hence of p.

From here, the argument is nearly the same as in Part II. Suppose, for notational simplicity, that there are only three attractive basic actions. Let these be $(\boldsymbol{\alpha}_1, \mathbf{a}_1)$, $(\boldsymbol{\alpha}_2, \mathbf{a}_2)$, and $(\boldsymbol{\alpha}_3, \mathbf{a}_3)$. System (5) can then be written as

$$\begin{pmatrix} \boldsymbol{\alpha}_1'\boldsymbol{\alpha}_1 & \boldsymbol{\alpha}_1'\boldsymbol{\alpha}_2 & \boldsymbol{\alpha}_1'\boldsymbol{\alpha}_3 \\ \boldsymbol{\alpha}_2'\boldsymbol{\alpha}_1 & \boldsymbol{\alpha}_2'\boldsymbol{\alpha}_2 & \boldsymbol{\alpha}_2'\boldsymbol{\alpha}_3 \\ \boldsymbol{\alpha}_3'\boldsymbol{\alpha}_1 & \boldsymbol{\alpha}_3'\boldsymbol{\alpha}_2 & \boldsymbol{\alpha}_3'\boldsymbol{\alpha}_3 \end{pmatrix} \begin{pmatrix} \dot{c}_1 \\ \dot{c}_2 \\ \dot{c}_3 \end{pmatrix} = \begin{pmatrix} \boldsymbol{\alpha}_1'\boldsymbol{\sigma} \\ \boldsymbol{\alpha}_2'\boldsymbol{\sigma} \\ \boldsymbol{\alpha}_3'\boldsymbol{\sigma} \end{pmatrix}. \tag{6}$$

Recall that $\boldsymbol{\alpha}_i$ is the sum of its invariant core $\boldsymbol{\alpha}_i^c$ and the feedback: $\boldsymbol{\alpha}_i = \boldsymbol{\alpha}_i^c + \boldsymbol{\Omega}\mathbf{a}_i$. Since $a_{11} = p$, each element of $\boldsymbol{\Omega}\mathbf{a}_1$ is an L, and all elements of $\boldsymbol{\Omega}\mathbf{a}_2$ and $\boldsymbol{\Omega}\mathbf{a}_3$ are K's. But then each element of $\boldsymbol{\alpha}_1$ is an L, and all elements of $\boldsymbol{\alpha}_2$ and $\boldsymbol{\alpha}_3$ are K's. It follows that $\boldsymbol{\alpha}_1'\boldsymbol{\alpha}_1$ is a Q, that $\boldsymbol{\alpha}_1'\boldsymbol{\alpha}_j = \boldsymbol{\alpha}_j'\boldsymbol{\alpha}_1$ is an L for $j = 2, 3$, and that all other $\boldsymbol{\alpha}_i'\boldsymbol{\alpha}_j$ are K's. Denote the elements of $\boldsymbol{\alpha}_1$ by $L_1, L_2, \ldots$; then $\boldsymbol{\alpha}_1'\sigma = \Sigma\alpha_{1k}\sigma_k = \Sigma L_k\sigma_k$. In now obvious notation, the other two $\boldsymbol{\alpha}_j'\boldsymbol{\sigma}$ have the form $\Sigma K_k\sigma_k$. So (6) is

$$\begin{pmatrix} Q & L & L \\ L & K & K \\ L & K & K \end{pmatrix} \begin{pmatrix} \dot{c}_1 \\ \dot{c}_2 \\ \dot{c}_3 \end{pmatrix} = \begin{pmatrix} \Sigma L_k\sigma_k \\ \Sigma K_k\sigma_k \\ \Sigma K_k\sigma_k \end{pmatrix}.$$

Solving by Cramer's Rule shows that $\dot{c}_1$, $\dot{c}_2$, and $\dot{c}_3$ have the form $\Sigma L_k\sigma_k/Q_o$, $\Sigma Q_k\sigma_k/Q_o$, and $\Sigma Q_k\sigma_k/Q_o$, where Q_o is the determinant of the coefficient matrix.

Consider one of the numerators—say, $\Sigma Q_k\sigma_k$. Define A_k, B_k, and C_k through $Q_k = A_kp^2 + B_kp + C_k$. Then $\Sigma Q_k\sigma_k = \Sigma(A_kp^2 + B_kp + C_k)\sigma_k = (\Sigma A_k\sigma_k)p^2 + (\Sigma B_k\sigma_k)p + (\Sigma C_k\sigma_k)$. Since all A_k, B_k, and C_k are constants, and all σ_k are t-functions, the coefficients $\Sigma A_k\sigma_k$, $\Sigma B_k\sigma_k$ and $\Sigma C_k\sigma_k$ are t-functions too. Call them $A(t)$, $B(t)$, and $C(t)$. We have now proved that both $\dot{c}_2$ and $\dot{c}_3$ have the form

$$\dot{c}_i = Q(t)/Q_o = \frac{A(t)p^2 + B(t)p + C(t)}{Dp^2 + Ep + 1}, \quad i = 2, 3. \tag{8}$$

By the same reasoning,

$$\dot{c}_1 = L(t)/Q_o = \frac{B(t)p + C(t)}{Dp^2 + Ep + 1}. \tag{9}$$

The rest of the theorem, concerning the cumulative-response function, is obvious. P.O.C.

Discussion. (*i*) The short-response function of Part II had, among its special cases, the own-price and cross-price demand functions as well as the own-price and cross-price supply functions, both for the consumer and for the producer. One of those cross-price demand functions was the quasi-Engel function. The long-response function of Theorem 1 includes, among its special cases, the dynamic versions of the same nine testable results.

For an example, let ($\boldsymbol{\alpha}_1$, $\mathbf{a}_1$) be "buying a gallon of milk." Let the milk element of $\mathbf{a}_1$ be $+1g$, and the money element, p. Milk is good 5. Since $p = a_{11}$, by convention, money must be good 1. The rate $\dot{q} = \dot{c}_1 a_{15}$ at which the agent buys milk depends on the price of milk according to a function of the form $L(t)/Q_o$, for every t. This $L(t)/Q_o$ is thus the own-price demand function (dynamic version). So long as p is fixed, $L(t)/Q_o$ is just a t-function. In that case then, the agent's demand rate for milk obeys a t-function from $t = 0$ on. (See curve CD in Figure 1.) If p does change at some $t_o > 0$, and retains its new value for all $t > t_o$, the demand rate will again obey a t-function, provided time is reset to zero at t_o. The postchange t-function will ordinarily differ from the prechange one.

For another example, let p have the same meaning, and suppose that "buying a loaf of bread" is one of the basic actions. The rate at which the agent buys bread depends on the price p of milk according to a function of the form $Q(t)/Q_o$, for every t. So long as the milk price remains fixed, every $Q(t)/Q_o$ is just a t-function.

(*ii*) What has just been said about the milk-price demand for bread applies of course to all cross-price demand functions. It applies, in particular, to all quasi-Engel functions (i.e., all cross-price demand functions in which p represents the wage).

(*iii*) Coefficients $A(t)$ through E in (3) are dimensioned. For particulars, see Question 6 at the end of this chapter, and also Chapter 7, Discussion of Theorem 1, point (*vii*).

(*iv*) Because the parameters in (3) depend on unobservable quantities, like the elements of $\boldsymbol{\xi}(0)$ and of $\boldsymbol{\Omega}$, their values should be regarded as obtainable solely by estimation, rather than by computation or direct observation. Chapter 10 illustrates how such estimation might be performed.

(*v*) Suppose that two or more elements of $\mathbf{a}_1$ are variable. With only small and obvious changes, Theorem 1 remains true. Details are like those in Chapter 7, Discussion of Theorem 1, point (*xii*).

(*vi*) The long-response function's denominator, $Q_o = Dp^2 + Ep + 1$, is the same for all flow rates. Because of it, every sum of flow rates obeys the long-response function too. Of course, the sum must be defined—the flow rates in the sum must all be measured in the same units. These remarks hold also for sums of flows, since the cumulative-response function has for all flows the same denominator $Q_o = Dp^2 + Ep + 1$.

Adding a flow rate to a flow will always be impossible, because the units do not match.

(*vii*) Many of the formulas derived could be taken further if the driver rate were specified. We examine two possibilities: a constant driver rate, and a driver rate that is constant except for a sudden, momentary spike.

A constant driver rate means $(\dot{\boldsymbol{\beta}}(t), \dot{\mathbf{b}}(t)) \equiv (\dot{\boldsymbol{\beta}}(0), \dot{\mathbf{b}}(0))$. Note that $\dot{\mathbf{b}}(t) \equiv \dot{\mathbf{b}}(0)$ implies $\dot{\boldsymbol{\beta}}(t) \equiv \dot{\boldsymbol{\beta}}(0)$, since $\dot{\boldsymbol{\beta}} = \boldsymbol{\Omega}\dot{\mathbf{b}}$.

Assuming a constant driver rate is not as unrealistic as it may seem. Many people lead a routine existence, with each week resembling the next. To them, $\dot{\mathbf{b}}(t)$ fluctuates about a constant mean, implying that the assumption of a constant $\dot{\mathbf{b}}(t)$ paints a fairly reliable picture of their lives.

When $\dot{\mathbf{b}} \equiv \dot{\mathbf{b}}(0)$, the t-function simplifies, from $e^{-\gamma t}[K^0 + \int_0^t e^{\gamma\tau}\sum_i K_i\dot{b}_i(\tau)d\tau]$ to $e^{-\gamma t}[K_0 + \sum_i K_i\dot{b}_i(0) \int_0^t e^{\gamma\tau}d\tau]$, easily seen to be of the form $e^{-\gamma t}K_1 + K_2$.

Tracing the proof of Theorem 1, you find that if $\dot{\mathbf{b}} \equiv \dot{\mathbf{b}}(0)$, Eqs. (8) and (9) simplify to

$$\dot{c}_i = \frac{e^{-\gamma t}Q_1 + Q_2}{Q_o}, \quad i = 2, 3, \tag{10}$$

$$\dot{c}_1 = \frac{e^{-\gamma t}L_1 + L_2}{Q_o}. \tag{11}$$

All Q's and L's in (10) and (11) are independent of time.

From the second paragraph of Theorem 1 follows, given (10) and (11), that the general flow rate $\dot{q}$ obeys $f(p,t) = (e^{-\gamma t}Q_1 + Q_2)/Q_o$. It also follows that if $\dot{q} = \dot{c}_1 a_{11}$ $(= \dot{c}_1 p)$, the Q's in the numerator lack a quadratic term. And it follows that if $\dot{q}$ is any other element of $\dot{c}_1\mathbf{a}_1$, the Q's lack a constant term.

Integrating (10) and (11) from 0 to t gives

$$c_i = \frac{(1 - e^{-\gamma t})Q_1 + tQ_2}{Q_o}, \qquad i = 2, 3, \tag{12}$$

and

$$c_1 = \frac{(1 - e^{-\gamma t})L_1 + tL_2}{Q_o}. \tag{13}$$

Differentiating (12) and (13) with respect to t will show that the Q_1 in (10) and the L_1 in (11) are γ times the Q_1 in (12) and the L_1 in (13).

Back to (5), copied here for convenience:

$$\underline{\mathbf{A}}_o{}'\underline{\mathbf{A}}_o\dot{\mathbf{c}}_o = \underline{\mathbf{A}}_o{}'\boldsymbol{\sigma}, \quad \text{with } \boldsymbol{\sigma} = -\gamma e^{-\gamma t}[\boldsymbol{\xi}(0) + \int_0^t e^{\gamma\tau}\dot{\boldsymbol{\beta}}(\tau)d\tau].$$

When $\dot{\mathbf{b}} \equiv \dot{\mathbf{b}}(0)$, this equation becomes

$$\underline{\mathbf{A}}_o{}'\underline{\mathbf{A}}_o\dot{\mathbf{c}}_o = \underline{\mathbf{A}}_o{}'\boldsymbol{\sigma}, \quad \text{with } \boldsymbol{\sigma} = -\gamma e^{-\gamma t}\boldsymbol{\xi}(0) - \dot{\boldsymbol{\beta}}(0)(1 - e^{-\gamma t}).$$

Premultiplication by $\underline{\mathbf{A}}_o(\underline{\mathbf{A}}_o{}'\underline{\mathbf{A}}_o)^{-1}$ gives $\underline{\mathbf{A}}_o\dot{\mathbf{c}}_o = \boldsymbol{\Pi\sigma}$, that is,

$$\underline{\mathbf{A}}_o\dot{\mathbf{c}}_o = \dot{\boldsymbol{\alpha}} = e^{-\gamma t}[-\gamma\boldsymbol{\Pi}\boldsymbol{\xi}(0) + \boldsymbol{\Pi}\dot{\boldsymbol{\beta}}(0)] - \boldsymbol{\Pi}\dot{\boldsymbol{\beta}}(0). \tag{14}$$

As t goes to infinity, $e^{-\gamma t}$ goes to zero, implying that $\dot{\boldsymbol{\alpha}}$ goes to $-\boldsymbol{\Pi}\dot{\boldsymbol{\beta}}(0)$ and $\dot{\boldsymbol{\xi}} = \dot{\boldsymbol{\alpha}} + \dot{\boldsymbol{\beta}}$ goes to $-\boldsymbol{\Pi}\dot{\boldsymbol{\beta}}(0) + \dot{\boldsymbol{\beta}}(0)$:

$$\dot{\boldsymbol{\xi}}(\infty) = (\mathbf{I} - \boldsymbol{\Pi})\dot{\boldsymbol{\beta}}(0).$$

The asymptotic velocity of the state of mind is thus constant, and perhaps null. It is null if $\dot{\boldsymbol{\beta}}(0) = \boldsymbol{\Pi}\dot{\boldsymbol{\beta}}(0)$, in which case $\boldsymbol{\xi}$ converges to stationarity. Matters are more interesting if $\dot{\boldsymbol{\beta}}(0) \neq \boldsymbol{\Pi}\dot{\boldsymbol{\beta}}(0)$. What happens then is illustrated in Figure 2, except that all velocities have been multiplied by dt. When $\dot{\boldsymbol{\beta}}(0) \neq \boldsymbol{\Pi}\dot{\boldsymbol{\beta}}(0)$, the path of $\boldsymbol{\xi}$ converges to a line; asymptotically, $\boldsymbol{\xi}$ travels along that line with uniform velocity $(\mathbf{I} - \boldsymbol{\Pi})\dot{\boldsymbol{\beta}}(0)$. In this last case,

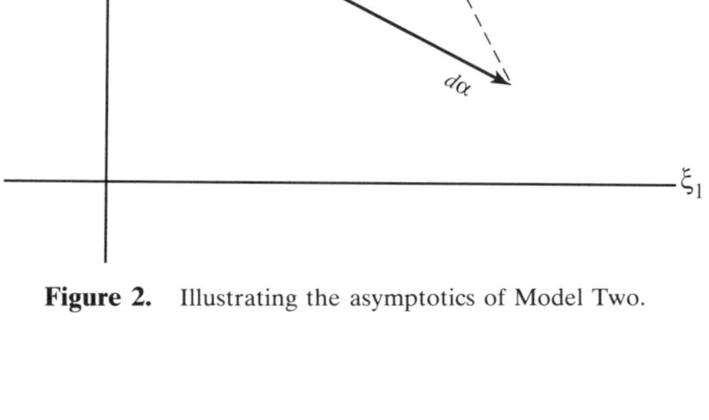

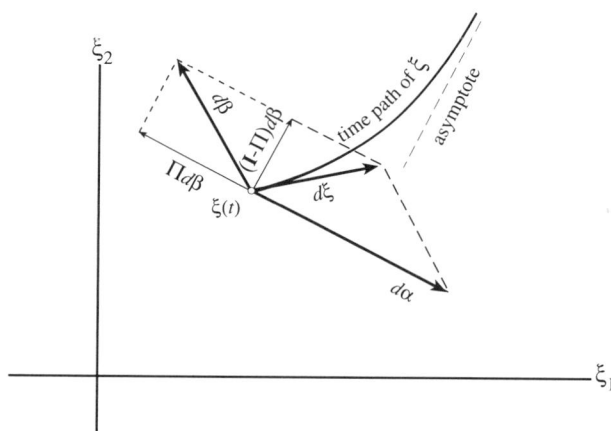

Figure 2. Illustrating the asymptotics of Model Two.

the agent's actions nullify only part of the exogenous $\dot{\boldsymbol{\beta}}(0)$, namely, $\boldsymbol{\Pi}\dot{\boldsymbol{\beta}}(0)$. The rest, $(\mathbf{I} - \boldsymbol{\Pi})\dot{\boldsymbol{\beta}}(0)$, goes uncountered. All of this makes solid intuitive sense.

Equation (14) is set in the unobservable world of the mind. To find its observable counterpart, recall that $\dot{\boldsymbol{\beta}} = \boldsymbol{\Omega}\dot{\mathbf{b}}$, and define

$$\mathbf{P} = \mathbf{A}_o(\underline{\mathbf{A}}_o'\underline{\mathbf{A}}_o)^{-1}\underline{\mathbf{A}}_o'.$$

This $\mathbf{P}$ looks like a projection matrix, but is not. It would be a projection matrix if its right side began with $\underline{\mathbf{A}}_o$, rather than $\mathbf{A}_o$.

Premultiplying (14) by $\mathbf{P}$ gives $\mathbf{A}_o\dot{\mathbf{c}}$, that is, $\dot{\mathbf{a}}$:

$$\dot{\mathbf{a}} = e^{-\gamma t}[-\gamma\mathbf{P}\boldsymbol{\Pi}\boldsymbol{\xi}(0) + \mathbf{P}\boldsymbol{\Pi}\dot{\mathbf{b}}(0)] - \mathbf{P}\boldsymbol{\Pi}\dot{\mathbf{b}}(0).$$

Asymptotically, $\dot{\mathbf{a}} = -\mathbf{P}\boldsymbol{\Pi}\dot{\mathbf{b}}(0)$.

Some stock-taking is in order. We are in the middle of the seventh (and last) point of the Discussion to Theorem 1. As said at the beginning of point (*vii*), many of the formulas derived earlier could be taken further if the driver rate were specified. One possibility is to specify the driver rate as constant. The analysis of that case is now done. A second possibility is to assume the driver rate constant except for a sudden spike. The analysis of that case is next.

Suppose that at some instant t_o the agent experiences an abrupt change in his surround. Maybe he receives an inheritance; maybe he is involved in an accident or some other traumatic event; maybe he attends a play that moves him deeply. How is his behavior—that is, $\dot{\mathbf{a}}$—affected? It will be shown that *the effect of the sudden change wears off at a negative-exponential rate.* This is the last of the ten testable results promised.

The proof involves the delta function $\delta(t_o)$ discussed in Chapter 2, MT 26. More particularly, it involves Eq. (11) of that chapter, which is

$$\int_{-\infty}^{+\infty} \delta(t_o - \tau)f(\tau)d\tau = f(t_o). \tag{15}$$

At time t_o, the vector $\dot{\mathbf{b}}$, constant until then, suddenly and briefly increases by $\Delta\dot{\mathbf{b}} = \delta(t_o)\mathbf{z}$, with $\mathbf{z}$ belonging to A. All elements z_i of $\mathbf{z}$ are constant. Some z_i may be zero. The scalar $\delta(t_o)$ equals $1/\epsilon$ for all t between t_o and $t_o + \epsilon$, and is zero for all t outside that interval.

Consider again (5),

$$\underline{\mathbf{A}}_o'\underline{\mathbf{A}}_o\dot{\mathbf{c}}_o = \underline{\mathbf{A}}_o'\boldsymbol{\sigma}, \text{ with } \boldsymbol{\sigma} = -\gamma e^{-\gamma t}[\boldsymbol{\xi}(0) + \int_0^t e^{\gamma\tau}\dot{\boldsymbol{\beta}}(\tau)d\tau].$$

Premultiply by $\mathbf{A}_o(\underline{\mathbf{A}}_o'\underline{\mathbf{A}}_o)^{-1}$, to get

$$\mathbf{A}_o\dot{\mathbf{c}} = \dot{\mathbf{a}} = -\gamma e^{-\gamma t}\mathbf{P}[\boldsymbol{\xi}(0) + \int_0^t e^{\gamma\tau}\dot{\boldsymbol{\beta}}(\tau)d\tau].$$

To bring in the changing $\dot{\mathbf{b}}$ and get rid of the unobservable $\dot{\boldsymbol{\beta}}$ at the same time, use $\dot{\boldsymbol{\beta}} = \boldsymbol{\Omega}\dot{\mathbf{b}}$. This gives

$$\dot{\mathbf{a}} = -\gamma e^{-\gamma t}\mathbf{P}[\boldsymbol{\xi}(0) + \int_0^t e^{\gamma\tau}\boldsymbol{\Omega}\dot{\mathbf{b}}\,(\tau)d\tau],$$

or

$$\dot{\mathbf{a}} = -\gamma e^{-\gamma t}\mathbf{P}\boldsymbol{\xi}(0) - \gamma e^{-\gamma t}\mathbf{P}\boldsymbol{\Omega}\int_0^t e^{\gamma\tau}\dot{\mathbf{b}}(\tau)d\tau. \tag{16}$$

When $\dot{\mathbf{b}}$ changes (at t_o) to $\dot{\boldsymbol{\beta}} + \delta(t_o)\mathbf{z}$, the action rate ($\dot{\boldsymbol{\alpha}}$, $\dot{\mathbf{a}}$) changes also. Our interest lies, this time, with $\dot{\mathbf{a}}$ rather than $\dot{\boldsymbol{\alpha}}$; $\dot{\mathbf{a}}$ becomes $\dot{\mathbf{a}} + \Delta\dot{\mathbf{a}}$, say. By (16), $\Delta\dot{\mathbf{a}} = -\gamma e^{-\gamma t}\mathbf{P}\boldsymbol{\Omega}\mathbf{z}\int_0^t e^{\gamma\tau}\delta(t_o - \tau)d\tau$. By (15), this equals $-\gamma e^{-\gamma t}\,\mathbf{P}\boldsymbol{\Omega}\mathbf{z}e^{\gamma t_o}$ if $t_o < t$, and $\mathbf{0}$ if $t_o > t$. (That $\Delta\dot{\mathbf{a}} = \mathbf{0}$ if $t_o > t$ should be obvious on interpretation: events still to happen do not affect current behavior.) Shortening the constant vector $-\gamma\mathbf{P}\boldsymbol{\Omega}\mathbf{z}$ to $\boldsymbol{\zeta}$ puts the conclusion in the form

$$\Delta\dot{\mathbf{a}} = e^{-\gamma(t-t_o)}\boldsymbol{\zeta} \quad \text{for } t > t_o, \tag{17}$$

completing the proof. P.O.C.

Worth nothing is that the rate γ at which the effect of a sudden event wears off is the same γ that appears in the motion law. Roughly, an agent with a relatively large γ—a Type A personality, say—acts faster but also forgets faster. It is of course possible that Type A personalities have more to forget in the first place. Whether they do depends on the relation between γ and the observation matrix $\boldsymbol{\Omega}$. The argument goes as follows. Suppose two agents, equipped with different $\boldsymbol{\Omega}$'s, have the same $\dot{\mathbf{b}}$ and observe the same spike $\delta(t_o)\mathbf{z}$ in $\dot{\mathbf{b}}$. Each thus experiences a spike $\delta(t_o)\boldsymbol{\Omega}\mathbf{z}$ in his $\dot{\boldsymbol{\beta}}$. And it may well be that the agent with the larger γ is also the one who is more affected, in the sense that his induced spike, $\delta(t_o)\boldsymbol{\Omega}\mathbf{z}$, has larger elements.

SUMMARY

Let $(\boldsymbol{\alpha}_1, \mathbf{a}_1)$ be attractive, and suppose that $a_{11} = p$ can vary parametrically. A change of p, occurring at time 0, affects the general flow rate $\dot{q}$ for all $t \geq 0$. The long-response function, $\dot{q} = f(p,t)$, says how: $f(p,t) = Q(t)/Q_o$, the quotient of two quadratic forms in p. Its numerator, $Q(t) = A(t)p^2 + B(t)p + C(t)$, is different for different flow rates. Its denominator, $Q_o = Dp^2 + Ep + 1$, which is positive-definite, is the same for all flow rates $\dot{q}$.

If $\dot{q} = a_{11}\dot{c}_1$ (for instance, if $\dot{q}$ is an own-price demand rate), $A(t) \equiv 0$. If $\dot{q}$ is any other element of $\mathbf{a}_1\dot{c}_1$ (for instance, if $\dot{q}$ is the rate at which the agent pays for $a_{11}\dot{c}_1$), $C(t) \equiv 0$.

Coefficients $A(t)$, $B(t)$, and $C(t)$ are functions of t. Except for the two special cases in the last paragraph, their analytical form is unknown unless the driver is specified. Two specifications were examined. First, if the driver rate is constant, each of $A(t)$, $B(t)$, and $C(t)$ is the sum of a constant multiple of $e^{-\gamma t}$ and a constant. Second, if the driver rate has a sudden spike at time t_o, the effect on the action rate wears off at a negative-exponential rate.

The cumulative-response function, $q = F(p,t)$ with $F(p,0) = 0$, is the integral from 0 to t of the long-response function.

Questions

1. Why does the tenth result—Eq. (17)—not follow from Model One?
2. Verify that each element of $\boldsymbol{\sigma}$ is indeed a t-function.
3. Does $\boldsymbol{\sigma}$ belong to A? X? A^0? R^m? E^m?
4. Prove that if $\mathbf{k}$ is a vector of constants, $\mathbf{k}'\boldsymbol{\sigma}$ is a t-function. Find the place in the text where this was used.
5. See the Discussion of Theorem 1, point (*ii*). Describe in general terms what the graph of the quasi-Engel function looks like.
6. How are the coefficients in (3) dimensioned?
7. Find the time paths of $\dot{\mathbf{a}}$ and $\dot{\mathbf{x}}$ if $\dot{\mathbf{b}}$ is constant ($\dot{\mathbf{b}} = \dot{\mathbf{b}}(0)$). What do the paths look like asymptotically?

10

A Test

This chapter tests the cumulative-response function. Indirectly, it also tests the short- and long-response functions, for the long-response function is the time derivative of the cumulative-response function, and the short-response function is found from the long-response function by fixing t.

As with all testing, the big question is where to get the data. The variable p needs to take on quite a few different values; while it does so, none of the parameters may change. Such demanding requirements are likely to be met only in the laboratory. Even then, few human subjects are willing to cooperate for as long as it takes. Will animal subjects do?

Intuition says no. Intuition says that animals do not have enough in common with people and bolsters that judgment with arguments from physiology, ethology, philosophy, and perhaps an extra science or two. Logic, on the other hand, says yes. Logic says that whether people and animals have enough in common is not a physiological or ethological or philosophical issue, at least not to a model builder. To a model builder, the issue is mathematical, and the conclusion obvious: human behavior and animal behavior have the same *mathematical* structure—that is, are captured by the same *mathematical* model—unless there is a *mathematical* distinction between the two.

There is, to date, no mathematical distinction between human and animal behavior. It seems fair to predict that there never will be. And if that is indeed so, then tests with animals say as much about human behavior as do tests with *homo sapiens.* If a model fits the behavior of pigeons, it is as encouraging as when it fits the behavior of people; if a model fails for mice, it must fail, sight unseen, for men.

Logic has now made its point, but intuition is still protesting. Intuition imagines a human being and an animal, inspects the two, and finds them so different as to sweep logic aside. Does intuition have a case?

Not really. Intuition is looking at living beings, which is the wrong thing to do. The one who matters is the model agent. And the model agent is not a living being. He is a robot. If we had set out to construct a theory of animal behavior, the model animal would have been a robot too. The question is thus, Is the agent-robot constructed according to the same principles as the animal-robot, or are there some essential engineering differences?

Maybe you find the idea that people and (other) animals are robots not entirely convincing. Maybe, when the agent-robot was first introduced, back in Model One, your intellect perceived him as the windup doll he really is, but your mind's eye saw him checking out power tools at Sears. If so, there is a more convincing argument. It comes from Model Two.

In Model Two, the central character is not the agent but the brain. The mind's eye is thus much less inclined to conjure up either living beings or robots, and much more inclined to see the protagonist as an organ of the sort you find depicted in biological or medical handbooks. A side benefit of this shift of focus is that it undercuts the belief that people have free will, or the ability to choose, or a utility function: pictures of the brain show no evidence that there exists a lobe in which free will originates, or a place where you might find the ability to choose, or a location where a utility function could be hiding out.

Back to the issue that started all this: do tests of animal behavior tell us anything about human behavior, and vice versa? The answer is now much more clear-cut: so long as there is no mathematical definition of the difference between human brains and animal brains, we must regard the two as operating according to the same principles. This means that hypotheses about human behavior can validly be tested on animals, and vice versa.

A 1951 article by two biologists, Israel Weiner and Eliot Stellar, describes an experiment involving the consumption of salt water by rats. Six rats were suddenly deprived of food and tap water. After a 15-hr fast—no breakfast, no lunch—they were given access to water with some salt in it ("test fluid"). For one hour, (the "test period"), the rats could drink all they wanted. Food remained out of reach.

At the end of the test period began another fast, without food, water, or test fluid. The purpose of this second fast, which lasted for 2 hr, was to keep the rats from learning to ignore the salt water and wait for Prime Time—the day's final 6 hr, when food and water were again freely available.

The experiment lasted 52 days. Each day was the same as the next, except for variations in the salt concentration in the test fluid. The salt concentration, p, measured in centigrams of salt per cubic centimeter of water, was changed every four days. In all then, p took on 13 different values, ranging from an insipid 0 *cg/cc* to a pleasant 0.8 *cg/cc* to an odious 3.5 *cg/cc.*

During the daily test periods, Weiner and Stellar measured every 5 min how much each rat had drunk. The observed quantities—which were flows q, not flow rates $\dot{q}$—were rounded to the nearest 0.5 *cc,* and then averaged over each 4-day period and over the six rats. In this way, the researchers found 156 values of q: 13 sequences (one for each p) of 12 intake figures each (one for every 5-min period).

Figure 1 shows 156 points, depicted as little circles. Each point has a p-coordinate, a t-coordinate, and a vertically measured q-coordinate. For 100 of the 156 points, the coordinates can be inferred from diagrams in the Weiner–Stellar article. For the remaining 56 points, the coordinates came from Professor Stellar, who was kind enough to send me all the original observations and give me permission to use them.

In the experiment, the "average rat" is the agent. Time begins at the start of the first test period. Every 24 hr after that, time is reset to zero. Implied in that practice is the assumption that every time a test period begins, the agent's state is the same point as it was 24 hr earlier: $(\boldsymbol{\xi}(0h), \mathbf{x}(0h)) = (\boldsymbol{\xi}(24h), \mathbf{x}(24h)) = (\boldsymbol{\xi}(48h), \mathbf{x}(48h)) = \cdots$. The assumption is probably not met, which damages the fit. On the other hand, the data were averaged over every four days, which improves the fit. The data were also averaged over the six rats; whether that helps or hurts the fit depends on the six γ's and the six Q_o's. It helps if γ and Q_o are about the same for all rats. Otherwise it hurts.

Let salt be good 1, measured in *cg*. Water, measured in *cc*, is good 2. Time is from here on measured in minutes. The variable basic action, "drinking test fluid," is $(\boldsymbol{\alpha}_1, \mathbf{a}_1)$; its observable part is $\mathbf{a}_1 = (p, -1cc, \ldots)'$.

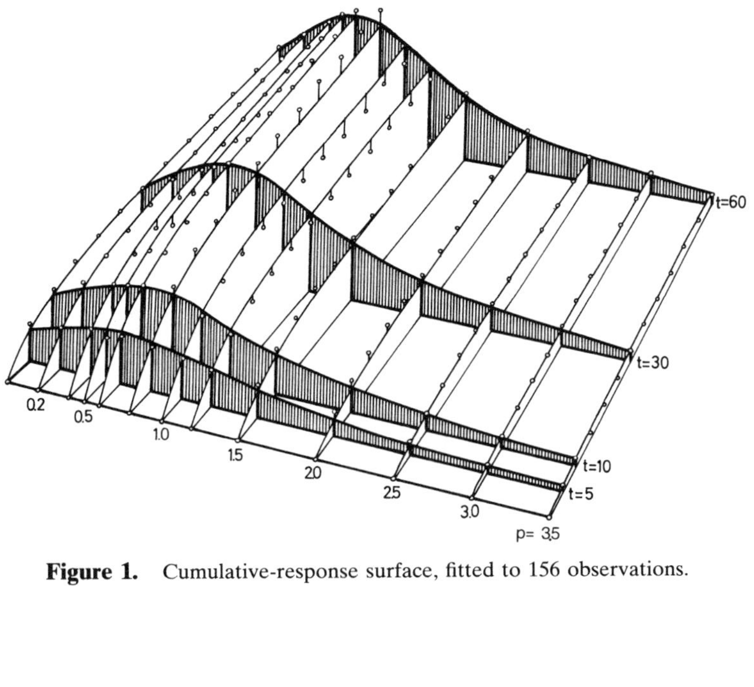

Figure 1. Cumulative-response surface, fitted to 156 observations.

Since ($\boldsymbol{\alpha}_1$, $\mathbf{a}_1$) is attractive—all rats drank test fluid—the first element of $\mathbf{c}_o$ is c_1. *Assume, for simplicity, that the driver rate is constant.*

By last chapter's Eq. (13), c_1 depends on p and t according to

$$c_1(p,t) = \frac{(1 - e^{-\gamma t})L_1 + tL_2}{Q_o} = \frac{(1 - e^{-\gamma t})(Ap + B) + t(Cp + D)}{Ep^2 + Fp + 1}. \tag{1}$$

When rats drink test fluid, the quantity of *salt* they ingest—call it q'—is $p \cdot c_1(p,t)$, and the quantity of *water* they ingest—call it q''—is $1 \cdot c_1(p,t)cc$. This observation suggests three ways to test Model Two.

The first way is to compute how much *salt* there is in every consumed quantity of test fluid—the q'-values—and then fit the function $p \cdot c_1(p,t)$ to the points (p,t,q').

The second way is to compute how much *water* there is in every consumed quantity of test fluid—the q''-values—and then fit the function $1 \cdot c_1(p,t)$ to the points (p,t,q'').

The third way is to use the given *test fluid* intake figures—the q-values—and fit the proper function to them. This is the most accurate method, because it requires no manipulation of the original data. But what is "the proper function"? Although test fluid consists of salt and water, q is not the sum of q' and q''. It cannot be: q' is measured in *cg* and q'' is measured in *cc*.

There is, fortunately, an easy answer. To be able to add quantities of salt to quantities of water, all we have to do is express them in the same unit. The preferred unit is the *cc,* since Weiner and Stellar measure test fluid that way. It goes as follows.

The specific gravity of salt is 2.16, meaning that the *weight* of 1*cc* of salt is 2.16*g,* or 216*cg*. Equivalently, the *volume* of 1*cg* of salt is (1/216)*cc.* The quantity of salt ingested, which has a *weight* of q' (*cg*) thus has a *volume* of $q'/216$ (*cc*). Adding the salt volume to the water volume gives the test fluid volume: $(q'/216) + q'' = q$. From $q' = p \cdot c_1$ and $q'' = 1 \cdot c_1$ now follows that $q = (1 + p/216)c_1$, with $c_1 = c_1(p,t)$ given by (1). The function to be fitted is thus

$$q(p,t) = (1 + p/216)\frac{(1 - e^{-\gamma t})(Ap + B) + t(Cp + D)}{Ep^2 + Fp + 1}. \tag{2}$$

Equation (2) expresses the cumulative demand for test fluid as a function of salt concentration and time.

A parenthetical note: although (2) could be written as

$$q(p,t) = \frac{(1 - e^{-\gamma t})Q_1 + tQ_2}{Q_o}, \tag{3}$$

it would be misleading to do so; for it might suggest that (3), and therefore

(2), is an example of the usual cumulative-response function, $F(p,t)$. It is not. If (3) were a representation of (2), we would be able to conclude that Q_1 and Q_2 have the factor $1 + p/216$ in common, which would probably be false. It would probably be false because the Q_1 and Q_2 appearing in the cumulative-response function have no common factor, at least not necessarily.

Equation (2) can be fitted to the observations by the least-squares method. This requires finding the parameter values that minimize the sum of squared residuals,

$$S_1 = \Sigma[q - q(p,t)]^2.$$

Calculus is no help here, but the computer is. The estimated (2) is found to be

$$q(p,t) = (1 + p/216)\frac{(1 - e^{-0.15t})(3.28p + 8.23) + t(0.00p + 0.07)}{1.08p^2 - 1.12p + 1}. \tag{4}$$

To see how well (4) fits the observations, define the goodness-of-fit measure $r^2 = 1 - S_1/S_2$, where S_2 is the "total variation," $\Sigma(q - q_{avg})^2$. One finds that $S_1 = 170.38$, $S_2 = 5151.67$, and $r^2 = 0.97$.

Of the seven coefficient estimates in (4), only 8.23 seems unusually large. To find out if there is an identifiable reason, we take $p = 0$, with an eye to isolating the offending coefficient. This leaves the flow $q(0,t) = (1 - e^{-0.15t})(8.23) + t0.07$. Differentiation with respect to t gives the flow rate $\dot{q}(0,t) = (0.15e^{-0.15t})(8.23) + 0.07$. Comparing now $\dot{q}(0,0) = (0.15)(8.23) + 0.07$ with $\dot{q}(0,\infty) = 0.07$, you see that the rats drink fast initially, but not eventually. The relatively large 8.23 thus reflects that the rats were thirsty at the beginning of the test period. No wonder—in the preceding six hours they had had nothing to drink.

In conclusion, a story of disappointment.

Equation (2) used that the specific gravity of salt is known. Suppose, however, that its value—call it g—is unknown. The number of unknown parameters then goes from seven to eight, g being the eighth. Naturally, we should be able to estimate not only the original seven parameters but also g. That is to say, it should be possible to estimate the specific gravity of salt by observing how much a rat will drink when given a salt-and-water mix of varying concentration.

It should be, but it was not. Or rather, the Weiner–Stellar data did yield an estimate $\hat{g}$, but it was as good as useless: it took only minuscule changes in the estimated coefficients of Q_1 and Q_2 to make $\hat{g}$ a hundred times as large, or a hundred times as small.

Disappointing though the outcome may be, it should not be allowed to obscure the message underneath. The message is that physical constants like g can in principle be found through experiments like Weiner and Stellar's. More generally, the natural and social sciences have a non-empty intersection.

Reference

Weiner, I. H., and Stellar, E. (1951). "Salt Preference of the Rat Determined by a Single-Stimulus Method." *Journal of Comparative and Physiological Psychology* **44,** 394–401.

11

Afterword

This chapter reviews, looks ahead, compares, contrasts, and ruminates.

Two models were discussed. Model One, concerning individual economic behavior, is an introductory theory, designed to span the gap between traditional economics and Model Two. Model Two, the main theory, concerns all individual behavior, and is thus of much greater scope. Both models are positive rather than normative.

Central to Model One are the motion law and the driver. Together, these two model ingredients determine how the endowment moves. The motion law depicts the agent as choosing not a bundle but a direction—the direction in which he wants his endowment to go. The driver is a vector embodying the exogenous influences that affect the endowment.

Like Model One, Model Two is governed by a motion law and a driver. The difference is that, this time, the two model ingredients determine the movements of the state of mind, rather than of the endowment. Except for interpretation, the motion law of Model Two is identical to that of Model One.

Model Two outperforms Model One in every way. Model One outperforms traditional theory in every way. For instance:

(*i*) Model One offers nine testable results. More precisely, Model One produces the short-response function, whose special cases include the consumer's and producer's demand and supply functions, both own-price and cross-price. Among the cross-price demand functions is the quasi-Engel function, which describes how the agent's demand for a good depends on the wage. (The Engel function in the traditional sense was found to be a misconception, for two reasons: first, it is not a function; second, its independent variable, income, is a monetary concept and so does not belong in the vocabulary of theory.) Encouragingly, all these special cases of the short-response function have graphs of the form that neoclassical theory says they ought to have. Even more encouraging is that at the moment when Model One introduced its motion law, neither the analytical form of these functions nor the shapes of their graphs could be anticipated.

Model Two generalizes the nine testable results, and adds a tenth. It manages to do so by choosing as its objective function a minimand, which it then specifies. Most of the testable results are special cases of the long-response function, $f(p, t)$, itself a generalization of the short-response function, $f(p,0)$. Model Two also finds that the effect of a sudden change wears off—is forgotten—at a negative-exponential rate, in agreement with longstanding belief.

(*ii*) Model One captures most individual economic behavior in one theory. Traditional economics, by contrast, offers several theories—a few for the producer, a few for the consumer-as-demander, and a separate theory for the consumer-as-supplier-of-labor-power. Model Two does still better: it captures most individual behavior, including behavior commonly viewed as noneconomic.

(*iii*) Models One and Two are dynamic, made so by the combination of motion law and driver. Continuous-time dynamic models are no novelty, of course. Some can be found in the older literature (Tintner, Klein, Koopmans); more recently, several have appeared in game theory and in the literature on adaptive economics. But most—perhaps all—of these theories have strong normative overtones, or are too hospitable to the Intrusive Agent, or both. Also most—perhaps all—of these theories are barren of testable results.

Worth noting is, further, that time does not appear in the objective functions of Models One and Two. This is a desideratum for all positive theories of behavior: a time-dependent objective function is an almost sure sign of normativity.

(*iv*) Model Two uses the state of mind as proxy for the living agent. Since the gap between the two is quite small, Model Two has no difficulty in concentrating on the proxy and keeping its animate owner out of the discussions. Model One manages to do the same, although not as easily. Traditional theory performs still worse: it fails to keep the Intrusive Agent out. More on this below.

(*v*) In both models, the motion law and the driver are defined so that the protagonist (Model One's endowment, Model Two's state of mind) always moves with finite speed. Neither model therefore has a need for stationary equilibrium. Both allow the agent to become richer, for example. Traditional utility theory is different. As was shown, traditional theory has the endowment move either not at all or with infinite speed. To put on the brakes and avoid explosive behavior, therefore, it must impose stationary equilibrium. Since actual behavior rarely if ever converges to stationarity (not counting death), Models One and Two substantially outperform traditional theory in this respect.

(*vi*) Models One and Two define all their terms mathematically. Not surprisingly then—and underscoring the essential simplicity of the behavioral mechanism—both theories have very small vocabularies. Some examples of terms found in traditional theory but not in Models One and Two: *consumer* and *producer,* both left out for lack of definition; *price,* which was replaced with "basic action element"; *money,* found to be an ordinary commodity and therefore not a theoretical notion; monetary concepts like *income, revenue, profit,* and *cost,* all of which are merely flow rates; and all *cognitive terms.* Cognitive terms were left out in part because they appear to be mathematically undefinable and in part because they tend to summon the Intrusive Agent.

Also absent from both vocabularies are all institutional notions. Of course, institutions affect the driver and so influence what the agent does; but they do not affect the mathematical structure of behavior. Physics offers a parallel: the sun affects the earth's path, but not the laws of gravity.

As few traditional notions as Model One has, Model Two has even fewer. In fact, Model Two begins with only two (endowment, commodity stock), then replaces "endowment" with "surround" and "commodity stock" with "aspect," and so winds up with no familiar economic terms at all. In the course of the book, therefore, we have been drifting steadily away from the traditional economic idiom.

If that seems undesirable, consider the benefits. Accompanying the disappearance of familiar terms has been the appearance of usable, testable results, many of them the object of decades or even centuries of largely fruitless search. It is hard to escape the conclusion that economic theories of individual behavior have been hampered in their development by their own language. It is equally hard to avoid the suspicion that the same is true for economic theory in general.

Model Two still needs a good bit of work. Perhaps its biggest weakness is the assumption of perfect divisibility, which is too hard on the intuition. To illustrate the point, compare a student who has one beer every day with a student who drinks 365 beers every January 1 and none at other times. Model Two cannot tell the two apart. It depicts both as drinking a steady trickle of beer, every second. Another example: as observed in the answer to Question 3 of Chapter 7, an agent living in a perfectly divisible world will undertake, during his lifetime, very few actions, possibly just one action. (If it were not for its period-analytical approach, neoclassical theory would reach the same conclusion.)

Allowing divisibility to be imperfect can be expected to produce additional testable results. But even if that were to prove false, benefits should still be substantial. Since imperfect divisibility is standard in the real world, many questions of interest to economists, and to social scientists in general, presume imperfect divisibility in their formulation. If Model Two were to assume imperfect divisibility, it should be able to handle such questions.

At present it cannot. (Neoclassical theory cannot handle them either, since it too is based on perfect divisibility; but because of its greater informality, it at least *appears* to have some of the answers. The economics of uncertainty offers a case in point, at least to the extent that it it a positive theory.)

Another weakness of Model Two is that it says nothing about learning, and very little about how the agent processes information. According to the theory, information reaches the agent as part of his $d\mathbf{b}$, and is next transformed into $d\boldsymbol{\beta}$. Perhaps so. But what if the agent hears a piece of information, and an hour later hears it again? The second message presumably has less effect than the first, but there is nothing in Model Two, as it now stands, to reflect that. Or take a tourist who visits a city he has not seen before. His first day will be full of new impressions. His second day will be full of old hat. According to Model Two, however, the two days affect him the same way. One solution to the dilemma is to stipulate that the register values—the $\xi_i(t)$—be finite, so that incoming information is deposited in registers only if they are not yet full; but that would require a complete overhaul of Model Two.

In comparing the performances of Models One and Two with standard theories of individual economic behavior, you may want to keep in mind that those standard theories do not perform quite so well as is commonly believed. The following three arguments are offered in support of this assertion.

First, the standard theories, which for present purposes are taken to be utility theory, the theory of the producer, and the theory of labor supply, are neither mutually exclusive nor exhaustive in their theoretical coverage. Nor are they well integrated. Hicksian utility theory, for instance, cannot handle supply and deals with the attendant difficulties by, among other things, stipulating that money is a noncommodity; but the theory of labor supply, although designed to resolve at least part of the problem, contradicts this by declaring money to be a carrier of utility.

Second, since the traditional consumer has no driver to spur him on, he rarely does anything. In fact, the only time he acts is when there is a change is the value of some parameter, in which case he adjusts his endowment instantaneously. Except for those moments, he does nothing at all. What causes this unrealistic behavior is that he is a utility-maximizing robot, and as such is incapable of changing his endowment so long as it maximizes utility. It follows that when neoclassical theory describes the consumer as buying and selling and working, it is not talking about its robot-consumer, the one with the utility function. Instead, it is talking about a living being—the Intrusive Agent. Small wonder then that the neoclassical picture of the consumer and his behavior seems so realistic. The never-shown true picture, which displays the behavior of the robot-consumer rather than the living one, does not look realistic at all.

A third imperfection of traditional theory is that it divides the time axis in periods but does not specify the period length. As a result, assertions like "The consumer buys two quarts of milk during the period" have no operational content. And this is not the only problem. According to period analysis, the endowment at the end of each period differs from that at the beginning of the next period. (Were this not so, there would be no need for period analysis.) The endowment's time path thus has discontinuities at every point where two periods meet. Those discontinuities have no counterpart in the real world.

Finally, a few examples to give you some idea of the practical, applicable side of Model Two.

Suppose you are the President of the United States and you wish to raise taxes. The time to do so is right after your election: since the effects of a traumatic event wear off at a negative-exponential rate, the voters are less likely to be still incensed by the time the next election comes around.

Or suppose you are a businessman. You may be able to use your knowledge of the theory to organize, interpret, and exploit information that you receive—information about, say, the short- or long-response function of a competitor or an important customer. Of course, observations made in an uncontrolled setting are not likely to give you enough information to compute anything as detailed as a response function's parameter values. But with luck, even vague and unspecific information can be useful. It might lead to, for instance, rough interval estimates of those parameter values.

Or suppose you are concerned about overpopulation and want to persuade people to have fewer babies. An economist's approach might be to raise prices—of diapers, say, or of baby food. A politician's approach would depend on where he lives. If he lives in a democracy, he might advocate tax increases—so much for the first child, so much for the second. Under an authoritarian regime, he would more likely propose that large families be outlawed and transgressors tossed in jail. Which way is best? Model Two offers a systematic way to go about the issue: if we want people to do anything, we must manipulate their $d\mathbf{b}$'s. Raising prices is a form of such manipulation. So is imposition of taxes. So is threatening with imprisonment. But there may be other, more efficacious ways, and it may not even occur to us to look for those *unless* we recognize $d\mathbf{b}$ as the crucial access road to people's minds.

A recent flier from Population Communications International (PCI), a United Nations affiliate, drives the point home. Seeking to halt the runaway growth of human population, PCI began, some years ago, to work with radio and television officials in several countries to produce soap operas with family-planning themes. According to PCI, the programs motivate audiences to have fewer children. In Mexico, Brazil, and Kenya, for example, fertility rates dropped between 24 and 34 percent when the soap operas were broadcast. Although PCI is careful not to claim a causal connection, its data strongly suggest that there is one. Which, in view of Model Two, is plausible: manipulating *d***b**'s, as those soap operas did, can be expected to have an effect.

There are other, similar examples. Advertising manipulates *d***b**. So does brainwashing. So does TV news. Journalists like to say that they do not make the news—they just report it. Model Two has little sympathy for this claim. To report the news is to manipulate the *d***b**'s of readers and viewers, and a manipulator is no idle bystander. It is well known, for example, that newspaper reports of suicides trigger more suicides. Conversely, when newspapers stop printing news about suicides—as they agreed to do in the Netherlands, many years ago—the number of suicides drops markedly. In the same way, Model Two implies that violence in movies affects the moviegoer. Model Two does not say, however, that violence begets violence—merely that it has an effect. As far as Model Two is concerned, violence may just as well beget antiviolence.

ANSWERS

CHAPTER 1

1. The function is $q = (p + 1)/(p^2 + p + 1)$. Elementary calculus shows that $p = 0$ is a maximizer and $p = -2$ is a minimizer. The maximum is 1; the minimum is $-1/3$. Letting p go to $+\infty$ and $-\infty$ shows the p-axis to be a horizontal asymptote. See Figure 1. Since the domain is limited to $p \geq 0$, everything to the left of the vertical axis is irrelevant.
2. You find that $B = 4/3$, $C = 2/3$, $D = 4/3$, and $E = 0$. For a graph, move the vertical axis in Figure 1 to the point $p = -\frac{1}{2}$, and then make that point the origin of the p-axis.
3. A matter of definition. A plausible approach is to regard inactivity as leaving the endowment unchanged. If the endowment is $\mathbf{x}$ before the inactivity begins and $\mathbf{x}$ when it ends, inactivity is reasonably defined as $\mathbf{x} - \mathbf{x} = \mathbf{0}$. Inactivity is then the difference of two endowments, and that makes it an action.
4. When units of measurement are ignored, John's initial endowment is the point (2, 5); his action is the vector $(1, -1)'$, where the prime signifies transposition; and the endowment resulting from his action is the point $(2 + 1, 5 - 1) = (3, 4)$. Altogether then, $(2, 5) + (1, -1)' = (3, 4)$. Taking measurement units into account (b for bottle, d for dollar), the equation becomes $(2b, 5d) + (1b, -1d)' = (3b, 4d)$.
5. This book's answer is given only in Chapter 5, but you may want to give it some thought now, and argue your opinion.
6. A midsize supermarket carries about 20,000 products. If a midsize supermarket is where you shop, a basket is a list of 20,000 quantities. Before you can *rank* all the market baskets that you can afford, you have to find out *which* baskets you can afford. This means that you must first find out the prices of all 20,000

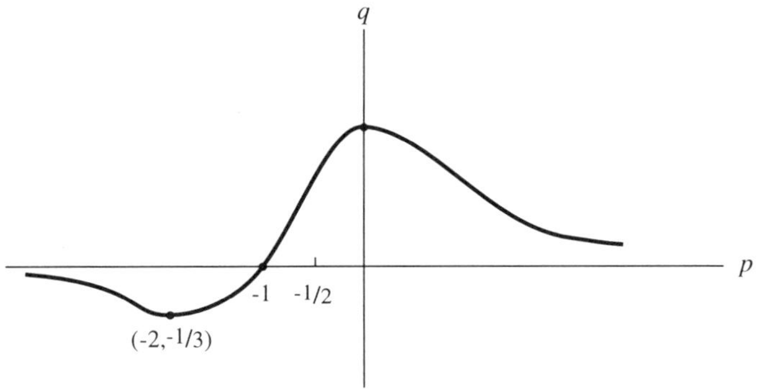

Figure 1

products (bring pencil and paper); next you must compute all affordable baskets (bring a calculator); finally, you must rank those baskets (bring lunch). None of this comes even close to what happens in the real world. If the thesis nevertheless seems plausible it is because we tend to think of flesh-and-blood consumers as decision makers. The consumer of theory, however, is not made of flesh and blood, and does not decide anything. He simply follows the dictates of theory. And theory equips him with neither the ability nor the need to rank baskets.

7. In this book, consuming a good is virtually the opposite of buying that good. Buying is an action. Actions produce and consume; they produce when they add to stocks and consume when they take away from stocks. Since buying adds to stocks, buying is producing.
8. Arguably, normative microeconomics is about decision making. Positive microeconomics is not.
9. Possibly true for normative microeconomics, false for positive microeconomics.
10. False. Market exchange predates property rights. Property rights make market exchange go more smoothly, but that is all.
11. The formal meaning of "Consumer Jones is indifferent between bundles $\mathbf{x}$ and $\mathbf{y}$" is $u(\mathbf{x}) = u(\mathbf{y})$. Satisfaction is an undefined term, not a theoretical notion.
12. We like to think of our actions as sometimes voluntary, sometimes involuntary; but the fact is, in the end we undertake them all. Absent a formal definition of free will (or an equivalent cognitive notion), the distinction between voluntary and involuntary actions is specious.

CHAPTER 2

1. $1/h$.
2. $e^{at} = 1 + at + \frac{1}{2}a^2t^2 + \cdots$. If a is measured in $1/h$, each term on the right is real, and so the entire right side is well defined and real. If a is not measured in $1/h$ (and t is measured in h), the right side is undefined.
3. Notation suggests that t is measured in units of time, but this is misleading; 3^t is defined only if t is real.
4. The function exists only if p is real; everything else leads quickly to contradiction. Multiplying two functions of the type described does not, as a rule, lead to a function of the type described. It follows that S is not a set with multiplication. But S is a set with addition and multiplication. This makes S a vector space.
5. They are different. For one thing, you cannot add (3 lbs., 4 gal.)′ to (2 gal., 7 lbs.)′.
6. One.
7. The null vector.
8. $\mathbf{A} + \mathbf{B}$ and $\mathbf{AB}'$ are, and the others are not.
9. Matrices don't have solutions.
10. You cannot multiply points by scalars (like c and $1 - c$), so $\mathbf{x}_1$ and $\mathbf{x}_2$ must be vectors. (Alternatively, you can regard $\mathbf{x}_1$ and $\mathbf{x}_2$ as points, and combine that with an agreement that $(1 - c)\mathbf{x}_1 + c\mathbf{x}_2$ is to be interpreted as meaning $\mathbf{x}_1 + c(\mathbf{x}_2 - \mathbf{x}_1)$. This is the traditional approach.)
11. $\mathbf{q}_1 + \frac{1}{2}(\mathbf{q}_2 - \mathbf{q}_1)$. This is of the form point + vector, and so represents a point. (But see the parenthetical remark in the answer to Question 10.)
12. $\mathbf{x}_1 + 1/n(\mathbf{x}_2 - \mathbf{x}_1) + 1/n(\mathbf{x}_3 - \mathbf{x}_1) + \ldots + 1/n(\mathbf{x}_n - \mathbf{x}_1)$. (But see the parenthetical remark in the answer to Question 10.)
13. False. You *set* $\mathbf{Ac} = \mathbf{0}$ (and then you count solutions).
14. The first two parts are true. The third one is absurd: $\mathbf{Ac} = \mathbf{0}$ *always* has a solution. (Or: every homogenous system is consistent.)
15. The columns of a low matrix, like $\mathbf{A}$, are always linearly dependent. Of the three inverses, only $(\mathbf{AA}')^{-1}$ exists. $\text{Det}(\mathbf{A}'\mathbf{A}) = 0$.
16. The columns of $\mathbf{A}$ have two elements each. They therefore belong to R^2, and so they certainly cannot form a basis for R^3. Since every basis for R^2 has two vectors in it, the columns of $\mathbf{A}$ do not form a basis for R^2 either. The two columns of $\mathbf{A}'$ have three elements each.

They thus belong to R^3. But they do not form a basis for R^3, because every basis for R^3 needs three vectors. (Since the two columns of $\mathbf{A}'$ are linearly independent, they do form a basis for a plane P, planes being two-dimensional. If you conjure up a picture, you'll see that P is a plane in R^3, containing the origin of R^3. Put differently, P is a two-dimensional subspace of R^3.)

17. Basis matrix,

$$\mathbf{A} = \begin{pmatrix} 1b & 0b \\ 0c & 1c \end{pmatrix}.$$

Dual-basis matrix,

$$\mathbf{A}^0 = \begin{pmatrix} 1/b & 0/b \\ 0/c & 1/c \end{pmatrix}.$$

18. $\mathbf{C}'\mathbf{B}'\mathbf{A}'$. $\mathbf{c}'\mathbf{B}'\mathbf{a}$. Every 1×1 matrix is symmetric.
19. The transpose is $\mathbf{V}^0\mathbf{K}'\mathbf{V}^{0\prime}$. Since $\mathbf{K}' = \mathbf{K}$, this equals $\mathbf{V}^0\mathbf{K}\mathbf{V}^{0\prime}$.
20. The diagonal elements of $\mathbf{I}$ are dimensionless ones. The off-diagonal elements are $0(c/b)$ (first row) and $0(b/c)$ (second row).
21. Nonsense question; $\mathbf{Ha}$ and $\mathbf{Hb}$ do not belong to V.
22. The elements are dimensioned like those of $\mathbf{H}$ in Question 20. If nonsingular, the Hessian matrix can serve as an inner-product matrix. Of course, it means that the inner product of two given vectors will vary from point to point, unless u is quadratic.
23. No, they belong to different spaces.
24. $\mathbf{x}$ can be any scalar multiple of $\mathbf{H}^{-1}\mathbf{b}$.
25. $(\mathbf{Ac}_1, \mathbf{Ac}_2, \mathbf{Ac}_3) = \mathbf{A}(\mathbf{c}_1, \mathbf{c}_2, \mathbf{c}_3) = \mathbf{AC}$. To be shown is that every linear combination of the columns of $\mathbf{AC}$ is a linear combination of the columns of $\mathbf{A}$, and vice versa.

    Every linear combination of the columns of $\mathbf{AC}$ has the form $\mathbf{AC}\boldsymbol{\mu}$ for some $\boldsymbol{\mu}$. This is a linear combination of the columns of $\mathbf{A}$, as you can see by writing $\mathbf{AC}\boldsymbol{\mu}$ as $\mathbf{A}(\mathbf{C}\boldsymbol{\mu})$.

    Every linear combination of the columns of $\mathbf{A}$ has the form $\mathbf{A}\boldsymbol{\nu}$ for some $\boldsymbol{\nu}$. This is a linear combination of the columns of $\mathbf{AC}$, as you can see by writing $\mathbf{A}\boldsymbol{\nu}$ as $\mathbf{AC}(\mathbf{C}^{-1}\boldsymbol{\nu})$. (The linear independence of the $\mathbf{c}_i$ ensures that $\mathbf{C}$ is nonsingular.) P.O.C.

    For a more intuitive argument, consider that performing column operations on $\mathbf{A}$ is equivalent to postmultiplying $\mathbf{A}$ by a nonsingular matrix (like $\mathbf{C}$). Performing column operations on $\mathbf{A}$ does not affect the linear span of the $\mathbf{a}_i$, any more than performing row operations on a system of equations affects the solutions of the system.

26. Since the equality holds for all $\mathbf{v}$ in R^3, it holds, in particular, for $\mathbf{v} = \mathbf{e}_1 = (1,0,0)'$, for $\mathbf{v} = \mathbf{e}_2 = (0,1,0)'$, and for $\mathbf{v} = \mathbf{e}_3 = (0,0,1)'$. Thus, $\mathbf{Pe}_i = \mathbf{A}(\mathbf{A}'\mathbf{A})^{-1}\ \mathbf{A}'\mathbf{e}_i$ for $i = 1, 2, 3$. Now if $\mathbf{M}$ is any matrix, $\mathbf{Me}_i$ is the ith column of $\mathbf{M}$. It follows that $\mathbf{P}$ and $\mathbf{A}(\mathbf{A}'\mathbf{A})^{-1}\mathbf{A}'$ have the same ith column, $i = 1, 2, 3$.

    The result would not hold if it were merely given that $\mathbf{Pv} = \mathbf{A}(\mathbf{A}'\mathbf{A})^{-1}\mathbf{A}'\mathbf{v}$ for *some* $\mathbf{v}$.

27. First do a column operation on $\mathbf{A}$: replace the first column with itself minus the second column. The resulting matrix is $\mathbf{B}$, say:

$$\mathbf{B} = \begin{pmatrix} 1 & 0 \\ 0 & 2 \\ 0 & 3 \end{pmatrix}.$$

    The columns of $\mathbf{B}$ span the same plane as do the columns of $\mathbf{A}$, so that $\mathbf{A}(\mathbf{A}'\mathbf{A})^{-1}\mathbf{A}' = \mathbf{B}(\mathbf{B}'\mathbf{B})^{-1}\mathbf{B}'$; but $\mathbf{B}(\mathbf{B}'\mathbf{B})^{-1}\mathbf{B}'$ is a lot easier to calculate than $\mathbf{A}(\mathbf{A}'\mathbf{A})^{-1}\mathbf{A}'$. You find that

$$\mathbf{B}(\mathbf{B}'\mathbf{B})^{-1}\mathbf{B}' = \frac{1}{13}\begin{pmatrix} 1 & 0 & 0 \\ 0 & 4 & 6 \\ 0 & 6 & 9 \end{pmatrix}.$$

28. The three vectors are linearly independent; therefore, $\mathbf{A}(\mathbf{A}'\mathbf{A})^{-1}\mathbf{A}' = \mathbf{I}$.
29. $(-2xe^{1-x^2-y^2}, -2ye^{1-x^2-y^2})'$.
30. $-(2/5)(3x + 4y)e^{1-x^2-y^2}$; $-4e^{-4}$.
31. Multiply $\mathbf{v}$ by $1/\|\mathbf{v}\|$. This is allowed, for $\|\mathbf{v}\|$ is a scalar, and so $1/\|\mathbf{v}\|$ is too. The result is a unit vector with the same direction as $\mathbf{v}$. The desired definition is now

$$D_{\mathbf{v}}u(\mathbf{x}) = \frac{\mathbf{v}'\nabla u(\mathbf{x})}{\|\mathbf{v}\|}.$$

32. $f(\mathbf{x} + h\mathbf{v}) = f(\mathbf{x}) + D_{\mathbf{v}}f(\mathbf{x}) + 1/2!\, D_{\mathbf{v}}D_{\mathbf{v}}f(\mathbf{x}) + 1/3!\, D_{\mathbf{v}}D_{\mathbf{v}}D_{\mathbf{v}}f(\mathbf{x}) + \cdots$.
33. $(-4e^{-4}, -2e^{-4})'$.
34. $b = -5$. The constraining line—call it L—is spanned by $\mathbf{a} = (1, 3)'$. Projection onto L is represented by

$$\mathbf{P} = \mathbf{a}(\mathbf{a}'\mathbf{a})^{-1}\mathbf{a}' = \frac{1}{10}\begin{pmatrix} 1 & 3 \\ 3 & 9 \end{pmatrix}.$$

    Let the given function be $f(x,y)$. The steepest constrained ascent is $\mathbf{P}\nabla f = (-e^{-4}, -3e^{-4})'$.

35. (You may find it helpful to view the contour surface $u(\mathbf{x}) = u(\mathbf{x}_o)$ as an indifference surface.) Abbreviate $\nabla u(\mathbf{x}_o)$ to ∇u. From $u(\mathbf{x}) = u(\mathbf{x}_o) + (\mathbf{x} - \mathbf{x}_o)'\nabla u + \cdots$ (Taylor) follows that the plane touching the surface $u(\mathbf{x}) = u(\mathbf{x}_o)$ at $\mathbf{x}_o$ is given by $(\mathbf{x} - \mathbf{x}_o)'\nabla u = 0$. To be shown is that $\mathbf{PH}^{-1}\nabla u$ is orthogonal to the intersection of the planes $\mathbf{x} = \mathbf{x}_o + \mathbf{Ac}$ and $(\mathbf{x} - \mathbf{x}_o)'\nabla u = 0$. That intersection, which is a line, is given by $\mathbf{x} = \mathbf{x}_o + \mathbf{Ac}^*$, say, with $\mathbf{c}^*$ satisfying $\mathbf{c}^{*\prime}\mathbf{A}'\nabla u = 0$ (or else the line won't lie in $(\mathbf{x} - \mathbf{x}_o)'\nabla u = 0$). To be shown is thus that $\mathbf{Ac}^*$ is orthogonal to $\mathbf{PH}^{-1}\nabla u$, or $\mathbf{c}^{*\prime}\mathbf{A}'\mathbf{H}(\mathbf{PH}^{-1}\nabla u) = 0$ for all $\mathbf{c}^*$ satisfying $\mathbf{c}^{*\prime}\mathbf{A}'\nabla u = 0$. Writing $\mathbf{P}$ as $\mathbf{A}(\mathbf{A}'\mathbf{HA})^{-1}\mathbf{A}'\mathbf{H}$ furnishes the proof.

    If the two planes coincide, their intersection is not a line but a plane. In this case, the vector $\mathbf{PH}^{-1}\nabla u$ both lies in the plane spanned by the columns of $\mathbf{A}$ and is orthogonal to that plane. That can happen only if $\mathbf{PH}^{-1}\nabla u = 0$.

    Note. Imagine a two-dimensional diagram showing an indifference curve and a point $\mathbf{x}_o$ on it. At $\mathbf{x}_o$ the indifference curve has a certain slope. You can characterize that slope (*i*) directly, as dx_2/dx_1; (*ii*) somewhat indirectly, as minus the MRS of good 1 for good 2; and (*iii*) indirectly, by describing the direction of ∇u. The indirect way might be called the umbrella method: you described the tilt of the umbrella's canopy by describing the direction in which the handle points.

    Imagine next a three-dimensional diagram, with an indifference surface and a point $\mathbf{x}_o$ on it. At $\mathbf{x}_o$, the indifference surface has a certain tilt, a certain slant. You can characterize that slant (*i*) directly, by listing dx_3/dx_1 and dx_3/dx_2, assuming both exist; (*ii*) somewhat indirectly, by using the MRS of good 1 for good 3 and the MRS of good 2 for good 3—that is to say, $|dx_3/dx_1|$ and $|dx_3/dx_2|$—assuming both exist; and (*iii*) indirectly, by describing the direction of ∇u.

    If there are n goods, you can characterize the slant of an indifference hypersurface (*i*) directly, by listing $n - 1$ differential quotients, assuming they all exist; (*ii*) somewhat indirectly, by listing $n - 1$ marginal rates of substitution, assuming they all exist; and (*iii*) indirectly, by describing one ∇u. The choice seems clear.

37. A *circle* is not a convex set. The *disks* $x^2 + y^2 \leq 1$ and $x^2 + y^2 < 1$ are convex, but that is a different matter.

CHAPTER 3

1. The Bright Puzzle Piece Fallacy.
2. The premise contradicts itself. Being a profit maximizer, the producer is already making the biggest possible profit, by definition. Doubling output thus will not increase profit.

3. It is a purely mathematical assumption, meaning that the utility function is independent of time.
4. All other uses of his land consist of planting θ acres ($0 \le \theta < 1$) with wheat and $1 - \theta$ acres with corn. Given what he is doing now, the next-best option is to let θ be the largest number less than 1. Since no such number exists, opportunity cost is undefined, at least in theory. In the real world, divisibility is not perfect; there, the next-best option is to plant one ear of corn and for the rest wheat. The opportunity cost is then a fraction below $800.
5. See Part II.
6. He will not. To make him drink, the theory needs an extra ingredient. See Part II.
7. If $n_1 = n_2 = 1000$, no utility maximizer will migrate. If $n_1 \neq n_2$, everyone shuttles back and forth between the two cities, and does so infinitely often in every arbitrarily small time interval. Equilibrium cannot be attained; it has to be there from the start. And there had better be not a single birth or death. Note that the Polykeynesians would behave more realistically if they were not all identical.

CHAPTER 4

1. Neither. A steak is not an endowment; nor is it a demanded bundle. There is thus no such thing as the utility of a steak.
2. The Hicksian consumer lives in a world in which commodities are perfectly divisible. He thus buys a fraction of the CD and a fraction of the book.
3. That eating too much ice cream makes you sick has nothing to do with utility. Utility is a function of endowments or demanded bundles, not of quantities eaten. Nor is utility another word for pleasure, gastronomic or otherwise.
4. Discussed in the next chapter.
5. Suppose u is real-valued. Let goods 1 and 2 be beer, measured in bottles (b), and tuna, measured in cans (c). The marginal utility of beer is then measured in $1/b$, and its marginal utility per dollar d is measured in $1/bd$. Arguing the same way for tuna, you find that its marginal utility per dollar is measured in $1/cd$. The marginal utilities per dollar thus cannot be equal. The Equimarginal Principle remains valid, of course. It is its description in terms of marginal utilities per dollar that is wrong.

6. The Equimarginal Principle says that, in equilibrium, marginal utilities are proportional to prices. Since all prices are positive, all marginal utilities must have the same sign. Nothing is lost by taking that sign to be positive.

   (That more is better than less is not the reason that marginal utilities are specified as positive. It is the *interpretation* of the positivity.)

7. Let "buying a bottle of beer" be **a**. A slide along the budget line is a slide in the direction of **a**. In that direction, the derivative of the utility function is $D_{\mathbf{a}}u = \mathbf{a}'\nabla u/\|\mathbf{a}\|$. The consumer loves beer, meaning $\mathbf{a}'\nabla u$ is positive at first. The slide comes to a halt when $\mathbf{a}'\nabla u$ is zero. It is thus $D_{\mathbf{a}}u$ that diminishes, not $D_{\mathbf{e}_1}u$.

8. In the Hicksian world, money is not a good, and so should not be on the vertical axis. Besides, it is hard to see how the points in the diagram might represent demanded bundles.

9. If it seems that the consumer is ultimately a demander, it is because Hicksian theory depicts him that way. (Being unable to deal with supply, Hicksian theory has no choice.) You could indeed argue that everything the consumer does has but one purpose, but it is not consumption. It is utility maximization.

   The idea that the consumer is ultimately a demander is a cousin of the idea that there are such things as final goods (in addition to primary goods and intermediate goods). The thought behind these notions is that life is a sequence of tasks, each with a well-defined end; once a task is done, we begin the next one. According to this view, the time axis is divided into a sequence of periods, one for each task. But such a subdivision is too arbitrary. It goes against the Principle of Least Astonishment. This is why Model One leaves the time axis unpartitioned and treats individual behavior as a journey without stops, without milestones, without an "ultimate goal." This is also why Model One makes no room for primary goods, intermediate goods, and final goods.

10. The distinction between consumers and producers is a theoretical issue. Theoretical issues should be settled on theoretical grounds. Any appeal to a legal notion like ownership is wholly beside the point. It is similar to the Scientist's having trouble defining "industry" and calling the Internal Revenue Service for help.

11. The argument confuses utility with usefulness and is thus wrong; but its conclusion may be right. Whether it is depends on the definition of "characteristics." If a characteristic is a point, Pareto's model applies with only a change in interpretation. If a characteristic is a

nonnegative vector, Hicks's model applies with only a change in interpretation. If a characteristic is neither a point nor a nonnegative vector, it may be possible to build a new model on it.

12. Most economists would probably regard money as an input. The profit-maximizing producer maximizes the inflow of that input. Since he does not maximize the inflow of any other input, like capital or labor, the asymmetry is obvious. The conclusion is not affected if you regard money as part of capital.
13. Apart from the obvious confusion of utility with usefulness, this is merely a rewording of the argument that money is wanted not for its own sake but for what it can buy.
14. Not true; utility theory is not asked to offer an explanation of why people have milk in their refrigerators, either. (And if asked, it would not give one. Theories describe; they do not explain.)
15. One of the functions of a car is to transport its owner from A to B. One of the functions of the telephone is to pass along information. One of the functions of orange juice is to quench thirst. One of the functions of money is to serve as a medium of exchange. If we find it acceptable that Pareto's theory ignores the functions of cars, telephones, and orange juice, we should find it acceptable that it ignores the functions of money.

    As for the uselessness of Pareto's theory when it comes to explaining such things as the properties of the demand for money and the process of monetization of an economy, this is as it should be. Theories describe; they do not explain.
16. The "therefore" is misplaced. Describing and analyzing the role of money is a technical task, just as describing and analyzing the role of cars is a technical task. The latter is probably best left to an engineer, the former to a banker. But determining the right theoretical treatment of money calls for different skills. The right theoretical treatment is based on the right definition—the right mathematical definition—of money, and that makes it the economic theorist's province.

    The fictitious quotes in Questions 15 and 16 present a theoretical issue as if it were a practical one. But those are very different things. A theorist who seeks to define money needs a bit of logic, a bit of theory, a bit of methodology; but he does not have to know how a bank works. Some physicists know everything about electricity but cannot find the fuse box.
17. It is true that if the money supply were suddenly doubled, every dollar would just as suddenly be worth less: you, the car buyer, would have to give up more dollars to buy a car. But it is also true that if

the stock of cars were doubled, car sellers would have to lower their prices to sell the sudden flood. It means that every car is now worth less: you, the car seller (and money buyer), must give up more car to buy a dollar. The statement in quotes is thus wrong.

18. To see what the argument is worth, consider the following parallel: "Imagine an economy in which everyone communicates telepathically. Such an economy has no justifiable use for telephones; but it does have as much use for commodities as the kind of economy in which we live. It follows that telephones are not a commodity."
19. The conclusion that money is different from commodities does not follow. What does follow is that money makes certain actions go more smoothly. Money is thus well-equipped to perform a certain task. The same can be said for just about every commodity.

    It is, incidentally, not always true that barter transactions involve substantially higher costs than do trades in which commodities are exchanged for money. If that were so, barter would be a bit of a rarity. But I remember reading, several years ago, that barter accounts for as much as 40% of world trade.
20. Circular. Besides, the statement mistakes a theoretical issue for a practical one. From a theoretical point of view, the sole reason for selecting a numeraire is mathematical: it normalizes the price vector, by setting one of its elements equal to 1.

    Model One is formulated without reference to prices. After this chapter, therefore, the selection of the right numeraire is academic.
21. This is another attempt at basing a theoretical definition of money on the role of money in the real world. Apart from that, the statement is false: if the unit of account is a pound of salt, then the value of a pound of salt, expressed in terms of the unit of account, is fixed—it will always be a pound of salt (Assuming that this is the right interpretation of the antiquated and undefined term "value").
22. Confuses utility with usefulness. Besides, whether money is a commodity is a theoretical issue; it cannot be settled by something as concrete as the observation that people hold cash.
23. True, but do not despair. One day it will be.

CHAPTER 5

1. See Figure 2, below.
2. Let ϵ be the p-elasticity of the demand rate for beer. To be shown is that $-1 < \epsilon < 0$. Since pq increases, $d(pq)/dp > 0$ or $q + p(dq/dp) > 0$. Division by q gives $1 + \epsilon > 0$, etc.

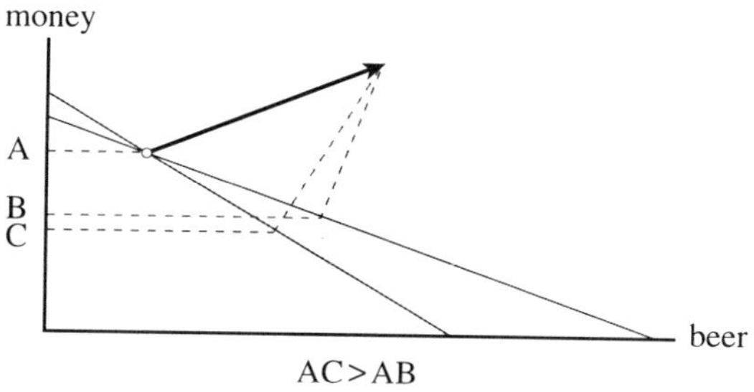

Figure 2

3. The definition of ϵ is $(p/q)(dq/dp)$, not $(p/q)(\Delta q/\Delta p)$.
4. The extremizers are $p = 1$ and $p = 3$. The extrema are $g(1) = 1$ and $g(3) = 7/3$. The horizontal asymptote is given by $g(p) = 2$. There are no zeros. See Figure 3.
5. It is easy to verify the handy formula

$$\frac{d}{dp}\left(\frac{Ap^2 + Bp + C}{Dp^2 + Ep + F}\right) = \frac{1}{(Dp^2 + Ep + F)^2}\begin{vmatrix} A & B & C \\ D & E & F \\ 1 & -2p & p^2 \end{vmatrix}.$$

Expanding the determinant with respect to the third row gives

$$p^2(AE - BD) + 2p(AF - CD) + (BF - CE). \qquad (*)$$

This quadratic form has at most two zeros, unless $AE - BD = AF - CD$

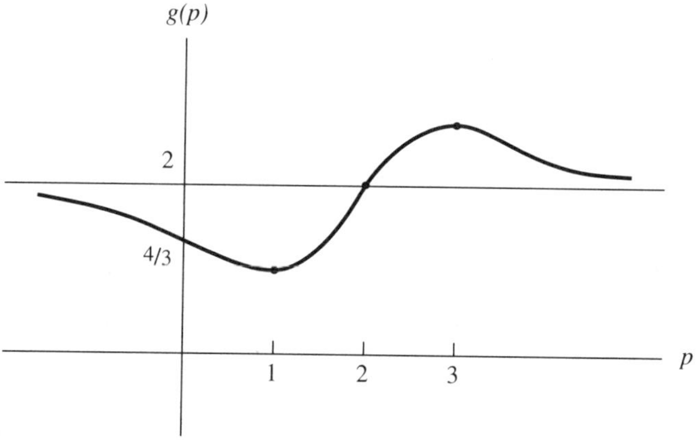

Figure 3

$= BF - CE = 0$. In this last case, g is constant, so that g has a unique extremum and infinitely many extremizers (namely, every value of p), and, if $g \equiv 0$, infinitely many zeros.

Because its denominator is positive definite, g is continuous everywhere. The continuity implies that if g has two extrema, they cannot be both maxima, nor both minima.

6. Being a demand function, $f(p)$ must be positive for all $p \geq 0$. Since the denominator is positive definite, this means $Bp + C > 0$ for all $p \geq 0$. Taking $p = 0$ gives $C > 0$; taking p large gives $B > 0$. Further, if the demand curve is to bend backward, $f'(0)$ must be positive. By (*), in the answer to the preceding question, this means $B - CE > 0$.
7. The limit of $f(p)$ is $0/D = 0$. The limit of $pf(p)$ is B/D.
8. Since $pf(p)$ converges to constancy (Question 7), ϵ goes to -1. The p-elasticity of the expenditure rate for beer, being $1 + \epsilon$, goes to 0.
9. The function $pf(p) = (Bp^2 + Cp)/(Dp^2 + Ep + 1)$—call it $h(p)$—is not the own-price supply function of money. It is a cross-price supply function, for p is the price of beer (in terms of money), not the price of money (in terms of beer). The price of money (in terms of beer) is $1/p$. The own-price supply function of money is thus $h(1/p) = (Cp + B)/(p^2 + Ep + D)$, which is indeed the quotient of a linear numerator and a quadratic denominator.
10. Let $\mathbf{H}^{-1} = (k_{ij})$. You find that $B = \gamma(k_{12}u_1 - k_{11}u_2)$, which can be positive. Without units, $\mathbf{H}^{-1} = \mathbf{I}$ and $B = -\gamma u_2$, which is negative.
11. γ is not a real number. It is a real multiple of $1/t$.
12. It is integration that has been done, not unification. When you integrate, you accept that there are two theories, and ensure that they do not contradict each other. When you unify, you reject the existence of two theories, and instead construct a single theory.
13. A living being has no utility function. The consumer-robot of theory does, but he does not talk to academics.

CHAPTER 6

1. The Scientist has the freedom to construct his world as he sees fit. The idea that reality determines the driver would occur only to the Visitor.
2. The solutions $\mathbf{p}$ of $\mathbf{A}'\mathbf{p} = \mathbf{0}$ are the vectors of the form $\lambda(-1, 7, 4)'$, with λ nonzero. If $\lambda > 0$, p_1 is negative. If $\lambda < 0$, p_2 and p_3 are negative.
3. False. $\mathbf{A}$ meets Definition 1.
4. There are infinitely many such actions. One of them is $2\mathbf{a}_1 + 3\mathbf{a}_2 = (11, 1, 1)'$.

5. Let the two actions be the columns of $\mathbf{A}$, set $\mathbf{Ac} = \mathbf{0}$, and solve. Actually, solving is not strictly needed. Showing that there is only one solution is enough.
6. If $k_o = 0$, the attractive facet is the origin of the action space A. In this case, the origin is $(0b, 0f, 0k)'$.
7. By (4), $\mathbf{A}_o\dot{\mathbf{c}}_o = \gamma\mathbf{A}_o(\mathbf{A}_o'\mathbf{H}\mathbf{A}_o)^{-1}\mathbf{A}_o'\nabla u$. Premultiply both sides by $(\mathbf{A}_o'\mathbf{H}\mathbf{A}_o)^{-1}\mathbf{A}_o'\mathbf{H}$. Alternatively, write the equation as $\mathbf{A}_o[\dot{\mathbf{c}}_o - \gamma(\mathbf{A}_o'\mathbf{H}\mathbf{A}_o)^{-1}\mathbf{A}_o'\nabla u] = \mathbf{0}$, and then conclude from the linear independence of the columns of $\mathbf{A}_o$ that $\dot{\mathbf{c}}_o - \gamma(\mathbf{A}_o'\mathbf{H}\mathbf{A}_o)^{-1}\mathbf{A}_o'\nabla u = \mathbf{0}$.
8. Solving $\mathbf{Ac} = \mathbf{v}_1$ gives $\mathbf{c} = (1/2, 3/2, 1)'$, so $\mathbf{v}_1$ is feasible. Solving $\mathbf{Ac} = \mathbf{v}_2$ gives $\mathbf{c} = (-1/2, 15/2, 5)'$, so $\mathbf{v}_2$ is not feasible. Solving $\mathbf{Ac} = \mathbf{v}_3$ gives $\mathbf{c} = (0, 3, 2)'$, so $\mathbf{v}_3$ is feasible.
9. Solve $\mathbf{Ac} = \mathbf{v}_i$ again. Using $\mathbf{a}_1c_1 + \mathbf{a}_2c_2 + \mathbf{a}_3c_3 = (-\mathbf{a}_1)(-c_1) + \mathbf{a}_2c_2 + \mathbf{a}_3c_3$ produces the three solutions without hard labor; they are $(-1/2, 3/2, 1)'$, $(1/2, 15/2, 5)'$, and $(0, 3, 2)'$. This time then, $\mathbf{v}_2$ and $\mathbf{v}_3$ are feasible, and $\mathbf{v}_1$ is not.
10. No, dt is not the same as Δt, and $d\mathbf{x}(t)$ is not the same as $\Delta\mathbf{x}(t)$. In fact, $\Delta\mathbf{x}(t) = d\mathbf{x}(t) + d^2\mathbf{x}(t)/2! + d^3\mathbf{x}(t)/3! + \cdots$ (Taylor).
11. Infinitely many. (There are only three *basic* actions.)

CHAPTER 7

1. There are no preferences in Model One.
2. Both Pareto's utility theory and Model One say that in certain circumstances your demand curve for apples slopes downward. As soon as you are told this, you can (just to be contrary) disprove the assertion by buying apples faster when their price goes up.
3. One. It is only if John's $\mathbf{A}_o$ were to lose a column that you might be able to argue that John had completed an action.
4. To prove $\mathbf{M}'\mathbf{M} = \mathbf{I}$, use $\mathbf{e}_i'\mathbf{e}_j = \delta_{ij}$. From $\mathbf{M}'\mathbf{M} = \mathbf{I}$ follows that $\mathbf{M}$ and $\mathbf{M}'$ are each other's inverse, proving $\mathbf{M}\mathbf{M}' = \mathbf{I}$.
5. Matrix $\mathbf{M}$ is $k_o \times k_o$. The columns of $\mathbf{A}_o$ are permuted. In fact, they are permuted in the same way that the columns of $\mathbf{I}$ were permuted in the formation of $\mathbf{M}$. For an example, take $\mathbf{A}_o = (\mathbf{a}_1, \mathbf{a}_2, \mathbf{a}_3)$ and $\mathbf{M} = (\mathbf{e}_2, \mathbf{e}_3, \mathbf{e}_1)$; then $\mathbf{A}_o\mathbf{M} = (\mathbf{a}_2, \mathbf{a}_3, \mathbf{a}_1)$, as you can easily verify.
6. Since postmultiplication by $\mathbf{M}$ merely reorders the columns of $\mathbf{A}_o$ and does not affect the action space itself, $\mathbf{H}$ and $\mathbf{H}^{-1}$ stay the same. But $\dot{\mathbf{c}}$ must be premultiplied by $\mathbf{M}^{-1}$ (or $\mathbf{M}'$, which is the same thing) if

$\mathbf{A}_o\dot{\mathbf{c}}_o$ is to stay the same ($\mathbf{A}_o\mathbf{M}\mathbf{M}'\dot{\mathbf{c}}_o = \mathbf{A}_o\dot{\mathbf{c}}_o$). The subspace spanned by the columns of $\mathbf{A}_o$ is unchanged if you merely reorder those columns/vectors, so $\mathbf{P}$ stays the same. Alternatively, replace each of the four $\mathbf{A}_o$'s in $\mathbf{A}_o(\mathbf{A}_o'\mathbf{H}\mathbf{A}_o)^{-1}\mathbf{A}_o'\mathbf{H}$ with $\mathbf{A}_o\mathbf{M}$; you will see that all four $\mathbf{M}$'s drop out. Since A is unaffected, A^0 is unaffected; ∇u thus stays the same. Both sides of (2) are premultiplied by $\mathbf{M}'$. To see the effect on Theorem 1, suppose the permutation turns $\mathbf{a}_1$ into $\mathbf{a}_5$. The only change in Theorem 1 is that $C = 0$ if $\dot{q} = \dot{c}_5 a_{51}$ ($= \dot{c}_5 p$) and $A = 0$ if $\dot{q}$ is any other element of $\dot{c}_5\mathbf{a}_5$.

7. Matrix $\mathbf{N}$ is $n \times n$. The rows of $\mathbf{A}_o$ are permuted.
8. Permuting the rows of $\mathbf{A}_o$ means permuting the n goods. Change $\mathbf{H}$ to $\mathbf{NHN}'$; that way, $\mathbf{A}_o'\mathbf{H}\mathbf{A}_o$ becomes $\mathbf{A}_o'\mathbf{N}'\mathbf{NHN}'\mathbf{N}\mathbf{A}_o = \mathbf{A}_o'\mathbf{H}\mathbf{A}_o$. Change $\mathbf{H}^{-1}$ to $\mathbf{N}\mathbf{H}^{-1}\mathbf{N}'$; that will turn $\mathbf{H}\mathbf{H}^{-1} = \mathbf{I}$ into $\mathbf{NHN}'\mathbf{N}\mathbf{H}^{-1}\mathbf{N}'$, which is $\mathbf{I}$. Nothing happens to $\dot{\mathbf{c}}_o$. Matrix $\mathbf{P}$ becomes $\mathbf{NPN}'$. The elements of ∇u must be permuted in the same way as the elements of vectors in A, so ∇u is premultiplied by $\mathbf{N}$. Equation (2) changes to $\mathbf{A}_o'\mathbf{N}'\mathbf{NHN}'\mathbf{N}\mathbf{A}_o\dot{\mathbf{c}}_o = \gamma\mathbf{A}_o'\mathbf{N}'\mathbf{N}\nabla u$, which on simplification becomes (2) again. To see the effect on Theorem 1, suppose the permutation turns good 1 into good 4. The only change in Theorem 1 is that $C = 0$ if $\dot{q} = \dot{c}_1 a_{14}$ ($= \dot{c}_1 p$) and $A = 0$ if $\dot{q}$ is any other element of $\dot{c}_1\mathbf{a}_1$.
9. The proof of Theorem 1 did not involve the sign of the marginal utilities; each $du(\mathbf{x})/dx_i$ may be positive, negative, or zero. Theorem 1 would thus remain the same if ∇u were changed to $-\nabla u$.

CHAPTER 8

1. $d\boldsymbol{\xi} = d\boldsymbol{\alpha} + d\boldsymbol{\beta} = (d\boldsymbol{\alpha}^c + \boldsymbol{\Omega}d\mathbf{a}) + \boldsymbol{\Omega}d\mathbf{b} = d\boldsymbol{\alpha}^c + \boldsymbol{\Omega}(d\mathbf{a} + d\mathbf{b}) = d\boldsymbol{\alpha}^c + \boldsymbol{\Omega}d\mathbf{x}$.
2. $\boldsymbol{\alpha} + \boldsymbol{\alpha}_o$ equals both $(\boldsymbol{\alpha} + \boldsymbol{\alpha}_o)^c + \boldsymbol{\Omega}(\mathbf{a} + \mathbf{a}_o)$ and $(\boldsymbol{\alpha}^c + \boldsymbol{\Omega}\mathbf{a}) + (\boldsymbol{\alpha}_o^{\,c} + \boldsymbol{\Omega}\mathbf{a}_o)$. Using $\boldsymbol{\Omega}(\mathbf{a} + \mathbf{a}_o) = \boldsymbol{\Omega}\mathbf{a} + \boldsymbol{\Omega}\mathbf{a}_o$ completes the proof of the first part. The second part is handled similarly.
3. Yes. To see why, reverse the proof of Question 2.
4. I believe it is not. Learning about Model Two constitutes input; this is part of $d\mathbf{b}$, and therefore part of the model. Reading Model Two changes you, and it is possible that, as a result, your behavior changes. But there is no reason to believe that Model Two describes only your old behavior, not the new. Nor then is there reason to believe that through your new behavior you have falsified Model Two.
5. For the purposes of this problem only, redefine the stress as $s(\boldsymbol{\xi}) = \|\boldsymbol{\xi}\|$. It is easy to verify that $\nabla s = \boldsymbol{\xi}/\|\boldsymbol{\xi}\|$, a unit vector. Thus, if $\mathbf{a}$ is a unit

vector, $D_\alpha s(\boldsymbol{\xi}) = \cos \phi(\boldsymbol{\alpha},\boldsymbol{\xi})$, regardless of the stress. Put differently, $D_\alpha s(\lambda\boldsymbol{\xi})$ is the same for all $\lambda > 0$. For an illustration, let $\boldsymbol{\alpha}$ be the unobservable part of "drinking a glass of water." Then $D_\alpha s(\boldsymbol{\xi})$ is the same everywhere along a ray through the origin of E^m. Thus, if your thirst doubles, and redoubles, and redoubles again, the rate at which a glass of water reduces the stress remains the same. Give the connotations of "stress," this is implausible. It does not follow that $\|\boldsymbol{\xi}\|$ is the wrong objective function. What does follow is that, were $\|\boldsymbol{\xi}\|$ chosen as the objective function, it had best be called something other than "the stress."

CHAPTER 9

1. Equation (17) is derivable only if the objective function is analytically specified. The objective function of Model One—utility—was not specified.
2. The ith element of $\boldsymbol{\sigma}$ is $\mathbf{e}_i'\boldsymbol{\sigma} = -\gamma e^{-\gamma t}[\mathbf{e}_i'\boldsymbol{\xi}(0) + \int_0^t e^{\gamma\tau}\mathbf{e}_i'\boldsymbol{\Omega}\dot{\mathbf{b}}(\tau)d\tau]$. All elements of the row $\mathbf{e}_i'\boldsymbol{\Omega}$ are constant, as is $\mathbf{e}_i'\boldsymbol{\xi}(0)$.
3. Since $\boldsymbol{\xi}(0)$ and $\boldsymbol{\Omega}\dot{\mathbf{b}}$ belong to R^m, $\boldsymbol{\sigma}$ does too.
4. All elements of the row $\mathbf{k}'\boldsymbol{\Omega}$ are constant, as is $\mathbf{k}'\boldsymbol{\xi}(0)$. This was used just before (8).
5. The graph is a surface, in a diagram with a horizontal p-axis, a horizontal t-axis, and a vertical $\dot{q}$-axis. Keeping the wage fixed, at $p = p_o$ say, amounts to cutting the surface with the vertical plane $p = p_o$; the intersection is the graph of a t-function. Keeping not p but t fixed, at t_o say, amounts to cutting the surface with the vertical plane $t = t_o$; the intersection is the graph of a function of the form Q/Q_o. In Part II, this Q/Q_o would have been the quasi-Engel function.
6. Suppose that p is measured in bottles (b) and $\dot{q}$ is measured in cans per hour (c/h). Since Q_o is real, D is measured in $1/b^2$ and E is measured in $1/b$. Further, $A(t)$ is measured in $c/(hb^2)$, $B(t)$ is measured in $c/(hb)$, and $C(t)$ is measured like $\dot{q}$.
7. From (5), $\dot{\mathbf{c}}_o = (\underline{\mathbf{A}}_o'\underline{\mathbf{A}}_o)^{-1}\underline{\mathbf{A}}_o'\boldsymbol{\sigma}$. Premultiply by $\underline{\mathbf{A}}_o$ to get $\mathbf{A}_o\dot{\mathbf{c}}_o = \dot{\mathbf{a}}$. Adding $\dot{\mathbf{b}} = \dot{\mathbf{b}}(0)$ gives $\dot{\mathbf{x}}$. The rate $\dot{\mathbf{a}}$ converges to $-\mathbf{A}_o(\underline{\mathbf{A}}_o'\underline{\mathbf{A}}_o)^{-1}\underline{\mathbf{A}}_o'\boldsymbol{\Omega}\dot{\mathbf{b}}(0)$.

INDEX

1-vector, 6
Ability to choose, 8, 9
Ability to rank bundles, 8, 9, 14
Accident, 165
Action, 6, 24, 106, 107, 146, 157
  between 0 and t as a pair of vectors, 148
  as a pair of vectors, 146, 157
  at t, 107, 118, 119, 121, 122, 126, 135, 148, 149, 151, 158
  at t, as a pair of vectors, 148, 149, 151
  between 0 and t, 107, 119, 148
  core of, 149, 153, 157, 161
Action element, 6
Action, feasible, 108, 110, 111, 113–115, 121, 148, 149, 153, 154
Action, involuntary, 14
Action matrix, 112, 114, 119, 121, 134
Action matrix unspecified, 119
Action, nonnegative, 70
Action rate, 107, 118, 119, 123, 136, 148, 158, 167
  at t as a pair of vectors, 148
Action space, 24, 63, 106, 113, 147
Action, voluntary, 14
Action without visible consequences, 147
Actions consume, 11
Actions produce, 11
Activity, 6, 78–80
Activity analysis, 6, 26, 63, 78–80, 101, 102, 104, 114, 115
Activity-analytical constraint, 78–80, 102, 104
Activity-analytical feasible set, 114
Activity, irreversible, 78
Activity, nonmanufacturing, 78
Activity, nonmarket, 7
Actuaries, 57
Adaptive economics, 175
Adding endowments, impossibility of, 24
Addition, 18
Additive group, 21
Adjusting
  ex ante, 154
  ex post, 154
Advertising, 179
After-tax earnings, 19
Agent, 102
Algebra, 21
Algebraic operation, 18, 21
Algebraic system, 21
Animal behavior, 153, 168, 169
  vs. human behavior, 168
Animate consumer, 8
Annihilation vs. orthogonality, 34
Anthropic, 7, 10, 51
Approximation, linear, 148
Array vs. matrix, 26
Aspect, 152, 157, 176
Assertion, 49
Assumption, 49
Asymmetric production function, 54
Asymmetric projection matrix, 36
Asymmetry in a theory, 54
Asymptotic velocity, 164
Attainable endowment, 67, 110, 112
Attractive $\boldsymbol{\alpha}_i$, 151
Attractive **a**, 151
Atttractive basic action, 119, 125, 126, 134, 135, 151, 158, 159, 161, 166, 170, 171
  as a pair of vectors, 151, 158, 159, 161, 166, 171
Attractive facet, 119, 121, 135, 151, 159
Autonomous energy drain, 96, 97
Average velocity, 106

Axiom, 49
Axiomatization vs. mathematization, 49

Backward-bending demand curve, 3, 105
Backward-bending labor-supply curve, 128
Bads, 60
Baking cookies, 7
Banks, 9
Barter, 53, 84
Basic action, 109–111, 114, 117–119, 122, 124, 128, 134, 135, 149, 151, 153, 158, 162
  attractive, 119, 125, 126, 134, 135, 151, 158, 159, 161, 166, 170, 171
  as a pair of vectors, 147–157
  unattractive, 119, 134
Basic-action element, 122, 123, 134
  variable, 134
Basic actions, dependent, 134
Basic activity, 79, 80
Basis, 28
Basis matrix, 29, 35
Beam-and-flashlight, 112
Behavior under uncertainty, 10, 11
Behavioral mechanism, 175, 176
Belief, 155
Between, analytical meaning of, 43
Big City, 62
Black Box, 142, 143
Bliss point, 144
Border, 9
Bound vector, 24
Boundary, 43
Bounded set, 43
Brain, 8, 141, 143, 154, 155, 169
Brainwashing, 179
Bread consumption, doubling of, 59
Bright Puzzle Piece Fallacy, 48, 52
Budget (hyper)plane, 70, 109–113, 118
Budget constraint, 3, 6, 53–56, 60, 61, 66, 69, 70, 72, 95, 101, 108
  asymmetry of, 54, 55
  circular definition of, 60
  Hicks's, 54, 55, 70
  Pareto's, 66, 69, 108
  symmetry of, 54, 55
Budget line, 71, 91–93, 97, 109
Buying faster, 91
Buying inputs, 78
Buying the opposite of consuming, 14
Capital, 2
  human, 53
Capital and labor, symmetric treatment of, 54
Capital flow, cross-border, 56
Capital goods, 53
Cardinality, 11
Cartesian product, 63
Cash balances, 84
Cave, 37
Certainty, 10
CES production function, 77
Choice, 9, 10
  as figure of speech, 9
Choice of basis, 29
Choosing
  a bundle, 3, 6
  to choose, 154
  a direction, 3, 6
Circle, 145
Circular definitions, 60
Circularity of definitions of money, 60
Circularity of definition of budget constraint, 60
Closed set, 43, 119
Closed input-output model, 98
Closed under addition, 19
Closed under multiplication, 18
Closed under scalar multiplication, 20
Cobb-Douglas, 2
Cobb-Douglas production function, 77
Coefficient, dimensioned, 162, 167
Coefficient matrix, 126, 127, 161
Cognitive, 7, 19, 51, 176
Coin, 51
Commodity, 24, 25, 53, 54, 63, 64
  defined, 64
  flow, 24, 25
  vs. good, 54
  vs. money, 53
  stock, 24
Compact set, 44
Compensation, 135
Cone, 80–82, 109–111, 113, 119, 121, 159
Congestion, 62
Connotations, 6, 67, 152
  irrelevance of, 6
  of utility, 67
Consistent behavior, 9
Consistent system, 27
Constancy of riches, 73
Constant driver, 107

Constant driver rate, 163, 165, 171
Constant elasticity of substitution, 77
Constant returns to scale, 56
Constant tastes, 61
Constrained indifference curve, 71, 118
Constrained maximum, 92, 96
Constrained utility maximum, 96, 116–118
  possible nonexistence of, 116, 117
Constraint, 2
  unified, 104
  uniqueness of, 102
Consumer as seller, 68
Consumer capable of ranking bundles, 8, 9, 14
Consumer demand, exogenous, 97, 98
Consumer goods, 52
Consumer on porch, 96
Consumer/producer dichotomy, 103
Consumer tries to maximize utility, 3, 91
Consumer ultimately a demander, 83
Consumer's cross-price demand function, 2, 122
Consumer's cross-price supply function, 2, 122
Consumer's demand function, 3
Consumer's own-price demand function, 2, 122
Consumer's own-price supply function, 2, 122
Consuming the opposite of buying, 14
Consumption activities, 52
Consumption by actions, 11
Consumption rate, 124
Continuity of preferences, 12
Continuous time, 2, 5, 10, 59, 90, 175
Continuous-time dynamics, 5, 10
Contour surface, 47, 145
Contract, 9
Converging path of ξ, 164
Convex, 43, 80, 109, 119, 148
Convex cone, 80, 109, 148
Coordinate axis, 28
Coordinate of an endowment, 6
Coordinate system, 28
Core of an action, 149, 153, 157, 161
Corner solution, 49
Cost, 9, 10, 61
  opportunity, 61
Costless information, 84
Country, 9
Coupon, 7
Cramer's Rule, 125, 127, 161
Crescend, 3
Cross-border capital flow, 56
Cross-border labor flow, 56
Cross-price demand function, 2, 94, 122, 124, 128, 131, 136, 162
Cross-price supply function, 2, 122, 124, 162
Cumulative demand, 171
Cumulative-response function, 158, 160, 162, 163, 167, 168, 172
Current endowment, 106, 108, 109, 112

Deciding to decide, 154
Decision, 10
Decision making, 14
Decrescend, 11, 145, 157
Deficient numerator, 126
Definition vs. interpretation, 6
Delta function, 42, 165
Demand, 9
  cumulative, 171
  derived, 2, 53
  excess, 80
  exogenous, 97, 98
  as a flow rate, 81
  for labor power, 76
  for leisure, 64, 72, 75, 76, 97
  for poverty, 75
  as a stock, 81
  and supply, 80, 81
    Marshallian interpretation of, 81
Demand curve, 3, 53, 81, 105
  backward-bending, 3, 105
  downward-sloping, 3, 81
Demand function, 1–3, 14, 94, 122, 124, 128, 129, 136, 162, 174
  cannot be linear, 54
  cross-price, 2, 94, 122, 124, 128, 129, 136, 162
  denominator of, 94
  dynamic version, 13
  form of, 3
  parameters of, 3
Demand rate, 81, 92–94, 104, 105, 122, 123, 130–134, 162
  converging to constancy, 13
  elastic, 104
  inelastic, 93, 104
  limit of, 105
Demanded bundle, 7, 8, 69–72, 75
Denominator of demand function, 94
Derivative of a function in the direction of a vector, 38, 39

Derived demand, 2, 53
Diagonal elements, 31
Dichotomy, 52, 55, 66
  false, 52
  vs. partitioning, 52
  valid, 52
Differential equation, 41
Dimension of a vector space, 25
Dimensioned, 19, 24, 95, 132, 162, 167
  coefficient, 162, 167
  coordinate, 24
  element, 24
  parameter, 132
  quantity, 95
Dimensionless, 19, 95
Dimensionless quantity, 95
Diminishing Marginal Utility, Law of, 147, 153, 155
Dining room, 76
Direction in which utility increases fastest, 3
Direction of feasible action, 115
Direction of steepest ascent, 39
Direction of steepest constrained ascent, 41
Directional derivative, 38, 39
Discount factor, 99
Discounted future pleasures, 99
Displacement, 20, 21, 23, 106
Disposable-income rate, 124
Distance, 44, 145
  between a point and a set, 44
Divisibility
  imperfect, 53, 176
  perfect, 49, 53, 90, 176
  strong, 90, 102
  weak, 90
Division, 18
Dollar flow, 19
Domain
  of Hicks's utility function, 69, 72
  of Pareto's utility function, 67
  of profit function, 77
  of short-response function, 134
  of utility function, 60, 69, 72
Dominant firm, 56
Doomsday, 115
Downward-bending labor supply curve, 128
Downward-sloping demand curve, 3, 81
Drifting endowment, 97
Driver, 97–99, 104, 106, 107, 112, 114–119, 121, 142, 143, 147, 148, 153–155, 157, 159, 167, 174–177
  constant, 107
  as feasible action, 114, 153
  as pair of vectors, 147, 148
  periodic, 107
  stochastic, 107
  at *t*, 107, 147
  between 0 and *t*, 107, 148
  between 0 and *t* as pair of vectors, 148
Driver rate, 107, 148, 163, 165, 167, 171
  as pair of vectors, 148
  constant, 163, 165, 171
Dual bases, 29
Dual-basis matrix, 29, 31, 46
Dual space, 25, 26, 32, 39
  main, 26, 32, 39
Durable goods, 53
Duration of economic period, 59, 66, 69, 75, 178
Dynamic, 5
Dynamic models, 175
Dynamic version of demand function, 13
Dynamic version of testable results, 13
Dynamics, continuous-time, 5, 10

Earth, 56, 61
Eating, 76, 96, 103
Echo of an action, 58
Economic fluctuations, 56
Economic period, duration of, 59, 66, 69, 75, 178
Economic vocabulary, 10
Edge of a cone, 111, 112, 121
Edible goods, 53
Efficient allocation, 9
Ego, 155
Egyptian priests, 51
Elastic demand rate, 104
Electrochemical, 4, 143, 155
Element of an action, 6
Endogeneity, 114
  and exogeneity mathematically distinguished, 114
Endogenous, 97, 114, 149
  energy loss, 97
  movement, 149
Endowment, 3, 5, 24, 67, 70, 79, 106–108
  attainable, 67, 110, 112
  current, 106, 108, 109, 112
  drifting, 97
  initial, 5, 67, 70, 79, 106, 108
  motion of, 3, 7, 12, 89, 107
  speed of, 12, 92, 100, 115, 117
  stationary, 97

vs. surround, 152
at *t*, 106
(time) path of, 5, 7, 9, 10, 90, 106, 118, 133
Endowment coordinate, 6
Endowment set, 24, 63, 79
producer's, 79
Endowment velocity, 93–95, 97, 105, 106, 120, 164
Energy, 64, 69, 72, 75, 76, 96, 97, 103, 111, 114, 124, 129, 130, 147
supply of, 72
Energy deficit, 97
Energy drain, autonomous, 96, 97
Engel curve, 132
Engel function, 2, 132, 174
English language, 52
Equal-stress contour, 145
Equilibria, multiple, 10, 80
Equilibrium, 2, 62, 100, 101, 104, 149, 175
absence of, 101
general, 2
irrelevance of, 101
moving, 101
static, 101
stationary, 100, 175
stochastic, 101
Equimarginal Principle, 82
Erg, 64, 75
Estimation, 93, 133, 162
Ether, 155
Euclid, 19, 51
Excess demand, 80
Exchange, 60, 84
network of, 84
Exogeneity, 114
and endogeneity mathematically distinguished, 114
Exogenous, 10, 96–98, 104, 105, 107, 114, 120, 143, 148, 149, 174
Exogenous change, 143, 148
Exogenous consumer demand, 97, 98
Exogenous energy loss, 96, 97
Exogenous factors, 10
Exogenous influences, 97, 99, 104, 105, 107, 120, 174
Expectations, 9, 10
Expenditure, 9
Expenditure rate, 93, 105, 124, 128
limit of, 105
Experiment, 173
Explicit cost, 77
Explosive behavior, 101, 175
Exponential decay, 13, 165, 166, 175, 178
Extreme close-up, 115

Facet, attractive, 119, 121, 135, 151, 159
Fallacy, Bright Puzzle Piece, 48, 52
False dichotomy, 52
Falsifiability, 136
Family Pak, 110, 111, 113, 121
Family planning, 178
Fat City, 62
Feasible, 78, 108–111, 113–115, 119, 121, 135, 148, 149, 151, 153, 154
Feasible action, 108, 110, 111, 113–115, 121, 148, 149, 153, 154
direction of, 115
length of, 115
as pair of vectors, 148
Feasible activity, 78–80
Feasible set, 79, 80, 101, 106, 108–111, 114, 115, 117, 121, 135, 148
defined, 114
Feasible set unbounded, 80, 115
Feedback, 143, 146, 147, 149, 157, 161
defined, 149
Fertility rate, 178
Fifth principle of model building: Avoid Circularity, 60
Final bundle, 5
Final endowment, 5, 106
Final goods, 53
Financial instruments, 9, 53
Finished product, 98
Finite endowment speed, 100, 115
Finite speed, 80, 100, 104, 115, 175
Firm wholly owned by household, 84
First principle of model building: Define Mathematically, 48
Fixed input prices, 56
Fixed output price, 56
Flashbulb, 42
Flashlight, 112
Flat set, 34
Flow, 6, 106, 107, 122, 158, 163
Flow rate, 10, 81, 106, 107, 122, 123, 126–130, 132, 133, 136, 158, 160, 163, 166
Flow rates
can sometimes be added, 133
measured in same units, 133
are unobservable, 133
Followers vs. Leader, 56

Fork in endowment's time path, 9, 10
Fourth principle of model building: Avoid Arbitrariness, 57
Free access, 79, 80, 115
Free disposal, 79
Free vector, 24
Free will, 155
Full column rank, 27
Future, 9, 68, 98, 99, 166
Future event, 166
Future expenses, 68
Future utility, 99

Game theory, 175
Gasoline rationing, 7
General equilibrium, 2
Geometry, 51
Geranium, 66
Giffen behavior, 152
Giffen curve, 152
Giffen goods, 3, 54
Good, 54
  vs. commodity, 54
  definition of, 64
  vs. money, 54
Goodness of fit, 172
Gossen, H., 11
Government, 9
Gradient, 26, 91, 93, 150

Hessian matrix, 27
Hicks, J. R., 12, 54, 55, 60, 63, 69–72, 75, 97, 177
Hicks's budget constraint, 54, 55, 70
  asymmetry of, 54, 55
  symmetry of, 54, 55
Hicks's model, 71
Hicks's utility domain, 69, 72
Hicks's utility theory, 63, 69, 75, 97, 177
Hicksian week, 69
Hiring a worker, 77
Homogeneous system, 27
Horizontal *p*-axis, 3, 123, 129
House of Calculus, 90
House painter, 103
Household production function, 105
Household sector, 53
Human capital, 53
Human vs. animal behavior, 168
Hunger, 143, 145
Hyperplane, 113

Idempotence, 35
Identical firms, 55
Imperfect divisibility, 53, 176
Imperfectly divisible goods, 53
Imputed price, 111, 121
Inability to buy, 81
Inability to sell, 81
Inactivity, 14, 24, 97
Inanimate consumer, 8
Income, 2, 9, 10, 53, 75, 132, 135, 174
Income effect, 132
Income elasticity, 132
Income-inferior, 131
Income-normal, 131, 132
Income rate, 124, 130, 132
Inconsistent behavior, 9
Indeterminate period length, 100
Indifference, 14
Indifference contour, 71
Indifference curve, 10
  constrained, 71, 118
Indifference map, 71, 72
Indifference surface, 70, 117, 145
Individual behavior, 58
Industrial sector, 53
Inedible goods, 53
Inefficient allocation, 9
Inefficient behavior, 5
Inelastic demand rate, 93, 104
Infeasible, 78, 111
Inferior good, 131
Infinite endowment speed, 100
Infinite speed, 175
Infinite wealth, 80, 101
Infinite wealth in finite time, 101
Infinitely rich, 115
Infinity of prices, 114
Information, 143, 177, 178
Ingested quantities, 67
Inheritance, 71, 165
Inhomogeneous system, 27
Initial endowment, 5, 67, 70, 79, 106, 108
Inner product, 17, 29, 33, 36, 132, 145
  nonstandard, 29, 33, 36
  standard, 17, 29, 145
Inner-product matrix, 31, 32, 36, 94, 145
Input, 7, 54, 77, 123, 142, 143

Input link, 142, 146–148
  defined, 148
Input markets, 56
Input prices, 56
Input-output model
  closed, 98
  open, 98
Inputs, symmetric treatment of, 54
Instant, 19, 21, 63
Institutional, 7, 9, 10, 51, 176
Integrated theory vs. unified theory, 105
Intensity of preferences, 12
Intention, 10
Interactive behavior, 58, 148
Intermediate goods, 53
Interpretation vs. definition, 6
Intrusive Agent, 175–177
Intrusive Consumer, 8, 9
Inverse-square law, 11
Involuntary action, 14
Irrational, 5, 8, 9, 96
Irrational behavior, 5, 9, 96
Irreversible, 78, 111
Irreversible activity, 78
Ivory Tower, 49, 51

Jigsaw puzzle, 48
Joint output, 7
Joint purchase, 7
Joint sale, 7
Jump discontinuity in endowment's time path, 5

Keeping the stockholders happy, 102
Klein, L. R., 175
Knowledge, 10
Kolmogorov, A., 49, 51
Koopmans, T. C., 175

Labor, 75; *see also* Labor power
  and capital, symmetric treatment of, 54
  as a bad, 76
  as primary good, 76
  supply of, 72, 75
Labor flow, cross-border, 56
Labor input, 124
Labor power, 2, 64, 72, 75, 76, 96
  demand for, 70
Labor supply, theory of, 63, 75, 76, 97, 177
Labor-supply curve, 129, 130
Labor-supply function, 2, 129
Labor-supply model, 75
Laboring, 76
Lancaster, K. J., 84
Law of Diminishing Marginal Utility, 147, 153, 155
Law of motion, 91, 92, 95, 97, 98, 104–106, 108, 115, 117, 118, 120, 126, 136, 141, 142, 146, 150, 159, 166, 174, 175
Laws, 9
Leader vs. Followers, 56
Learning, 177
Least-squares method, 172
Leisure, 64, 72, 75, 76, 97
Lemma, 49
Length of economic period, 59, 66, 69, 75, 178
Length of feasible action, 115
Length of steepest ascent, 39
Length of steepest constrained ascent, 41
Liechtenstein, 56
Life insurance, 57
Limit of demand rate, 105
Limit of expenditure rate, 105
Limit of price elasticity, 105
Linear approximation, 148
Linear dependence, 27
Linear form, 125, 134, 160
  in two variables, 134
Linear function, 37
  matrix representation of, 37
Linear independence, 27
Linear span, 46
Linear system, 125
Linear transformation, 37
Linearity, 37
Literary models, 52
Location, 153
Locational change, 153
Locations in the plane, 19, 20
Logic, 49
Logically unexchangeable, 66
Long-response function, 122, 141, 145, 158, 160, 162, 163, 166, 167, 168, 175, 178
Lottery ticket, 10
Low matrix, 28

Main dual space, 26, 32, 39
Mainstream models, 63, 66

Manufacturing, 77, 78
Marginal utility, 26, 74, 82, 97
  per dollar, 82
  of income, 74
  of money, 74
  negative, 60
  unit of measurement of, 26
Market behavior, 1, 53, 109
Market exchange, 14
Market place, 152
Market price, 111
Market value, 77
Marshall, A., 123
Marshallian interpretation of demand and supply, 81
Marshallian model, 81
Marshallian price-quantity diagram, 81
Mathematization vs. axiomatization, 49
Matrix representation of a linear function, 37
Matrix vs. array, 26
Maximand, 3, 145
  vs. minimand, 145
Maximum age, 57, 58
Maximum, constrained, 92, 96, 116–118
Measurement unit, 19, 94, 106, 108, 114
Medium of exchange, 60, 65, 84
Methodology, 48
Mice in the pantry, 96
Migration, 62
Mind, 4, 13, 141, 165
Minimand, 11, 145
  vs. maximand, 145
Model building, 2
Model ingredient, 106, 174
Monetary concept, 53, 64, 65, 174
Monetary exchange, 53
Monetization of an economy, 84
Money, 9, 53, 54, 60–68, 72, 74–76, 84, 85, 93, 94
  circular definitions of, 60
  vs. commodity, 53, 66
  definition of, 64
  directly exchangeable, 66
  vs. good, 54
  nominal, 9, 67, 68, 84
  as nongood, 72, 75, 76
  real, 68, 84
  the only supplied good, 65
  used but not used up, 65
Money balances, 68, 85
Money/commodities dichotomy, 66
Money illusion, 74
Money not wanted for its own sake, 60, 65
Money-supply function, 94
Money-supply rate, 93, 94
Moneyness, 84
Monopolistic firm, 97, 98
Monopoly profit, 102
Mortality tables, 57, 58
Motion, 107
Motion law, 91, 92, 95, 97, 98, 104–106, 108, 115, 117, 118, 120, 126, 136, 141, 142, 146, 150, 159, 166, 174, 175
  for Model One, 91, 92, 97, 115, 120, 126
  for Model One, reformulated, 120
  for Model Two, 150, 159
  for neoclassical theory, 118
Motion of a particle, 154
Motion of the endowment, 3, 7, 12, 89, 107
Mount Everest, 95
Movies, 179
Moving equilibrium, 101
MT, 18
Multiple equilibria, 10, 80
Multiplication, 18
  by a scalar, 18, 20
Multiplicative group, 21
Mutual observation, 148
Myopic Law, 99, 154
  vs. Rational Law, 154

Natural sciences, 6, 173
Negative marginal utility, 60
Negative-exponential rate, 13, 165, 167, 175, 178
Network of exchange, 84
Neuron, 143
Newton, I., 3, 11
Next period, nonexistence of, 60
Nile, 51
Nominal balances vs. real balances, 68
Nominal money, 9, 67, 68, 84
Nominal money stock, 84
Nondurable goods, 53
Noneconomic behavior, 175
Nonexistence of next period, 60
Nonexistence of profit maximum, 57
Nonmanufacturing activities, 78
Nonmarket activities, 7
Nonmarket behavior, 53
Nonmatrix array, 27

Nonmonetary concepts, 53
Nonmonetary transaction costs, 7
Nonnegative action, 70
Nonnegative linear combination, 114, 119, 151
Nonnegative point space, 63, 64
Nonprimary goods, 53
Nonstandard inner product, 29, 33, 36
Nonstandard norm, 32
Norm, 17, 32; *see also* Length
Norm of steepest ascent, 39
Norm of steepest constrained ascent, 41
Normal good, 91, 131
Normative theory, 5, 64, 99, 174
Null vector, 22
Numeraire, 84, 85
n-vector, 6

Objective function, 67
  unified, 104
  uniqueness of, 102
Observable consequences, 143
Observable input, 142
Observable output, 142
Observable part, 147
Observation matrix, 27, 148, 166
Obtuse angle, 155
Off-diagonal elements, 31
Offering for sale vs. selling, 128
Oil well, 96
One good, one price, 60
Open input–output model, 98
Operation, algebraic, 18, 21
Ophélimité, 66
Opportunity cost, 61
Optimization, 10
Ordinality, 11, 70
Origin, 22
Orthogonal, 33
Orthogonal projection, 34
Orthogonality vs. annihilation, 34
Output, 2, 77, 142
Output link, 142, 143, 146, 147
  defined, 147
Output price, 2, 56
Output rate, 124, 134
Outputs, two or more, 7
Overeating, 144
Overpopulation, 178
Own-price demand function, 2, 94, 105, 122, 124, 128, 134, 136, 162
Own-price demand rate, 166
Own-price supply function, 2, 105, 122, 124, 129, 136, 162
Ownership, 9

Paint, 103
Palm trees, 58
Pantry, 76
Pareto, V., 11, 12, 76
Pareto's budget constraint, 66, 69, 108
Pareto's handling of supply, 69
Pareto's utility domain, 67
Pareto's utility theory, 63, 66, 76, 89, 93, 97, 101, 136
Parmenides, 61
Particle, motion of, 154
Partitioning vs. dichotomy, 52
Party Pak, 110, 111, 121
Path of $\boldsymbol{\xi}$, converging, 164
Path of the endowment, 5, 7, 9, 10, 90, 106, 118, 133
Paying taxes, 7
Perception of the future, 99
Perfect competition, 55–57
Perfect divisibility, 49, 53, 90, 176
Period analysis, 5, 6, 10, 59, 102, 106, 176, 178
Period length, 59, 66, 69, 75, 100, 178
  indeterminate, 100
Periodic functions, 107
Permutation matrix, 136
Perpendicular, 33, 35; *see also* Orthogonal
Pharmacist, 65
Physical constants, 172
Physiology, 155
Plane geometry, 51
Planning, 10
Point, 21
Point set, 21
Point space, 23, 24, 34, 36, 37, 43, 45, 63, 64, 147
  nonnegative, 63, 64
Pointed cone, 80, 109–111, 113
Pointed, convex, polyhedral cone, 109
Points written as vectors, 24
Polyhedral cone, 80, 109, 174
Possession, 9
Postulate, 49
Potential utility gain, 12
Powers of a matrix, 35
Prediction, 10

Preference, 9–12, 62, 103
  revealed, 62
Preference-aversion curve, 152
Preference intensity, 12
Preference ordering, 12
Present utility, 99
Price, 10
Price change, interpretation of, 123
Price elasticity, 105
Price index, 68
Price is a quotient of two action elements, 123
Price maker, 59
Price of capital, 2
Price taker, 59
Price vector, 25, 91, 94, 114
Price vector not unique, 114
Primary good, 53, 76
Prime, 17
Principle of Least Astonishment, 57–59
Principles of model building
  Avoid Arbitrariness, 57
  Avoid Circularity, 60
  Beware Dichotomies, 52
  Define Mathematically, 48
  Small Is Not Zero, 55
Prism, 80
Private goods, 53
Probability, 49, 51
Probability theory, 51
Problem of the Intrusive Consumer, 8
Procrustes, 76
Producer behavior, 1, 6
Producer/consumer dichotomy, 103
Producer goods, 52
Producer's cross-price demand function, 2, 122
Producer's cross-price supply function, 2, 122
Producer's endowment set, 79
Producer's own-price demand function, 2, 122
Producer's own-price supply function, 2, 122
Production activity, 6, 7, 52, 53
Production by actions, 11
Production *ex nihilo,* 79, 115
Production function, 54, 77
  household, 105
Production process, 7, 77–79, 114, 123, 134
Productive economy, 53
Profit, 9, 10, 53, 76
  monopoly, 102
Profit function, 76, 77
Profit maximization, 53, 77, 78
Profit maximum, nonexistence of, 57
Projection, 34–37, 92, 93–95, 118, 120, 125, 135, 150, 151, 159
  onto budget line, 93, 94
  onto budget plane, 95, 118
  onto facet, 118, 135, 150, 151, 159
  onto feasible set, 118, 135, 150, 151
  onto plane, 125
  of point onto set, 36, 37
  onto subspace, 35
  of vector onto set, 36
Projection matrix, 35, 36, 150, 165
  asymmetric, 36
  symmetric, 35
Projects, consumer as undertaker of, 5, 6
Property, 9
Property rights, 14
Protagonist of Hicks's utility theory, 89
Protagonist of Model One, 7
Protagonist of Model Two, 13
Protagonist of Pareto's utility theory, 89
Protagonist of producer theory, 89
Protagonist of labor-supply theory, 89
Public goods, 53
Pure theory, 49, 53, 64
Pure-exchange economy, 53
Purpose, 10
Pythagorean theorem, 32

Quadratic form, 125, 134, 160
  in two variables, 134
Quadratic utility function, 11
Quadrilateral, 51
Quasi-Engel function, 2, 122, 130–132, 136, 162, 167, 174
Quasiconcavity, 108
Quiet life, 102

Raising taxes, 178
Random, 10
Randomness, 10
Rank of action matrix, 113
Rational, 8
Rational, bad, myopic, good, 100
Rational behavior, 9

Rational Law, 99, 153, 154
  vs. Myopic Law, 154
Rationality, 10, 154
Rationing, 7
Rats, 169
Ray, 113, 116
Real analysis, 44
Real money, 68, 84
Real money stock, 84
Real balances vs. nominal balances, 68
Real-balance approach, 68
Register, 143, 146, 153
Regression analysis, 27
Repeated trials, 51
Response function
  cumulative, 158, 160, 162, 163, 167, 168, 172
  long, 122, 141, 145, 158, 160, 162, 163, 166, 167, 168, 175, 178
  short, 122, 124–126, 134, 136, 158, 162, 174, 175, 178
Restaurant owner, 103
Retailer, 78
Returns to scale, 56
Revealed preference, 62
Revenue, 9, 10, 77
Revenue rate, 124
Rights, 9
Ring, 21
Risk, 9
River current, 97
Robinson Crusoe, 58
Robot, 8, 9, 95, 96, 102, 103, 168, 169, 177
  uniqueness of, 102
Robot-consumer, 8, 9, 96
Role switching, 102
Roof, 37
Rowboat, 97

Sailing, 6
Sales rate, 124
Salt concentration, 169
Salt water, 169
Satisfaction, 14, 67
Satisficing, 102
Savings, 9
Scalar multiple, 20
Scalar multiplication, 18, 20
Scarce means, 14
Scientist, the, 49, 50, 136, 152
Scitovsky, T., 102
Second principle of model building: Beware Dichotomies, 52
Seller, consumer as, 68
Selling a unit of output, 77
Selling output, 77, 78
Selling vs. offering for sale, 129
Sensations, 143
Sequentiality, 97
Set of instants, 20
Set with addition, 19–21
Set with multiplication, 18, 19, 21
Set with scalar multiplication, 20
Short-response function, 122, 124–126, 134, 136, 158, 162, 174, 175, 178
Sigmoid, 132
Signal, 143
Slope of a surface in the direction of a vector, 12, 39, 92
Slutsky equation, 1, 3, 53, 135
Slutsky, E. E., 1
Small is not zero, 55
Small vs. zero, 55
Soap operas, 178, 179
Social behavior, 58, 59, 148
Social science, 6, 155, 173
Specific gravity, 171, 172
Specifying the action matrix, 119
Speed, 12, 90, 92
  of endowment, 12, 92, 100, 115, 117
Spike, 42, 163, 165, 167
Stackelberg, H. von, 56
Stagnant societies, 97
Standard inner product, 17, 29, 145
Standard norm, 17, 32
State at *t*, 9, 146, 157, 170
State of mind, 13, 141–144, 146, 156, 157, 164, 174, 175
  asymptotic velocity of, 164
Statement, 49
Static equilibrium, 101
Stationarity, 164, 175
Stationary endowment, 97
Stationary equilibrium, 100, 175
Steepest ascent, 39, 40, 46, 150
  direction of, 39
  norm of, 39
  as a vector, 39
Steepest constrained ascent, 41, 47, 92, 94, 99, 116–118, 150
  direction of, 41
  length of, 41
  norm of, 41

Steepest constrained descent, 150
Steepest descent, 150
Steering the endowment, 3, 6
Stellar, E., 169
Stimuli, 154
Stimulus, 142
Stochastic driver, 107
Stochastic equilibrium, 101
Stochastic process, 107
Stock, 6
Store of value, 65
Straight-line demand curve, 53
Stress, 145–147, 150, 155–157
Stress slope minimization, 145
Strict quasiconcavity, 108
Strong divisibility, 90, 102
Submarine, 66
Submaximum utility, 91, 104
Suboptimal behavior, 5
Subspace, 22, 23
Subtraction, 18
Sudden event, 42, 166, 175
Suicide, 179
Sum of flow rates, 163
Sum of flows, 163
Supply, 9, 73, 75
  of output, 2
  Pareto's handling of, 69
Supply curve, upward sloping, 81
Supply function, 2, 122, 124, 128, 136, 162, 174
  cross-price, 2, 122, 124, 162
  of money, 94
  own-price, 2, 105, 122, 124, 128, 136, 162
Supply rate, 81, 92–94, 123
  of money, 93, 94
  as absolute value, 81
Supplying by consumers, 72, 76
Supplying of energy, 72
Supplying of labor, 72, 75
Surplus, 97
Surround, 152, 153, 157, 165, 176
  vs. endowment, 152
Symmetric matrix, 30
Symmetric projection matrix, 35
Symmetry, 5
  in indices, 54, 55
  of interpretation, 55
  in a theory, 54–56
  of theory of gravitation, 56
t-function, 159–163, 167
  defined, 160
Tall matrix, 28, 35
Tasks, consumer as undertaker of, 5, 6
Tastes, 61
Tax payment rate, 124
Taxes, 9, 178
Taylor expansion, 37
Taylor series, 38, 44
Tea-drinking consumer, 68
Technological constraint, 77
Technology, 79, 84
Technology matrix, 26, 79
Test, 13
Test fluid, 169, 171
Test period, 169
Testable results, 1, 2, 10, 11, 13
  dynamic version, 13
Tests of animal behavior, 169
Theorem, 49
Theoretical (a)symmetry, 54
Theoretical vocabulary, 6, 9, 10, 52, 53, 91
Theory of gravitation, 3, 56
Theory of labor supply, 63, 75, 76, 97, 177
Theory of leisure demand, 75, 97
Theory of the firm, 59
Theory of the producer, 59, 63, 76
Third principle of model building: Small Is Not Zero, 55
Thirst, 143, 145
Time, 5, 19, 20, 23, 63, 64
  as a continuous variable, 2, 5, 10, 59, 90, 175
  defined, 63
Time axis, 19, 20, 63
Time flow, 20, 63
Time line, 19
Time path, 5, 7, 9, 10, 90, 106, 118, 133, 144, 167
  of ξ, 144
  of endowment, 5, 7, 9, 10, 90, 106, 118, 133
  uniqueness of endowment's, 10
Tintner, G., 175
Toaster, 111
Tomato plants, 96
Total variation, 172
Trading, 78
Transaction, 6, 7, 76, 77, 108, 114
Transaction costs, 7
Transitivity of preferences, 12

Transposition, 17
Trapezoid, 51
Traumatic event, 165, 178
Travel, 153
Triangle, 51
Trying to maximize utility, 3, 91
Tuna inheritance, 71
TV news, 179
Type A personality, 166

U.S. economy, 56
Unable to buy, 81
Unable to sell, 81
Unattainable endowment, 112
Unattractive basic action, 119, 134
Unbounded feasible set, 80, 115
Uncertainty, 8–11, 177
Unified constraint, 104
Unified objective function, 104
Unified theory, 104
  vs. integrated theory, 105
Uniform velocity, 164
Uniqueness of behavior, 111
Uniqueness of endowment's time path, 10
Uniqueness of objective function, 102
Unit of account, 65, 85
Unit of measurement, 19, 94, 106, 108, 114
Unit vector, 37
Unit of time, 64
Unobservable, 157
Unobservable part, 146, 147, 149, 154
  of action, 146, 147, 149
  of driver, 147
Upward-sloping supply curve, 81
Usefulness, 67, 99, 103
Utility, 3, 106, 107
  differentiable, 107, 108
  future, 99
  not a measure of anything, 11
  not a maximand, 3
  always maximized, 91
  present, 99
  of a steak, 82
  as a "tainted notion", 12
Utility difference, 12
Utility function, 2, 60, 68, 69, 72
  asymmetric in indices, 68
  quadratic, 11
Utility maximization, 3, 91, 93, 95, 96, 118
Utility-maximizing action, 67, 118
Utility-maximizing demanded bundle, 71
Utility-maximizing endowment, 70, 75
Utility-maximizing location, 115
Utility maximum, constrained, 96, 116–118
Utility slope maximization, 3, 92, 95, 96
Utility theory
  Hicks's, 63, 69, 75, 97, 177
  Pareto's, 63, 66, 76, 89, 93, 97, 101, 136
Uzawa, H., 12

Valid dichotomy, 52
Value added, 77
Variable basic action, 125, 170
  elements, more than one, 134
Vector space, 21
Velocity, 90, 92, 94, 97, 106, 164
  asymptotic, 164
  average, 106
  uniform, 164
Velocity of endowment, 92–95, 97, 105, 106, 120, 164
Verbal economics, 49
Vertical p-axis, 123
Vertical translate, 127
Visitor, the, 50, 136, 152
Vocabulary of theory, 6, 9, 10, 52, 53, 91
Voluntary action, 14

Wage, 2, 122, 124, 129–132, 174
Wage-inferior, 131
Wage-normal, 131
Wage rate, 75
Weak divisibility, 90
Weaknesses of Model One, 153
Week, Hicksian, 69
Weekly expenditure for all other goods, 83
Weiner, I. H., 169
Wholesaler, 78
Widget manufacturer, 56
Willing to buy, 81
Willing to sell, 81
Windup doll, 95, 169
Working, 97, 129

Zero endowment speed, 100
Zero period length, 59, 60, 90, 98
Zero vs. small, 55